OUTRAGEOUS BETRAYAL

OUTRAGEOUS BETRAYAL

THE DARK JOURNEY OF WERNER ERHARD FROM EST TO EXILE

Steven Pressman

St. Martin's Press

New York

OUTRAGEOUS BETRAYAL:

THE DARK JOURNEY OF WERNER ERHARD FROM EST TO EXILE. Copyright © 1993 by Steven Pressman. All rights reserved. Printed in the United States of America. No part of this book may be used or reproduced in any manner whatsoever without written permission except in the case of brief quotations embodied in critical articles or reviews. For information, address St. Martin's Press, 175 Fifth Avenue, New York, N.Y. 10010.

Design by Richard Oriolo

Library of Congress Cataloging-in-Publication Data

Pressman, Steven.
    Outrageous betrayal : the dark journey of Werner Erhard from est to exile / Steve Pressman.
        p.   cm.
    ISBN 0-312-09296-2
    1. Erhard seminars training—History. 2. Erhard, Werner, 1936–
—Trials, litigation, etc. I. Title.
RC489.E7P74   1993
158—dc20
[B]   93-7433
                                                                       CIP

First Edition: September 1993

10 9 8 7 6 5 4 3 2 1

To the memory of
Robert Sillman and John J. Lindsay,
for their friendship and
inspiration

To Tracy and Roshann,
for making it all
worthwhile

Contents

Contents

Prologue

At her home in suburban San Jose, Janis Vivo, a slim and attractive brown-eyed woman of forty-two, poured the red wine into her glass and took a few sips, careful not to spill any on her stylish tan slacks and the white sweater that she wore over a plain white blouse. After setting the wine bottle and glass on the seat next to her, she picked up the tablet of lined white notebook paper and began to write in her clean, neat handwriting.

It was early in the afternoon on December 31, 1988, only a few hours before her friends would be dressing to go out and celebrate New Year's Eve. Vivo had already settled on her own plans for ushering in the new year, but they did not include party hats and champagne at midnight. Her husband, Stephen Wachter, a partner at a successful executive recruitment agency in Silicon Valley, had been out of town, visiting relatives in New York with the couple's two small children, and was not scheduled to fly back home until later that night. Vivo planned to be alone as she sipped again from her glass of wine and switched on the engine to the Toyota. As she began to write, deadly fumes of carbon monoxide began to dance around the garage that she had sealed tight with towels, which were stuffed along the bottom of the garage door.

The wine bottle sat at her side while the words began to spill out across the first sheet of paper. "There's not much point in explaining any of this," she wrote at the top of the page. "It never really makes any sense to anyone anyway."

Vivo was no longer happy working as an airline stewardess and instead had begun to imagine a far more fanciful life filled with riches and glamour. There had been strains in her marriage to Wachter, and the couple had been talking about a trial separation, though nothing definite had yet been decided. Wachter knew his wife seemed a little depressed but passed it off to her lingering concerns about her job and the future of their marriage.

"I just really don't want to be left out, or alone," Vivo wrote on the notebook paper, while the poisonous air continued to fill the garage. "I guess I would have always felt like I just wasn't doing something right, just not quite good enough, and not having enough balls to figure out what that would be."

Only a few months before Vivo thought she had finally discovered a place to find some answers for her confused life. Some of the executives and other employees at her husband's company had become enthusiastic about a program called the Forum, a two-weekend self-awareness seminar offered by a San Francisco company, Werner Erhard & Associates. For years Werner Erhard had been one of the country's most famous pop gurus, recruiting hundreds of thousands of people into a controversial get-in-touch-with-yourself program called est. Just about everyone from famous actors to bored housewives, it seemed, had gone through Erhard's "training," and huge numbers of them swore to the fantastic results they got from est. Lurking behind the shadows were the occasional rumors about the cultlike devotion that some of Erhard's most enthusiastic adherents felt for him as the "source" of est. Erhard himself had long been surrounded in a shroud of myth and mystery, revered by his legions of followers as a godlike figure despite his own dubious background as a onetime used-car salesman who had years earlier abandoned his first wife and four children.

Replacing est in 1985, the Forum likewise promised its participants dramatic "breakthroughs" in personal "transformation"—and all for only a few hundred dollars and the willingness to sit for hours at a stretch in hotel conference rooms. Erhard, Vivo heard, had figured out a way years earlier to force people to come to grips with a variety of problems in their lives and present a powerful way of teaching them how to live more fulfilling lives. The promise of a brighter future had certainly sounded tantalizing to Janis Vivo.

After going through the Forum in 1988, Vivo became an immediate convert to Erhard's philosophy and quickly began to enroll in more of his self-awareness courses, signing up for an advanced six-day course and also registering in a program for those interested in becoming Forum leaders themselves. Vivo spent $900 on yet another Erhard program he called the Sales Course. In that one Vivo and other participants were told they would gain a "mastery . . . beyond merely responding to wants and needs."

Though she had not received any new job offers by the end of the year, Vivo immersed herself further in the Erhard network of courses and programs and soon found herself surrounded by a new circle of friends who shared her enthusiasm about the "transforming" work of Werner Erhard.

In early November Vivo began a new $290 course called the More Time Workshop that required her to write out the goals she wanted to achieve in her life over the next week, the next month, the next year, and well into the future. Vivo wrote in her diary that during the first week alone, she wanted to obtain a new job, a piano, $100,000 in cash, and the marital separation agreement she and her husband had been talking about.

She also desired a new car, preferably a cream-color Jaguar. She wanted to get herself into better physical shape. She hoped to enroll her children's nanny in the Forum. She wanted to begin leading courses herself in the Erhard network. She wanted to amass a personal fortune of at least $10 million. She hoped to learn fluent Russian and to own a vacation home in Northern California's scenic wine country. She wanted a "great sex life forever" and still another vacation cabin in the mountains.

Beyond such physical and material comforts, Vivo described in her diary her desire for a "personal relationship" with Werner Erhard and other executives at Erhard's company; she wanted to be "acknowledged" for her participation in the network. When she was asked as part of the course to outline her goals for her "last month on earth," Vivo wrote that she wanted to "clean up the environment, end hunger in the world, provide for my children's lives [and] end war in the Middle East."

Three days before she settled into her Toyota and switched on the engine in a sealed garage, Vivo had mailed in a check for $1,450 to cover the balance of her $1,800 enrollment fee in another course offered by the network. This one was called Presentation, Negotiation, Enrollment, and was one of Erhard's advanced courses that "inquires into what's needed to produce and sustain real accomplishment in our dealings with others—the unstated principles that govern the simplest as well as the most complex human interactions." By then she had spent nearly $6,400 pursuing the kind of lofty improve-your-life promises held out on every page of the catalog of courses offered by Werner Erhard & Associates.

After taking a few more sips of wine as the Toyota's exhaust system continued to pump deadly fumes into the still air of the garage, Vivo signed her name at the bottom of the page, but she still had a few more things to write. "P.S. over," she wrote in the bottom corner, and turned to the other side of the sheet of notebook paper. The handwriting was still neat, but there was just a trace of unsteadiness—

evidence that the wine and suffocating air were taking their predictable toll on Janis Vivo's body.

"Please do the Forum," she urged one friend. "You're very special to me." After running out of room, and with her handwriting showing more signs of sloppiness now, Vivo wrote a note to her children along the side margin. "I love you guys deeply. You are my hearts. I never wanted to hurt you and I felt that someday I might." Vivo said she wanted her three-year-old daughter to inherit her pearls and to wear them at her high school graduation.

Halfway down the page she struggled to write her final words, knowing by now that her time was running short. She scribbled the pen across the width of the page. The handwriting was messy but the words were unmistakable. "Werner," the dying woman scrawled in handwriting that was now barely legible, "thanks for keeping me alive this long."

Megan Carryer, the young nanny from New Zealand who took care of Vivo's children, arrived home in the late afternoon, after a weeklong holiday vacation at Lake Tahoe. Surprised to find the front door unlocked, Carryer was immediately drawn to the garage, where she heard the sounds of a running engine and a car radio. After prying open the garage, she was stunned to find Janis Vivo's lifeless body reclining against the driver's seat of the Toyota, her hands crossed over her chest. A corked bottle of red wine, three-quarters empty, was lying on the floor of the passenger's side. On the seat, Carryer saw an empty wineglass next to a few pages of notebook paper. The wine had spilled across the first page of Vivo's suicide note, bleeding the ink through to the other side and leaving a blotchy red-purple stain across the top of the paper. Trying her best to remain calm, Carryer gingerly reached into the car, turned off the engine and the radio, and ran to a neighbor's house to call the 911 emergency line. Fire officials arrived a few minutes later and at 5:40 P.M. pronounced Janis Vivo dead. An autopsy performed by the coroner's office for Santa Clara County placed the time of her death about two hours earlier and the cause as carbon monoxide poisoning. After flying home from New York that evening, Vivo's husband, Stephen, was greeted solemnly at the airport by a friend who had arranged to pick up him and the children after hearing what had happened to Janis. "Jan killed herself," the grim-faced friend told Wachter, who reacted to the sad news almost with a numb sense of resignation. He knew his wife had been terribly unhappy; he was not completely surprised to know she had just taken her own life.

Wachter also was not surprised when he came across Werner Erhard's name in his wife's detailed suicide note. Janis had even urged him to enroll in the Forum, insisting that it had been such a positive experience for her and undoubtedly would prove the same for him. He also had seen how the Erhard network had come to dominate her life, providing her with a new circle of friends seemingly intent on little more than increasing her own participation. But it was not until he read her diary entries that Stephen Wachter realized with a chill just how powerful was the influence Werner Erhard had exerted in his wife's life. And perhaps in her death as well.

Not long after Janis Vivo's suicide, Wachter considered filing a lawsuit claiming that Erhard and his network bore some responsibility for what happened. Instead, Wachter contacted Erhard's San Francisco headquarters himself, saying he had spoken to an attorney but preferred to settle the matter privately. Wachter's decision could not have pleased Werner Erhard more. For years lawsuits had generated nothing but bad publicity for him and his work, even though no jury had ever found est or the Forum legally responsible for any injury. Courtroom fights just weren't good business when it came to selling the wonders of personal transformation.

Wachter soon struck a private deal with Erhard's in-house attorney at Werner Erhard & Associates. While disclaiming any legal responsibility for Janis Vivo's death, Erhard agreed to pay a small amount of money—no more than several thousand dollars—to Wachter. In exchange, Wachter promised never to file a lawsuit accusing Erhard or his company of any role in his wife's death.

A young woman had died, and a sympathetic jury or a lawyer's skillful negotiation might have forced Erhard to pay a hefty financial restitution to her husband and children. Instead, Werner Erhard had managed to slip off the hook. Stephen Wachter even received a full refund for the course his wife had not lived long enough to complete.

From Car Lots to California

I need to see that I

am a con man before I can

see my true value.

—Werner Erhard

Jack Rosenberg, with his thin pursed lips and handsome features, gazed out the window of the westward-bound airplane and watched the Pennsylvania landscape rush by below while he fled farther and farther from his past as an unhappy twenty-four-year-old family man and frustrated car salesman. As the plane cruised toward Indianapolis on this late May day in 1960, Rosenberg idly flipped through a year-old copy of *Esquire* magazine, brushing quickly past a profile of comedian Jonathan Winters and a story about a new play, *J.B.*, by Archibald MacLeish. After browsing through a short photo essay on the scenic California coastline, Rosenberg focused his attention on one of the main features in the magazine—an article entitled "The Men Who Made the New Germany."

Spread over several pages, the article profiled in words and photographs sixteen prominent Germans from the varied fields of politics, industry, science, and the arts. All of them were linked by their common devotion to the *Wirtschaftswunder*—the economic miracle—that had been fueling the country's recovery in the decade and a half that had passed since the destruction of the Nazi war machine. Among the profiled luminaries, Rosenberg found himself particularly intrigued by two men. The first, Werner Heisenberg, had been a Nobel Prize–winning atomic scientist whom the Nazis had left unharmed and undisturbed during Hitler's reign, perhaps, as *Esquire* wrote, because they were "intellectually incapable" of penetrating his detached ivory tower.

The second profile that caught Rosenberg's attention was that of Economics Minister Ludwig Erhard, a jovial, cigar-smoking public servant whom the magazine described as "one of Bonn's best brains" and a current favorite to become the nation's next chancellor. *Esquire* considered Erhard, with his keen understanding of the nation's economic situation and a proven ability to get along with a range of German industrialists, to be nothing less than "the living symbol of the boom."

Rosenberg played around with the sounds of the German names mentioned in the pages of the magazine. And then it came to him. Werner Erhard. It sounded both powerful and exotic, a blending of scientific intellectualism and respected statesmanship. Werner Erhard. He definitely liked the sound of it, and injected another note of Aryan purity into the mixture by picking a good, solid German name: Hans. Werner Hans Erhard. Nobody back in Philadelphia, he thought to himself, would ever imagine that Jack Rosenberg would change his name to Werner Hans Erhard. He had been worried ever since making his plans to leave Philadelphia that whatever name he picked, an

2

uncle of his in the city's police department would be able to track him down. But this name was good.

He turned to the pregnant woman sitting beside him, the same woman with whom he had driven to the Newark, New Jersey, airport earlier that day to board a flight to escape to a new life. He asked her what she thought of the name he had picked out. She smiled and nodded in agreement and told him she had picked a new name for herself. Ellen Virginia Erhard was easy enough to pronounce and even had a bit of a poetic lilt to it. Of course, there'd be family back in Philadelphia looking for June Bryde as well as for Jack Rosenberg, so it was important to shed identities and pick up new ones once the plane landed in Indianapolis. A few hours later, when the plane touched ground, a new future lay ahead for Werner and Ellen Erhard.

Jack Rosenberg figured he had every good reason in the world to leave behind the city of his birth and the family that had created such a heavy burden for him. He had been married for more than six years to a high school sweetheart, a slim dark blonde named Patricia Fry, who had discovered that she was pregnant right around the time she and Jack graduated from Norristown High School in June 1953. Tall and attractive, Pat Fry had found herself instantly attracted to the lanky and sharp-featured Rosenberg, whose infectious laugh and penetrating blue eyes caught her attention in the senior year homeroom that they shared at high school. She spent chilly autumn football nights that year clad in the blue and white uniform of the school's majorettes, twirling her baton and step-dancing to the brassy rhythms of the school band. Rosenberg had transferred to Norristown for his senior year, after his family moved to the nearby town of Plymouth Meeting from one of the closer Philadelphia suburbs. Rosenberg signed on to the staff of the school newspaper, the *Hi-Eye*, and also got a small role playing a basketball player in the senior class production of *Our Miss Brooks*. Friends at the school sometimes wondered what the shy and unassuming majorette saw in the brash and arrogant Rosenberg, while others were even more curious when the two announced their plans to be married at the Fry family church a few months after graduation.

About fifty guests sat in the dark-wood pews lined up beneath the high-vaulted ceiling at the Trinity Evangelical and Reformed Church for the wedding of Patricia Fry and Jack Rosenberg on September 26, 1953. The following March, Pat gave birth to a daughter named Clare Susan Rosenberg. Less than a year later, another baby girl arrived and was named Anita Lynn. A son, Jack Rosenberg, Jr., was born in 1958 and a fourth child, Deborah, arrived at Christmas 1959. For Jack Rosenberg, the immediate demands of being a husband and a father directly out of high school forced him into a succession of dead-end jobs that paid little and offered even less hope for the future. For a while, he worked at an employment office and later took a job at a meat packing plant. After that, he helped out at one of the Philadelphia restaurants in which his father worked as a waiter and a manager. After leaving there, Rosenberg signed on with a local construction company, where his job involved working up estimates for customers interested in remodeling their homes or businesses. Finally Rosenberg thought he'd try his hand at selling cars. He liked the business of selling and quickly discovered a knack for the high-pressure, slick-talking tactics that have long been the hallmark of aggressive auto salesmen in America.

His fledgling success on the car lots only seemed to encourage Rosenberg's increasing alienation from his family. Feeling flush with a little money in his pocket, he much preferred the bellicose carousing and womanizing favored by his fellow salesmen to the mundane domestic isolation that awaited him at home with his wife and growing family. It was a pattern that would be repeated over and over again long after Jack Rosenberg transformed himself Werner Erhard.

Rosenberg was the grandson of Nathan Rosenberg, an immigrant Jewish tailor, and his wife, Clara, both of whom had arrived from Russia at the turn of the century and settled into a small brick row house on Mountain Street—one of an endless series of narrow, cobblestoned streets in South Philadelphia that marked the city's Orthodox Jewish ghetto. These were the neighborhoods of peddlers and butchers and hatmakers, Old World Jews with ethnic-sounding names like Tannenbaum and Abromovitz and Zopolonsky—and Rosenberg. By the depression year of 1933, Nathan and Clara's son Joe was twenty-three years old, living with his parents and working as a waiter.

That was the year he met Dorothy Clauson, whose similarities with Joe Rosenberg began and ended with her own job as a waitress. With solid WASP roots grounded in New England, the Clausons lived on one of the tree-lined streets of Germantown, in northwest Philadelphia, and worshiped faithfully at the local Episcopalian church. Despite their differences, Joe Rosenberg and Dorothy Clauson embarked on a whirlwind courtship that culminated in their marriage in August 1933. At the Rosenbergs' insistence, the couple was married by an Orthodox rabbi, though only after Joe had insisted that his wife indeed was Jewish despite her decidedly non-Jewish name and appearance.

Within months, however, the marriage ran into trouble, and Joe and Dorothy separated in 1934. Their respective families awaited the anticipated divorce, undoubtedly relieved that the odd union would soon be at an end. Instead, Dorothy informed her husband early in 1935 that she had "accidentally" gotten pregnant, which led to an uneasy reconciliation. Three years after their son Jack was born on September 5, 1935, Joe Rosenberg resolved one thorny family problem by converting to Christianity. Though Jack continued to see his Jewish relatives, his own religious upbringing took place within the walls of the Clauson family church, the Church of the Holy Nativity in Germantown, where he was baptized John Paul Rosenberg in February 1945, at the age of nine.

From his earliest years, Jack's strained relations with his parents were shaped indelibly by the knowledge that he had never been planned, and his insecurities as an unwanted child were exacerbated because his parents did not have their other children—a daughter and two sons—until long after their oldest had reached his teens.

Married himself and employed selling Ford Mercurys and Lincolns for a prominent Philadelphia auto dealer, in 1959 Rosenberg met an attractive and quiet blonde named June Bryde, who lived in the city with her family while working as a secretary in a local real estate office. Jack and June quickly began seeing each other, although Rosenberg at first neglected to inform her that he was married with children. Several months into the affair, June discovered she was pregnant. Rosenberg responded to the news by arranging to get a phony driver's license and other pieces of identification under the name of Jack Frost, which he had already been using on the car lot because he thought it was an easier name for customers to remember. The false name was part of his plan to steal away from the city and marry June out of town. The fact that he already was married to another woman did not deter him.

Unfortunately for Rosenberg, his wife, Pat, and his mother learned about his affair, which succeeded only in increasing his hostility toward both of them. Soon he had a new plan to get away from his family and Philadelphia. On March 29, 1960, he and June—who now knew about Rosenberg's double life—drove the seventy miles that separated Philadelphia from Bel Air, Maryland, not far from the Pennsylvania border. That afternoon he and June applied for a Maryland marriage license under the names of Curt Wilhelm VonSavage and Celeste Marie Radell. On the application for the license, Rosenberg accurately listed his age as twenty-four and his occupation as that of a salesman. But VonSavage, he wrote, had been born in New Jersey and currently lived in the small New Jersey town of Phillipsburg. Three days later, on April 1, a Methodist minister in Bel Air united the covert couple in marriage. Jack Rosenberg had committed bigamy. Wedding vows completed, the couple returned to Philadelphia, where June Bryde quietly resumed her job at the real estate office while Rosenberg continued selling cars and living with Pat and the children in an apartment in Hatboro, a commuter town north of Philadelphia off the turnpike.

Not long after, "Jack Frost" abruptly announced to his boss he was quitting and moving out of town. On May 25, 1960, Rosenberg picked up June from her real estate office and drove to the Newark airport, where they left the car in the parking lot and boarded a flight to Indianapolis. More than a dozen years would pass before Rosenberg's family would hear from him again. By the time they landed a few hours later, Jack Rosenberg and June Bryde were ready to begin new lives as Werner and Ellen Erhard.

After arriving in Indianapolis, the couple boarded a train to St.

Louis, where Erhard found work selling used cars at two or three different lots around the city. He and Ellen also made arrangements with an attorney to give up the baby she was carrying for adoption immediately after the birth. Meanwhile, Erhard had struck up a friendship with another fast talker named Orlando Gaut, who soon convinced Erhard to give up the car business and travel out west with him for a new venture selling correspondence courses in the operation of heavy construction equipment. Erhard was growing restless in St. Louis so the idea of moving on caught his fancy even though he did not even own a car. He solved that dilemma by packing Ellen and their meager belongings into a Buick Special that he had agreed to sell on consignment and simply taking off.

Driving west in a stolen car without much money, the Erhards often spent the night in the Buick. Once Ellen woke up to the jarring sounds of Erhard yelling and banging on the car. The heater had not been working correctly, which had angered him so much that he pounded furiously on the car until he managed to punch the heater right out. On other nights the couple would check into a motel, only to steal away early in the morning without paying the bill. Erhard also avoided arrest by periodically screwing on new license plates that he had taken from one of the car lots back in St. Louis.

Although their original destination had been California, Gaut and Erhard were soon traveling in the Pacific Northwest, where they continued to sell the correspondence course, first in Seattle and then throughout the surrounding area. Eventually Erhard ended up in Spokane, where he abandoned the correspondence course venture with Gaut and found a new job selling *Encyclopedia Britannica*'s Great Books series to doctors, lawyers, and others along a route that stretched from Spokane back to Seattle. By 1963 Erhard had switched jobs again, this time taking a sales position for a division of *Parents* magazine that sold encyclopedias door to door.

Early that year a vacuum cleaner salesman named Michael Maurer answered one of Erhard's ads in a Seattle newspaper for sales representatives for a line of children's books. A smooth-talking pitch-man himself, Maurer soon found himself in the compelling presence of someone he instantly recognized as a master salesman. Erhard would persist with customers on whom other salesmen would long ago have given up. He simply refused to take no for an answer, grinding down his "marks" until they gave him an order. At one door, Maurer watched in awe as Erhard spent more than two hours with a reluctant couple who finally succumbed to his don't-tell-me-no pitch.

Erhard's territory for the *Parents* door-to-door sales operation extended throughout the Northwest and into Northern California. At Erhard's request, Maurer traveled to San Francisco to open an office for *Parents* in the Bay Area. Before long Maurer's impressive sales figures prompted Erhard to abandon the Northwest territory and move to San Francisco. From there, he figured, he could oversee Maurer's sales efforts while trying to duplicate the same impressive results even farther south in Los Angeles.

Erhard and Maurer worked out of an office on the fourth floor of the Flood Building on Market Street, in the heart of the city's bustling downtown business district. Working with as many as 150 salespeople at a time, Erhard also regularly ran newspaper ads to recruit new people because of the high turnover rate. Bringing in thirty or forty people at a time, Erhard would pitch the promise of great results and handsome commissions, relying on his own smooth charm, energetic charisma, and flashing smile to convince them to work for him. For those who signed up, he would hold morning pep rallies in the office complete with high-spirited razzmatazz and cheery sing-songs. Out of the offices they would burst, belting out the words to "Happy Days Are Here Again" while getting ready to tackle another grueling day of door-knocking and bell-ringing on the streets of San Francisco and surrounding Bay Area communities.

Erhard rarely talked about his past, even when friends like Maurer would ask him about his background. Sometimes he would vaguely mention that he was from "back East" or had worked in the "car business." So far he seemed to have successfully shed his previous life. In Philadelphia, his first wife and family were left without a clue as to his whereabouts. As far as they could tell, Jack Rosenberg had simply vanished without leaving a trace.

During the next few years Werner and Ellen Erhard moved several times, once for Erhard to open a new sales office in Los Angeles and later to work in another office in Virginia, only a few hours' drive from his abandoned Philadelphia family. A daughter, Celeste, had been born in August 1963 and a second daughter, Adair, arrived in November 1964, after the Erhards had moved back to the Bay Area and into an apartment in Sausalito, a picturesque harborfront town in Marin County, just north of San Francisco.

Fifteen months later Ellen and Adair ended up unwittingly on the front page of the *Marin Independent Journal*, their photograph above a caption that read "Lucky Child." The accompanying article informed readers that the baby girl living in Apartment 204 of the Cote d'Azur apartment building in Sausalito had fallen, apparently by accident, more than forty feet from the deck of the Erhard apartment to the surf below. Amazingly, Adair had not suffered any serious injuries but had been cushioned from the blow by the incoming tide. Identifying Werner Erhard as a sales manager for *Parents*, the article reported that he had been home at the time of the incident but had been unaware that his infant daughter was playing with her older sister on the apartment deck.

The apparently successful transformation from a Philadelphia car salesman named Jack Rosenberg to a San Francisco book salesman named Werner Erhard did not change the old Rosenberg habit of romancing women to whom he was not married. He usually preferred to hire attractive women for his book sales force, and he rarely hesitated to seduce those whom he found sexually appealing. Between work and his extramarital socializing, Erhard had little time to spend with Ellen and his children, often seeing them only for a few minutes late in the evening after one of his employees—often one of the women he was seeing—drove him home from San Francisco across the Golden Gate Bridge. On some evenings the night security officer who patrolled the grounds of the Cote d'Azur would see Erhard arriving home well past midnight in the company of women who enjoyed parking with him and talking for a while before he went inside.

On the night of June 3, 1967, William LaValley, the night patrol officer, drove up to Erhard's car and asked him to turn off the car's headlights since the beams interfered with his patrol duties. Erhard exploded in anger at the request, jumping out of the car and threatening to toss the startled security guard over a railing and down a steep embankment to the water below. Erhard's companion, an attractive employee named Gonneke Spits, remained quiet in the car.

Sitting at the wheel of his own car, LaValley wrapped his arm tightly around the steering wheel and turned on a bright red light, forcing Erhard to back away. Later that night Erhard was arrested for battery and disturbing the peace by San Rafael sheriff's deputies. The battery charges were later dropped, leaving Erhard to pay a $44 fine and receive a sentence of six months' probation. A year later, however, the conviction was formally set aside, leaving Erhard's criminal record officially expunged. Around the same time, in June 1968, Ellen Erhard gave birth to her third child, a son she and her husband called St. John, whose name was more casually pronounced as "Sinjin."

The following year, after *Parents* magazine had decided to close down its door-to-door sales operation, Erhard took a similar sales job in San Francisco, this time for a large direct marketing company, the Grolier Society Inc., that sold encyclopedias and other children's educational materials door to door. For Erhard, the switch involved little more than a new office address. He took several members of his loyal sales force—including a few young women with whom he had been having occasional affairs—with him into the new job. Erhard set up shop on the second floor of a building in San Francisco's colorful North Beach district, directly above Enrico's Café, a longtime popular gathering spot located next to a nightclub that specialized in female impersonators.

In 1970 the California attorney general's office accused Grolier in two different lawsuits of using fraudulent and misleading techniques to sell its books, including outright lies and deceptive sales pitches aimed at tricking people into buying encyclopedias. Although Erhard was not named in the lawsuits, which ultimately resulted in an injunction against Grolier selling encyclopedias in California, the message seemed clear enough. By the time Erhard left Grolier in 1971, he had settled on a dramatically new product to sell.

T w o

THE CURIOUS
ROOTS OF EST

The problem is not that so many

people are constantly looking for enlightenment

these days, but that so many are

constantly finding it.

—R. D. ROSEN
Journalist, author of *Psychobabble*

I n the summer of 1966, while Werner Erhard was busy selling encyclopedias, *Look* magazine—one of the nation's most popular fea-
ture magazines with nearly 8 million subscribers—came out with a
special issue devoted entirely to California. Produced by some twenty
editors, writers, and photographers, *Look*'s California issue presented
a state on the cutting edge of culture and ideas in the United States.

Throughout its picture-filled pages, the magazine announced nothing less than a revolution within the borders of the nation's most populous and trend-setting state. Much of that revolution was being waged in the name of a fledgling phenomenon described by the magazine as the "human potential movement."

That phrase had actually been coined about a year earlier by George Leonard, *Look*'s West Coast bureau chief based in San Francisco. Leonard by then had developed a close friendship with Michael Murphy, a young dark-haired San Franciscan who, in 1962, had opened the doors to the Esalen Institute, billed as one of the country's first "growth centers" devoted solely to exploring the frontiers of the human psyche. Located along a rugged strip of Big Sur coastline a few hours south of San Francisco (and named for a tribe of Indians who once lived there), Esalen quickly established itself as the epicenter of the nascent human potential movement while Murphy became one of the movement's founding fathers. Leonard, a gangly and serious-minded Georgia native, and Murphy, a smiling, spirited California native, soon embarked on a giddy quest to promote their new movement.

In *Look*'s special California issue, spearheaded by Leonard, Murphy appeared on a page of photos headlined "Turned-on People." As he looked out across the expansive Pacific Ocean, there was no mistaking the connotation. The dramatic coastline, on which Esalen itself was perched, literally defined the edge of a nation while symbolizing the farthest stretches of its cultural, social, and moral boundaries.

Born and raised in Salinas, Michael Murphy was the grandson of a prominent local doctor whose practice included the delivery of some of the town's babies. One of Dr. Murphy's deliveries grew up to be the writer John Steinbeck, who is said to have modeled the two brothers in his novel *East of Eden* after Michael and his younger brother, Dennis. Michael Murphy's introduction to eastern spiritualism occurred in 1950, during his sophomore year at Stanford, when he wandered into a lecture on comparative religion. After further academic studies, the inquisitive Murphy spent eighteen months in an ashram (a spiritual center) in Pondicherry, India. The ashram, which accommodated some 2,000 people at a time, had been built by Sri Aurobindo, one of the giant spiritual figures in India who had died only a few years before Murphy arrived.

After returning to the United States, Murphy hatched a plan to turn a parcel of longtime family property at Big Sur into a center to explore his expanding interests in philosophy, psychology, and other disciplines relating to the human mind and spirit. At the time, some of the buildings on the Murphy property were occupied by a holy-roller evangelical sect. Writer Henry Miller lived nearby in a cabin and ambled down the road with his friends from time to time to soak in the natural baths on the Murphy land. To keep out unwelcome intruders, Murphy's elderly grandmother had hired a live-in caretaker (and future gonzo journalist) named Hunter Thompson to stand guard over the grounds. A young folk singer with long jet-black hair and a golden voice named Joan Baez occupied a neighboring cabin with her boyfriend.

Murphy's new center, known first as Big Sur Hot Springs, officially got under way in the fall of 1962 with a series of seminars entitled "The Human Potentiality." Within a few years the center had already become more widely known as Esalen and as a gathering place for the leaders of the growing human potential movement. Frederick Perls—he insisted that everyone call him Fritz—installed himself as Esalen's resident guru and established the place as a head-quarters for his brand of gestalt therapy. He arrived at Esalen in the spring of 1964, and within a few years he had managed to become one of the human potential movement's first gurus. His fame quickly spread, thanks in large part to a short poem he wrote called the "Gestalt Prayer" that soon found its way onto posters and cards, often accompanied by photographs of the bearded cherub himself. The poem, perhaps more than anything else Perls ever wrote, quickly became an anthem for the budding human potential movement.

Years later Werner Erhard would list Perls's gestalt therapy methods as one of the influencing forces in the creation of est. More significantly, Erhard also adapted some of the ways in which Perls—in contradiction to his own stated philosophy toward life—dealt with other people. "In one way," Walter Truett Anderson wrote of Perls in a 1983 book on Esalen, "he simply didn't give a damn what they thought: he would violate rules, behave outrageously, insult anybody, do whatever seemed to suit his own personal standards. But in another way, he was hugely needy, mad for approval, forever striving to look good. His hunger for love and attention matched his hunger for many other things." No more accurate description of Werner Erhard could have been written.

Alan Watts, a former Episcopalian minister and a disciple of Zen Buddhism, was another frequent visitor during Esalen's early years. Settling in San Francisco after leaving his native England in the 1950s, the irreverent and bohemian Watts had first shown up at Murphy's Big Sur lodge in 1962. By then Watts had already been identified by the media as Zen's leading Western interpreter and could be heard giving radio lectures or speaking to enthusiastic followers on board his Sausalito houseboat, not far from where Erhard years later would dock his own floating domicile.

Between 1965 and 1968, the growth of the human potential movement in California could be measured, at least in quantitative terms, simply by the expanding bulk of the Esalen catalog. The 1965 edition described twenty different programs available to Esalen's consciousness-seekers. Three years later the psyche-expanding curriculum had expanded to 120 courses. "You could take belly dancing at Esalen, and movement and sensory awareness," Adam Smith wrote in his 1975 book, *Powers of Mind.* "Or you could sit on the lawn and eat a single grape very slowly. Or you could find six or eight people rolling over and over each other in a sandwich, like kids do: it's all right to do that as a kid in our society, but not as an adult. It's all right to touch, said Esalen. It does your head good."

While Esalen was growing in popularity—and providing, as journalist Tom Wolfe once described, "lube jobs for the personality"—the American Association for Humanistic Psychology in August 1968 was holding its annual convention inside the Fairmont Hotel atop San Francisco's Nob Hill. Inspired by the guiding influence of Abraham Maslow, the humanistic psychology group had been formed in 1961 and was nurtured by the ideas and theories of free-spirited psychologists and writers that, besides Maslow, included Rollo May, Aldous

Huxley, Arthur Koestler, Lewis Mumford, and Carl Rogers. Rogers had placed his own indelible stamp on the human potential movement by stressing the psychotherapeutic use of small "encounter groups," which he once described as "the most significant social invention of the century." Years later, however, the prominent psychologist would place some distance between his own enthusiasm for group therapy and the ersatz mass-audience approach that Erhard would adapt for his ballroom-size est training sessions. "I've never been through est, and I don't think I want to," Rogers told a pair of interviewers in the mid-1970s. "Their goals are not too bad, actually, but their means are horrendously authoritarian. I feel that they have lost completely the distinction between means and ends."

Although California hardly held a monopoly on human potential activities in the United States, the state—and more specifically the San Francisco Bay Area—was more heavily saturated with the outward signs of the movement than any other single region in the country. From nude encounter sessions and gestalt therapy weekends to yoga classes and meditation groups, the seeker of an expanded human mind or spirit could find just about anything that the heart or mind or body desired by traveling down the mountainous coast to Esalen or merely wandering through the colorful streets of San Francisco. There one could find saffron-robed Hare Krishnas dancing through the streets with their tambourines, drums, and meditative chants. Or one might encounter a character who called himself "Sufi Sam" and who taught folk dances while introducing his audiences to the exotic tenets of Sufism, a mystical branch of Islam. Not many years later a newly elected California governor named Jerry Brown treated his surprised guests at an annual prayer breakfast to songs performed by a Sufi choir from Marin County.

Werner Erhard, living in the grueling world of door-to-door sales, was quick to recognize the potential of a symbiotic connection between the practice of commercialism and the free-flowing ideas from the human potential movement that seemed to be exploding all around San Francisco. He already had heard some of Alan Watts's radio talks and grew increasingly curious about the man's irreverent approach to Zen. In the conduct of his own life, Watts hardly came across as anyone's idea of a monastic-oriented spiritual traveler walking in the footsteps of devout Zen masters. Instead, he was a man who savored the pleasures of tobacco and drink and who made no secret of his various affairs with a stream of women while carrying on the life of a carefree bohemian aboard his houseboat docked near Erhard's Sausalito apartment. Erhard hoped to enjoy his own free-swinging life-style, though he would have to wait a few more years before indulging his own fantasies of life as an admired guru.

While the human potential movement was blossoming all around him, Erhard was busy learning about other strains of pop psychology and motivational theories, some of which had been around for decades.

His own evolution from book salesman to mind salesman would hinge on a pair of self-help books that he had discovered during his book-selling career. The first of the lot—Napoleon Hill's *Think and Grow Rich*—has established itself over the past seven decades as an American self-help classic ever since its original publication at the height of the Great Depression in 1937. Hill said he based his book's recipe for success on insights he received from the likes of Andrew Carnegie and hundreds of other wealthy American industrialists and moguls. "Be prepared, when you begin to put the philosophy of Think and Grow Rich into action," read a publisher's note that accompanied a 1960 paperback reprint of Hill's enormously successful book, "for a changed life which will not only ease the trials and stresses of living but will also prepare you for the accumulation of material riches in abundance."

By the time Werner Erhard concocted his own prescriptive program for self-improvement, he simply added his name to a litany of self-help promoters that stretched back far into American history.

Not surprisingly, the original American notions of self-help were integrally related to religious devotion. In colonial times, Puritan leaders distributed pamphlets that offered self-improvement tips on leading good, honest, God-fearing Protestant lives. A century later Alexis de Tocqueville—one of the most astute observers ever to chronicle the American experience—discovered similar strains during his travels throughout the young United States in the 1830s. "Strange sects endeavor [in America] to strike out extraordinary paths of eternal happiness," wrote the wandering Frenchman. "Religious insanity is very common."

Throughout the nineteenth century, the swelling American population had available to it a myriad of self-help books on topics that ranged from homemaking and sexual purity to methods for achieving business and commercial success as the society grew more industrialized and urban and complicated. By the close of the century, a crop of modern "positive thinkers" had arisen, preaching the miracles of "mind cures" and other mental and spiritual therapies aimed at lifting individuals out of the morose existence of daily life. Years before Norman Vincent Peale touted his *Power of Positive Thinking*, Americans were being introduced to a bevy of "mind-cure principles" that, stripped to their core, bore uncanny resemblances to the basic tenets of movements that would burst forward decades later led by the curious likes of Scientology founder L. Ron Hubbard and the "source" of est, Werner Erhard.

The mind-cure movement of the nineteenth century had much in common with its twentieth-century counterparts. Concerned largely with the well-being of an individual, the mind curists cared little for the overall state of the society or the common good. The philosopher William James, in particular, called to task the nineteenth-century positive thinkers for failing to grapple with the existence of evil. Instead, James often observed how the various mind-cure groups seemed to share a revealing emphasis on self-absorption, on feeling good, on instant gratification. "The mind-cure principles," wrote James in 1902, "are beginning to so pervade the air that one catches their spirit second hand. One hears of 'The Gospel of Relaxation,' of the 'Don't Worry Movement,' of people who repeat to themselves 'Youth, health, vigor!' when dressing in the morning."

Had James lived in San Francisco in the 1960s and 1970s, he would have realized quickly that the American zeal for self-absorption, self-love, and instant cures of the soul remained as vibrant and appealing as ever. After all, some of the same themes that marked the mind-cure movement were reflected as well in the human potential offshoots of the positive-thinking theories of the earlier twentieth century. With their reliance on an ersatz spirituality, all of these groups helped to fill a unique American hunger for achieving a sense of innocence lost. But always an innocence attached to individual needs, not the collective good of the society. "The problem is that these movements don't teach you to weep for the world, only to weep for yourself," a friend once remarked to the author Sam Keen. Such sentiments very closely matched those ascribed to the mind-cure groups of a previous century.

As the twin strains of mind cure and positive thinking converged in the person of Werner Erhard, he looked to the simplistic ideas of Napoleon Hill as a rich source of homilies and tenets that eventually would work themselves into both the core tenets of est and into Erhard's own thirst for fortune and power. "Wishing will not bring riches," wrote Hill in a passage from *Think and Grow Rich* that surely must have piqued Werner Erhard's interest. "But desiring riches with a state of mind that becomes an obsession, then planning definite ways and means to acquire riches, and backing those plans with persistence which does not recognize failure, will bring riches."

Hill's book also played an influential role in helping to formulate many of the key ideas that Erhard later worked into est and his other self-awareness courses. Beginning in 1971, Erhard started to amass his own personal fortune by telling at first hundreds, and then later thousands, and then later still hundreds of thousands of people that there are no such things as "victims" in the world, whether they are people set upon by muggers in dark alleyways or hospital patients suffering from cancer and other debilitating diseases.

A particularly disturbing example occurred years later when, during an est session, Erhard set about convincing a Holocaust survivor and est participant that she—along with family members who had perished in a Nazi death camp—was "responsible" for her own predicament. Neither the Nazis nor Hitler, Erhard said later, created the woman's "experience" of the concentration camp. They were only an illusion. The reality, said Erhard, was that she had created her Holocaust experience.

But Erhard's core message was not new, even though he would come to call himself the inventor of a new form of transformation.

18

Napoleon Hill already had presaged Erhard's pivotal argument in his book. "There are millions of people," wrote Hill, "who believe themselves 'doomed' to poverty and failure, because of some strange force over which they believe they have no control. They are the creators of their own 'misfortunes,' because of this negative belief. . . ."

Erhard also likely discovered in Hill's writing on the "magic of self suggestion" other vital secrets that would come to play a crucial role in enabling Erhard to gloss over some of the darker aspects of his personal life. "It is a well-known fact," wrote Hill, "that one comes, finally, to believe whatever one repeats to one's self, whether the statement be true or false. If a man repeats a lie over and over, he will eventually accept the lie as truth. Moreover, he will believe it to be the truth."

Werner Erhard must have been absolutely thrilled when he reached the chapter in Hill's book that outlined the author's thoughts on the "power of the master mind," which included his key theory about the "driving force" of sex. "Sex energy," wrote Hill, "is the creative energy of all geniuses. There never has been, and never will be a great leader, builder, or artist lacking in this driving force of sex." Hill also made it clear, in a passage that certainly could not have escaped Erhard's rapt attention, just how important sexual energy was to the business of selling. "Master salesmen attain the status of mastery in selling," he wrote, "because they either consciously or unconsciously transmute the energy of sex into sales enthusiasm."

Erhard, with his own record of seduction and sexual conquests, undoubtedly found in Hill's motivational writing a rationale for his own sexual exploits. After all, sex—at least in the get-rich formula of Napoleon Hill—amounted to little more than part of a salesman's arsenal of weapons in the ongoing battle to sell more, to be more productive, to be more successful.

The other book to which Erhard paid close attention was published in 1960, years after Hill's self-help classic. Written by a plastic surgeon named Maxwell Maltz, *Psycho-Cybernetics* was billed as a revolutionary fusion of the "new science" of cybernetics with traditional theories of human psychology. Cybernetics, Maltz told his readers, dealt with the hows and whys of machines—how they work and why they do the things they do. By applying the science of machines to the human mind, Maltz argued that men and women could learn to lead happier, more productive, more successful lives aided by a series of mental exercises and processes that ranged from learning a "happiness habit" to dehypnotizing themselves of false beliefs.

Cybernetics had indeed emerged as a new legitimate science during World War II—a field of scientific inquiry, prompted by the U.S. government's immediate need to master the mechanical intricacies of modern warfare. Defined as the study of "communication and control in the animal and the machine," its name had been coined by a mathematician at the Massachusetts Institute of Technology named Norbert Wiener. After the war ended, the new science of cybernetics produced amazing new breakthroughs in automatic control systems, ranging from self-triggering toasters to automatic washing machines.

Maltz, of course, had little interest in toasters and washing machines when he grafted assorted theories of human psychology onto the machinistic application of cybernetics. He wrote that people could easily change their own self-image. The key, he said, was to focus on "experience" rather than on things people have learned intellectually. Again, those same terms would later be mirrored in Erhard's programs, in which trainers and later Forum leaders would harshly ridicule participants for using words such as "I think" or "I feel." Paramount to the est philosophy was the idea of direct experience. In fact, Erhard turned that crucial distinction into a successful selling point to get paying customers into hotel ballroom seats. Est graduates for years were admonished never to tell others about what occurred inside est training sessions. It was okay only to "share" their "experience" without explaining any of the details of the training. A decade earlier Maltz had included an identical message in his book: "This book," he wrote in the preface to *Psycho-Cybernetics*, "has been designed not merely to be read but to be experienced."

After he started est, Erhard told interviewers he had spent the decade of the 1960s toiling away in the field of "executive development," which explained his enthusiastic interest in a range of motivational theories and disciplines that ranged from Napoleon Hill and Dale Carnegie to Maxwell Maltz and the founders of the human potential movement. Although the truth was that, from 1962 through the end of the decade, Werner Erhard had earned his living as a sales manager, he had only to step out of his office to see the signs of a human potential movement sweeping across San Francisco, if not quite the rest of the country.

As the 1960s came to a close, Erhard was about to make more discoveries that would pave the way for his own entrance into the human potential movement. Werner Erhard, a former car salesman peddling books door to door, now stood on the verge of becoming Werner Erhard, the guru.

Three

ERHARD AND THE SCIENTOLOGISTS

I have a lot of respect for L. Ron Hubbard,

and I consider him to be a genius and perhaps less

acknowledged than he ought to be.

—WERNER ERHARD

P eter Monk was a civil engineer by training, but it was for an entirely different purpose that he poked his head into the doorway
of a jewelry shop in Sausalito one day in the late 1960s and made an
unusual request in his refined English accent.

"I'm looking for some chairs," Monk asked of those standing
inside the shop. "Do you know where I might find some good, sturdy
folding chairs?"

Flat broke at the time, Monk was living aboard a friend's houseboat in Sausalito and trying to make good on a plan to offer local courses in an ersatz religion he had joined called Scientology. Using an overextended credit card, Monk had rented a small office in Sausalito and now was walking along Bridgeway Avenue, near the center of town, popping his head into each store and wondering if anyone might be able to help him out with a few extra chairs.

A native of Toronto, Monk had been raised in England but migrated to the San Francisco Bay Area in 1959. It wasn't long after his arrival that he began immersing himself in a variety of esoteric psychology movements that were spreading throughout the area as part of the 1960s' Age of Aquarius. It hardly came as an accident, then, that Monk found himself fascinated with the Scientology movement, which he first discovered not in San Francisco but back in England, during a seven-week vacation in the mid-1960s. Intrigued by the thoughts and ideas that Scientology offered, Monk wasted no time enrolling himself in an introductory program called the communications course. Soon after Monk decided to train further at the London headquarters of Scientology's founder, a former science fiction writer named L. Ron Hubbard. Increasingly excited about his new studies, Monk found himself coming up with ideas about spreading the gospel to wider audiences. What better way, he thought to himself, than to find a good salesman back in the States who could be trained in Scientology and then put his expertise to work to sell the wisdom of L. Ron Hubbard? Excited by his plan to combine Scientology and entrepreneurial skills, Monk returned to the Bay Area in 1968, ready to find his salesman and start selling Scientology.

Fortunately for Monk, Michael Maurer, the former vacuum cleaner salesman who now worked for Werner Erhard, happened to be shopping at the Sausalito jewelry store in which Monk asked about folding chairs. Maurer mentioned that he had some packed away in storage and that Monk might be able to use them once they were shipped out to the Bay Area. The two men fell into a discussion of Monk's plan to introduce Scientology to the area, and Maurer was fascinated as he listened to Monk spell out the seeming wonders of

Hubbard's philosophy, complete with tantalizing promises of human transformation and mind-curing miracles.

As he began dabbling in Scientology, Maurer knew this was exactly the kind of discovery that should be shared with his friend Werner Erhard. After all, he knew that Erhard was always watching out for new motivational theories to try out on his teams of booksellers— Erhard's own personal lab rats back at the office.

Just as Maurer expected, Erhard was quickly taken by Scientology—the organization, the wealth of materials that screamed out Hubbard's name at every turn, the tantalizing technology and courses that spread the Hubbard gospel to his flocks that gathered under the Scientology banner. Erhard wasted no time in asking Maurer to set up a meeting with Monk. Maybe the three of them could figure out some way to do business together, Erhard thought.

But first Erhard decided he would learn much more about Scientology itself. In the late summer of 1968, Monk agreed to lead Erhard through a series of "auditing" sessions, an integral part of Scientology akin to going to confession or confiding secrets to a private therapist. But Hubbard's own view of the path toward spiritual and mental enlightenment called for more than mere confessional words. Years earlier he had introduced to his followers a strange contraption that he called the e-meter, a crude version of a lie detector that, he claimed, revealed through the brain's electrical charges deeply embedded traumatic memories known in Scientology jargon as engrams. Ultimately, Hubbard proclaimed, the objective of Scientology was to clear one's brain of disturbing engrams through a rigorous course of auditing along with other costly training courses and methods. According to Hubbard, by clutching onto two tin cans, attached by wires to a set of flickering needles, anyone could be trained to free him- or herself of the menacing engrams.

Hubbard was hardly the first person to realize that a machine could be used to measure skin response to such things as excitement and emotional stress. But he proved to be the most successful one ever to turn the relatively simple device into a hugely lucrative source of income. The original e-meter had been invented by one of Hubbard's early adherents, and the machine quickly was incorporated into the Scientology auditing procedure. By the time Werner Erhard met Peter Monk, Scientology had branched off into the field of franchise auditors, permitting those who were "trained" to use e-meters to conduct auditing sessions, largely as a way of promoting Scientology and attracting new followers.

Impressed by Monk's auditing sessions, Erhard delved further into Scientology literature and lessons. Between August and December of 1968, he purchased several books from the San Francisco Scientology office and enrolled both himself and some of his sales employees in the introductory communications course. In October a local Scientology official wrote to Erhard asking him about his interest in joining the staff. Scientology had a place for enthusiastic new converts like Werner Erhard. Although Erhard did not respond to the offer, he continued to study Scientology over the next several months, gradually rising through the various training levels — "grades" in Scientology jargon — that marked the path toward ultimate enlightenment. When a routine letter was sent in August 1969 letting him know that he had passed "Grade II" in his Scientology studies, Erhard immediately responded with his own letter claiming that he had reached Grade IV.

It's likely by then that Erhard had learned something about Hubbard's background — or at least the official version of the life and career of its red-haired, ruddy-faced founder. After years of boldly concocting a colorful past for himself, Hubbard had given Scientology's true believers a portrait of himself as a brilliant writer, philosopher, creator, explorer, and excavator of the mind whose research and insights had unlocked the ultimate secrets of human existence. In the early 1950s, he had created and unveiled "the modern science of Dianetics," through which he claimed to have discovered the "hidden source of all psychosomatic ills and human aberration." Application of Dianetic principles, Hubbard told his followers in those early years, could help them cure everything from ulcers to the common cold.

Lafayette Ronald Hubbard, born in Tilden, Nebraska, in 1911, first made a name for himself churning out pulp fiction stories in the 1930s with titles such as *The Green Gods, Sea Fangs, Dead Men Kill,* and *The Carnival of Death.* For a time he savored visions of Hollywood glamour after Columbia Pictures bought one of his stories to turn into a Saturday matinee serial. It turned out to be the only script he ever sold to Hollywood. By the end of the 1930s, Hubbard had turned his writing career in the direction of science fiction and westerns. Interrupted by World War II, Hubbard served in the navy, later complaining to the Veterans Administration that his military service resulted in "suicidal inclinations" and a "seriously affected" mind. In later years he would be described, falsely, in Scientology brochures as an "extensively decorated" wartime hero who had been crippled and blinded in action, only to be miraculously cured through his own invented "religion" of Scientology.

After the war Hubbard resumed his writing career by returning to pulp stories, churning out such titles as *Blood on His Spurs, Killer's Law,* and *Ole Doc Methuselah.* His writing finally hit paydirt in 1950, when he touched off a short-lived national craze resulting from a piece he wrote for *Astounding Science Fiction* magazine in which he unveiled a new "science of the mind" that he called Dianetics. Hubbard quickly followed up his magazine story about his new discovery with a full-length book. In his rambling book, Hubbard spelled out his curious theories of engrams, auditing, and other Scientology practices.

Hubbard's amazing "discovery" of the new science of Dianetics became an immediate sensation, fed by his beguilingly simplistic notions of using the untapped power of the human brain to solve any world problem, from the threat of nuclear annihilation to the scourges of famine, disease, and poverty. Hubbard seized on the surprising success of Dianetics by quickly devising a lucrative way to mass-market his science fiction–tinged ideas. He announced a $500 course—a considerable sum in the 1950s—to train people to become Dianetics auditors, after which they would be equipped themselves to erase menacing engrams.

Almost overnight, "Dianetic groups" began forming on college campuses, while Dianetics parties became a sudden social fad. By July 1950 Hubbard's book hit the top of the *Los Angeles Times* bestseller list despite the mounting criticism aimed at Dianetics from groups such as the American Psychological Association. Writing in

The New York Times Book Review on July 2, 1950, psychologist Rollo May objected to Dianetics and like-minded blueprints to better mental health because of their "oversimplification of human psychological problems."

Despite the warnings, Hubbard's popularity continued to soar. Hollywood, populated by celebrities flush with both money and emotional problems, proved to be a fervent bastion of faddish support for Dianetics. Hubbard, always savvy about public relations, boosted his own image by surrounding himself in the early 1950s with a coterie of well-known celebrity names, among them the sons of film director Cecil B. de Mille and writer Ernest Hemingway.*

Like so many other American fads, however, Hubbard's Dianetics movement, which had shot so quickly to stratospheric heights, found itself on the descent after a matter of months. Word began to seep out that Hubbard was growing unyieldingly authoritarian, refusing to delegate power while growing increasingly suspicious of those around him. There were rumors that he had beaten and mistreated his second wife, and it was later revealed that he married his second wife without informing her that he had not divorced his first wife, a strikingly eerie parallel to Werner Erhard's bigamy. He started having affairs with women who worked on his staff or as volunteers. Adding to the troubles were some severe cases of psychotic behavior suffered by a few individuals going through Dianetics auditing.

Scrambling to keep his fledgling movement alive, Hubbard abandoned his Los Angeles headquarters and moved to Phoenix, where he claimed in 1951 to have discovered something even more powerful than Dianetics. He called his new discovery Scientology, which had at its core Hubbard's "scientifically validated evidence" of the existence of a human soul. The true self of an individual, he now argued, derived from an immortal, omnipotent entity that he called a thetan. These thetans had each inhabited millions of bodies over trillions of years, and Scientology offered a proven way of exploring someone's

---

*Throughout the years, Scientology has continued to court famous Hollywood celebrities, even operating a private club near its worldwide headquarters on Sunset Boulevard that has long catered to entertainment figures. Among Scientology's celebrity followers have been John Travolta, Kirstie Alley, Tom Cruise, and Nancy Cartwright, the cartoon voice of Bart Simpson.

past lives in an effort to search for the human soul, for thetan. In February 1954 Hubbard established the first Church of Scientology and by the beginning of the following year had moved his operation from Phoenix to Washington, D.C.

By 1959 Scientology had its first brush with U.S. authorities—in this case, the federal Food and Drug Administration—over Hubbard's promotion and sale of a vitamin compound he devised called Dianazene. Hubbard touted the vitamin as a sure-fire protection against radiation as well as skin cancer. But the FDA took a more critical view of Dianazene, seizing huge supplies of the tablets. In the spring of 1959, Hubbard decided to leave the country, moving himself and his family into a mansion outside London that he turned into a worldwide training center for Scientologists.

Hubbard wasted no time in assuming the role of feudal master and absolute king after ensconcing himself in the baronial atmosphere of Saint Hill Manor, his Sussex mansion. He issued a directive that everyone on his staff be checked regularly on official e-meters. He also ordered that slavish attention be paid to housekeeping tasks such as washing the fleet of cars or taking care of flowers. Hubbard got into the practice of auditing himself with an e-meter as soon as he awoke each morning.

By the mid-1960s Hubbard was again hearing the ominous sounds of footsteps marching after him. In October 1965 complaints about Scientology in Australia had prompted a blue-ribbon panel there to issue a scathing 173-page report that called the practice of Scientology a "serious threat to the community, medically, morally and socially, and its adherents sadly deluded and often mentally ill." The report also blasted the Hubbard Association of Scientologists International, which Hubbard had created in London in 1952, as "the world's largest organization of unqualified persons engaged in the practice of dangerous techniques which masquerade as mental therapy." The Australian government responded to the report in December by passing the Psychological Practices Act that effectively outlawed Scientology in that country. That legislative act, in turn, prompted calls within the House of Commons in Great Britain to probe the status of Scientology in that country. In the United States, Internal

Revenue Service agents began to investigate the legitimacy of Scientology's tax-exempt status as a "church."

Facing mounting legal pressures, Hubbard once again chose to uproot himself. This time he left terra firma altogether, opting for the high seas while carrying out a strange fantasy of establishing his own private naval mission, which he called the Hubbard Geological Survey Expedition. After installing himself as "commodore" of the fleet, Hubbard officially announced his resignation as president of the Church of Scientology so that he could devote all his attention to the floating party that he called the Sea Org. (Local Scientology offices were known as orgs, short for organizations.)

Peter Monk may have been one of the last Scientology enthusiasts to receive training at Saint Hill Manor. In July 1968 the British government declared Scientology to be "socially harmful" and imposed a ban on its students entering the United Kingdom. Within days the British home secretary announced that Hubbard had been classified as an "undesirable alien."

While Hubbard cruised warm waters, Werner Erhard continued to study Scientology while subjecting his staff to Hubbard's odd tenets and theories. Having completed the communications course, Erhard was now undergoing regular auditing sessions with Monk, during which he would clutch the two tin cans attached by wires to Monk's e-meter while answering a series of engram-searching questions. Not long before Erhard left *Parents*, Monk became known as Erhard's resident "ethics officer," a term used in Scientology circles to describe someone whose job involves keeping others in line with proper Scientology behavior.

Monk, taking his job quite seriously, once noticed that sales figues had taken a downward spiral and concluded that the problem stemmed solely from Erhard's breach of proper Scientology behavior. Marching into Erhard's office, he solemnly announced, "You've become a liability to your own organization" by violating some of Scientology's rigid rules. Erhard dutifully acknowledged his transgression and stood ready to accept his punishment. In this case, Monk ordered Erhard to announce his wrongful ways by wrapping a dirty rag around his arm and wearing it for several days. Coincidentally, *Parents* magazine published a long article entitled "The Dangerous New Cult of Scientology" only a few months after Erhard had moved on to a sales job at the Grolier Society. The article warned parents about the frightening authoritarian power that Scientology was exercising over its adherents.

After Erhard's move to Grolier, Peter Monk moved to Southern California for an engineering job and more advanced Scientology training. Erhard now found a place for Michael Maurer on the Grolier staff, putting him in charge of developing sales methods that incorporated Scientology. In June 1970 Erhard received a letter from a local Scientology official congratulating him and his Grolier Society employees "for applying Scientology tech[nology]."

Toward the end of 1970, however, the Scientology office stopped hearing from Erhard. Clearly, he had other plans for the material he had learned during his own training.

Erhard and Maurer teamed up with Monk, who had returned to the Bay Area, to market the basic communications course offered to new Scientology recruits. Monk would deliver the course, Maurer would handle the logistics, and Erhard would take care of the marketing. Why not, he thought, teach the course to a hundred or more people at once? Scientology would earn a percentage of the profits, while Erhard and his partners would pocket the rest. It seemed like a perfect idea.

Erhard's Scientology course never got off the ground. For Erhard quickly realized that once his customers completed the course, they would have no further need for him. Werner Erhard wanted more: namely a program and a marketing plan that would keep his customers coming back again and again.

A Door-to-Door
Mind Salesman

Mind Dynamics is a

beautiful and powerful

experience.

—Werner Erhard

E ven as he continued to explore with Erhard the intricacies of
Scientology, Peter Monk read with curiosity a local newspaper ad
in the fall of 1970 for a lecture that was to be given about a program
called Mind Dynamics. He tore out the ad and showed it to Erhard,
who instantly seemed interested. Mind Dynamics, as it turned
out, was about to lead to a much more rewarding opportunity than

Scientology for an ambitious and charismatic salesman named Werner Erhard.

Launched in the Bay Area only a few months earlier, Mind Dynamics was the hybrid creation of Alexander Everett, a former English schoolmaster whose own fascination with mind-cure principles had begun in the 1950s, when he worked in Kansas City for one of the Unity Schools of Christianity, a mind-cure offshoot. From there Everett had wandered down to Texas, where he found work as an assistant principal at an exclusive private school in Fort Worth. It was in Texas that Everett ran across a man named José Silva who years earlier had concocted something called Mind Control that purported to teach its adherents over the course of four twelve-hour sessions how to relax and harness the power of their minds. By controlling the brain's alpha waves, Mind Control held out the promise of extraordinary results, from waking up without an alarm clock to ridding the body of dangerously addictive habits.

By the late 1960s Everett had created a similar mental exercise program called Mind Dynamics. After offering a few courses in Texas, he soon realized that California, with its free-spirited environment, might provide a more hospitable climate for his metaphysical theories about brain waves. Everett settled in San Francisco in the early spring of 1970. Not long after he began selling for $200 a thirty-two-hour course on controlling the brain's alpha waves. By mastering Mind Dynamics, students supposedly could achieve almost any goal they set, from improving their IQs and ending insomnia to curing cancer while learning to avoid other life-threatening illnesses.

To reach more people, Everett needed a better marketing plan than simply the promise of untapped human potential. He found one in William Penn Patrick, a ruggedly handsome and self-confident master salesman, who presided at the time over a worldwide pyramid-sales network of companies that sold products ranging from motor oil additives to banana-flavored body lotion. Patrick, a former door-to-door salesman in Illinois, was impressed with Everett's seeming ability to motivate people and quickly realized that Mind Dynamics could play a part in expanding his own business empire. Together he and

Everett created the unlikely marriage of mass-marketing sales techniques and the human potential movement.

Six years earlier, at the age of thirty-three, Patrick had begun a pyramid-sales company called Holiday Magic that ostensibly sold a line of fruit-flavored cosmetics. Holding out the tantalizing promise of handsome profits, Patrick sold distribution franchises to thousands of men and women from coast to coast. More often than not, the hapless distributors ended up with basements or garages stacked to the ceilings with jars of avocado face cream or cases of Sta-Pro motor oil additive while they vainly searched for other "distributors" to keep the endless chain letter of marketing in motion. At the top of the pyramid stood Patrick, who amassed a fortune estimated at $200 million and lived on a 6,000-acre ranch north of San Francisco, where he pursued his hobby of restoring and flying vintage military airplanes.

Patrick's decision in 1970 to add Mind Dynamics to his stable of pyramid-sales companies came at a time when other pieces of his enterprise were coming under increasing legal attack. By then the California attorney general's office had received a rash of complaints about Patrick's business methods at Holiday Magic. Around the time he met Alexander Everett, Patrick had added an even more bizarre new program called Leadership Dynamics, which eventually created additional legal headaches. The four-day "sensitivity" course put participants through a physically and mentally abusive regimen in the name of offering them a "more creative and constructive life."

While Patrick and Everett were mapping plans to bring Mind Dynamics into the Patrick empire, an energetic red-headed housewife named Charlene Afremow was in the process of divorcing her husband and moving herself and two young sons from a Chicago suburb to the San Francisco area. A few years earlier Afremow had scraped together $5,000 to become a local Holiday Magic distributor, eventually rising to the top of the pyramid in the Chicago region. From there she eagerly accepted yet another promotion to the company's main headquarters in San Rafael, a few miles north of the Golden Gate Bridge in Marin County.

In California, Afremow found herself falling under the spell of

Alexander Everett. He mesmerized her with his ideas about the amazing untapped powers of the brain that Mind Dynamics could help unlock. After learning the program, Afremow eagerly agreed to become a Mind Dynamics instructor, paying Everett $1,000 for a two-week training course that would enable her to teach the same course to others. One of Everett's other students was a former East Coast life insurance salesman named Stewart Esposito, who had already become one of Patrick's Holiday Magic distributors. At the end of the course, Afremow was rewarded with a Mind Dynamics franchise of her own in Marin County. Esposito returned to the East Coast, where he began selling the franchises around New York and Boston. Before long both Afremow and Esposito would play major roles in the mind-expanding empire built by Werner Erhard.

Erhard started out as one of Charlene Afremow's students, enrolling in the second Mind Dynamics course she taught at San Rafael's Holiday Inn in December 1970. Erhard sat in the second row, hanging on every word Afremow uttered while intently studying her gestures and body language as she led the class through the mental exercises and long lectures that constituted the Mind Dynamics program. She had a feeling the man with the handsome face and dazzling smile somehow was destined to become one of her star pupils.

Erhard wanted to learn as much as he could about Mind Dynamics and the way in which the program was marketed. After completing Afremow's two-weekend course, he began showing up at smaller follow-up workshops she conducted out of her home in San Rafael. One of Afremow's assistants led Mind Dynamics sessions for young children, and Erhard eagerly enrolled his two young daughters, Celeste and Adair, in the program. Afremow was impressed with Erhard's enthusiasm; after all, she had put her own two young sons through Mind Dynamics.

Erhard never failed to ooze plenty of sweet charm around Afremow. He was always eager to compliment her, to tell her how much he admired the work she was doing and how he so much wanted to learn everything he could from her. Afremow was flattered by Erhard's attention and noticed that he had even begun showing some outward signs of the kind of transformation promised by Mind Dynamics. An incessant cigarette smoker, Erhard announced to Afremow he had quit smoking and also had appeared to lose some excess weight. But Afremow noticed other quirky habits about Erhard that puzzled her about him. He never drove himself anywhere, but instead relied on one of his attractive female assistants from the book business to do the driving. To Afremow, they seemed like more than just dutiful employees. They worshiped Werner Erhard, hanging on to his every word and always quick to carry out any little order he barked at them. At first, Afremow couldn't understand why they were so devoted. Yet she had to admit there was something very appealing about the man. She sensed in him a raw, magnetic power that he held over people, but a power that could be harnessed to do good for others. She wondered whether her own destiny might intersect with his.

In January 1971, with Afremow's sponsorship, Erhard paid his $1,000 training fee to Everett and was given the Mind Dynamics San Francisco franchise. He taught his first class a month later.

Erhard filled a room at the Holiday Inn near Fisherman's Wharf with thirty-two students, two of whom would come to play major roles in his burgeoning career. Gonneke Spits, an attractive and strong-willed native of Amsterdam, had first come to work for Erhard at *Parents* in 1966 and remained with him ever since. Laurel Scheaf, a statuesque former schoolteacher with short brown hair, joined Erhard's door-to-door staff about a year later. Now Erhard's "girls" were ready to take on their next assignment by filling up seats at his Mind Dynamics classes and recruiting others into the course.

Erhard wasted no time putting Afremow's Mind Dynamics recruiting concepts to work for himself. He began by hosting "guest seminars" in the homes of some of his employees. People who had already taken the Mind Dynamics course were invited to bring guests, who listened while the "graduates" praised the course. Afterward, the guests were treated to a far more aggressive sales pitch for the next monthly Mind Dynamics session Erhard was leading. At the end of the guest seminar, while Erhard chatted in the living room with some of his graduates, Gonneke Spits or Laurel Scheaf took up their posts in the bedroom, pressuring the new students into signing up for the $200 course.

37

While William Penn Patrick's pyramid scheme spread Mind Dynamics around the country, no one was more successful at selling the program than Werner Erhard. Though most sessions attracted twenty or thirty students, Erhard was filling his own classes with sixty to a hundred people. As the course became more widely known, Erhard began renting out hotel conference rooms, where he delivered free introductory lectures that always ended with the same high-pressure sales pitch he had used for years in the book business. Erhard used the lectures to hone his own skills as a showman, though one who still had some of the mannerisms of a slick-talking car salesman. After everyone had been seated, Erhard usually began the evening by running down the center aisle, bounding onto the stage, and launching into his presentation in a loud, high-pitched voice. A few minutes later, upon a prearranged cue, one of his employees often walked onto the stage to relieve Erhard of his sport jacket.

By early 1971 Erhard's part-time earnings as a Mind Dynamics instructor—he was still running the Grolier office—depended entirely on the commissions he received for each new student who enrolled in the course. To boost the number of students who signed up, Erhard added his own new marketing twist to the program. Only through their willingness to introduce others to the program, Erhard told his "graduates," could they really expect to gain its full results. "Graduates who take on the responsibility of telling others about the benefits of Mind Dynamics always increase their ability to apply the principles in their own lives," Erhard wrote in the group's monthly newsletter in April 1971. "You can insure your own continuing results by participating in the success of Mind Dynamics."

Erhard pressed each student for a firm commitment to bring five new people into the program. "Be especially alive and in tune with these people," said Erhard. "Make it your responsibility to talk to them about Mind Dynamics in such a way that they actually become interested in sharing the experience. Take them to the next available workshop or lecture." Above all else, Erhard told his students, do whatever was necessary to sell them on the merits of Mind Dynamics "so that these people are able to overcome their obstacles and actually be in the course."

A month after taking Erhard's Mind Dynamics course, one of his enthusiastic new adherents quickly recruited other friends into the next session. A few weeks later, still flushed with excitement about Erhard and Mind Dynamics, the same young woman appeared at Erhard's office on Kearny Street. Though she had not announced her arrival in advance, no one at the office seemed surprised to see her.

"Oh yeah, Werner said you'd be here," Laurel Scheaf said in a matter-of-fact tone. "He wants you in the field. So I'll see you Monday morning at eight o'clock."

The woman spent the weekend wondering what Scheaf meant by "the field." To her utter astonishment, she arrived bright and early Monday morning only to be sent back out on the street immediately as the newest member of one of Erhard's door-to-door book-selling teams. Until that moment, she had no idea that her inspiring Mind Dynamics instructor really sold books for a living.

As he had been doing for years, Erhard still began each new day of selling with a rousing pep talk and a round of hand-clapping and singing among the sales teams, who belted out Beatles' songs and other current tunes before hitting the streets. Always Erhard stressed the need to achieve good sales results. The goal was all that mattered. Sometimes he handed the women small acorns, which they had to place inside their bras or in their panties so that, as he told them, "when you sit down, you won't ever forget the goal."

There was a constant buzz of activity in the office above Enrico's. During the day, the book teams fanned out across the city ringing doorbells and meeting sales quotas. They returned in the afternoon to hit the phones, calling people to invite them to Erhard's lectures for Mind Dynamics. In the evenings, there was still more work to do— attending Erhard's guest lectures and signing up students for his next course.

In the late summer of 1971, Erhard assigned a new task to his loyal staff. For several nights he had them copying the names, addresses, and phone numbers of everyone who had taken his Mind Dynamics course or showed up at one of the introductory lectures. He was making plans, he told his staff, to invite everyone on the list to a very special lecture he was going to give in September. He confided to them that he was going to leave Mind Dynamics and begin his own program. "I want you to make me famous," Erhard told his excited staff members.

By then Erhard already had come across an interesting name for his soon-to-be announced new venture. Earlier in the year, a friend had handed Erhard a science fiction novel called *est: The Steersman Handbook*, written by an author named L. Clark Stevens. In his book, Stevens wrote that "est" stood for "electronic social transformation," and heralded the arrival of "est people" bent on transforming society. Erhard was excited about Stevens's message and made sure other staff members read the book. It wouldn't be long before he borrowed "est" to fit his own needs.

Although Erhard already had decided to start his own organization, he waited for several weeks before telling Alexander Everett and William Penn Patrick. Impressed with his sales results for Mind Dynamics, the two men during the summer had asked Erhard to become a partner, offering him a slice of the profits if he agreed to train new instructors around the country. Erhard had no interest in becoming partners with anyone. At the same time, he tried to recruit to his own staff a witty and spritely irreverent Australian named Stewart Emery, who also worked for Mind Dynamics.

Emery, a former advertising official in Australia with a full head of prematurely graying hair, first went to work for Holiday Magic in his native country in the late 1960s. He arrived in San Francisco in the summer of 1971 for further training and to discuss plans to export Mind Dynamics back to Australia.

When Emery attended one of Alexander Everett's Mind Dynamics lectures, somebody got up and began to ramble on about something Everett had said. An impatient Emery, annoyed at the interruption, stood up and yelled "Bullshit!" loudly across the room.

Word about the scrappy Australian quickly filtered back to Erhard, who made a point during the summer of introducing himself to Emery. The two hit it off immediately. With his impish grin and irreverent wit, Stewart Emery recognized immediately that Werner Erhard was something of a bullshitter, as talented salesmen often are. But there was also that energetic smile, ribald sense of humor, and air of self-promoting confidence that took over whenever Erhard was around. Emery figured that Werner Erhard was definitely somebody to watch.

Toward the end of August, Erhard asked Emery to come up and see him at the Grolier office in North Beach. After Emery arrived, Erhard told him Laurel Scheaf had heard in one of the Mind Dynamics courses that Emery had had some experience with "encounter sessions" in Australia. Emery replied that he had gone through the harsh Leadership Dynamics course that William Penn Patrick had begun earlier for his Holiday Magic employees. Erhard wondered if Emery might be willing to lead a private encounter session with him and his staff. Emery agreed, particularly after Erhard told him he was willing to pay $1,000 for the intensive weekend-long session. It was scheduled to take place the first weekend in September, in a small room Erhard had rented at the Canterbury Hotel in San Francisco.

By the time Erhard gathered his staff together for the session with Emery, the Leadership Dynamics course had become the target of lawsuits brought by participants who had signed up only to find themselves the unwitting victims of cruel physical and emotional abuse during the sessions. In some cases instructors ordered participants into closed coffins. Others were hung onto large wooden crosses for hours at a time. Still others were forced to take off all their clothes while fellow participants taunted them with cruel insults. In one session, a man was forced to perform fellatio on an artificial penis while women attending a separate Leadership Dynamics class were brought in to watch.*

Emery did not bring in coffins or crosses into the Canterbury Hotel. Nor did he conduct the session in the same bizarre manner that marked the Leadership Dynamics course. But the absence of the weird features of Leadership Dynamics did not prevent the weekend

*In depositions and other court documents, Patrick and other Leadership Dynamics officials acknowledged the accuracy of some of the charges leveled against them in several lawsuits that stemmed from the brutality of the courses. Asked about simulated sex with an artificial penis, Patrick responded: "Well, to put it bluntly, there are a lot of men that come to class that have forgotten how to use theirs in their marriage." Patrick also admitted that it was common practice to hit people during the sessions. "I slap my children from time to time. It serves a useful function," he told lawyers during his deposition. The lawsuits eventually settled out of court, and Leadership Dynamics soon after went out of business.

session from turning ugly and violent at one point. In asking Emery to lead the session, Erhard wanted to learn more about the hard-hitting "sensitivity" techniques William Penn Patrick had incorporated into his own company. Another one of Erhard's probable objectives was to measure the loyalty and commitment of his own staff. Sitting around a U-shaped table, Erhard decided to put Gonneke Spits to the test. He began shouting at her, deliberately trying to provoke her into betraying even the slightest doubts that she might have toward him. While he continued to shout at her, Erhard slapped her hard across the face. She staggered backward but still insisted that her loyalties belonged to Erhard. Others in the room watched in stony silence, hoping they would not be the recipients of Erhard's strange method of determining their own loyalties.

The dark moment of violence ended almost as abruptly as it had begun, and by the end of the marathon session, on Sunday morning, everyone in the room seemed to be in giddy and jovial spirits. Only the blackened eye and bruises clearly visible on Gonneke Spits's face betrayed some of the demons that lurked inside Werner Erhard.

Later that day Emery joined the others on Erhard's staff to celebrate Erhard's thirty-sixth birthday at his Marin County home. The festive atmosphere was heightened by a delicious lunch of fresh crab, salad, and sourdough bread, with plenty of white wine for everyone. Somebody was playing the guitar and Erhard was in a buoyant mood. Pulling Emery aside that afternoon, Erhard confided his plan to leave Mind Dynamics and start his own training course.

"We'd welcome you as a part of the staff," Erhard told Emery that afternoon. "And I want you to know that's very unusual because people usually have to go a very long route to be invited to be on staff. But your contribution to us these last few days has been of such a magnitude that you have earned the right in just two days to be part of the staff."

As Emery pondered his response, Erhard quietly added another inducement. "There's enough money in this thing," he told the Australian, "for us all to become millionaires."

To Erhard's surprise, Emery declined the offer. He explained how he felt obliged to remain with Mind Dynamics, and how it would not have felt right to leave Everett and Patrick after the support they had given him in Australia and in the United States. He thanked Erhard for the offer and politely asked if he could take a raincheck. Erhard assured Emery he could call anytime he changed his mind.

A few miles away, another birthday celebration was taking place on that same Sunday. It was Alexander Everett's fiftieth birthday, and his staff was honoring him with a party set up in the parking lot outside the Mind Dynamics office in San Rafael. Toward the end of the afternoon, Erhard appeared at the party but remained in the background, standing at the edge of the parking lot amid the balloons and the bunting and the gaily wrapped gifts that many had brought for Everett. Erhard had yet to tell Everett that he had definitely decided to leave Mind Dynamics to launch his own business. Finally Erhard walked up to Everett, handing him the present he had brought. Everett wished Erhard a happy birthday himself, but the two exchanged no other words.

Erhard's formal break occurred a little more than a week later. Even then, Erhard made sure to take full advantage of his popular standing within Mind Dynamics when it came to unveiling his new plans. He had earlier scheduled one of his regular Mind Dynamics lectures for the evening of September 13 in a ballroom at the Mark Hopkins Hotel atop San Francisco's Nob Hill. Hundreds showed up to hear him, many of them guests of Erhard's Mind Dynamics students. But that night Erhard was no longer interested, financially or otherwise, in touting the miracles and wonders of Alexander Everett's course on controlling the brain's alpha waves. At the appointed hour, he launched into his lecture, but without any of the usual theatrics that had always accompanied an Erhard performance. After finishing his obligatory remarks about Mind Dynamics, he revealed the real purpose of the night's session. He announced that he was quitting Mind Dynamics to begin his own self-awareness program. He had decided to call it Erhard Seminars Training, though he preferred that it be known only as est. He never mentioned that the word "est" had originated in an obscure science fiction novel.

As Erhard spoke, many in the audience began to realize that Everett himself was sitting in the ballroom, listening calmly and with a faint smile on his face while Erhard made his dramatic announcement. When Erhard finished, he turned toward Everett and motioned him forward toward the microphone. A few days earlier, after Erhard had finally broken the news directly to Everett, he invited Alexander to send a representative to the Mark Hopkins "to express whatever views you wish." Erhard had not expected to see Everett himself that evening.

"I want everyone here to know that Werner has worked with me for some time," Everett told the audience. "And I want everyone to know that he's a great person. I'm sorry that he wants to leave but that's his choice. And so I want you to know that I'm supporting him in anything that he does. And I back him all the way in creating his own organization."

Privately, Everett was furious with Erhard for working behind his back for months while he planned his break. But Everett knew there was little he could do to stop Erhard from going through with his plans. By then he knew enough about Erhard's past—and about how hard Erhard pushed his own staff—to realize that in Werner Erhard's world, things either had to be run his way or not at all.

A week after the evening at the Mark Hopkins, the *San Francisco Chronicle* published a four-column ad that featured a dramatic photograph of Erhard, dressed in a dark jacket and tie, his upraised hands framing a serious face that seemed to stare at newspaper readers with a hypnotic gaze. The ad announced the first course to be held later that October by "Erhard Seminars Training." The ad announced a new course to train people to "know and understand yourself and others."

For Werner Erhard, his big moment had finally arrived. For years he had been selling, but always for others. Now it was time to take center stage, with a new product to sell—a course that bore his own name. Erhard closed down his Grolier office at the same time that he announced his break from Mind Dynamics. In their place est was born, and was about to grow up very quickly.

A LESSON IN
TAX SHELTERS

The purpose of

est is to serve people.

It is not to make money.

—EST EXECUTIVE DON COX

B y the time he started est, Werner Erhard had every reason to believe that his new product would take off. Even before the first est training was held in San Francisco, Erhard already had made plans to maximize the profits that soon would be flowing in to his second-floor offices above Enrico's in North Beach.

Jack Rafferty, a onetime San Francisco nightclub promoter with a salty tongue and a devilish grin, had heard all about Werner Erhard from a friend who had taken Erhard's Mind Dynamics course and encouraged him to do likewise. Not long before Erhard announced his switch from Mind Dynamics to est, the white-haired Rafferty accepted Erhard's offer to help him promote his courses. As the plans for creating est were getting under way, Rafferty arranged for Erhard to meet an attorney friend named Harry Margolis who knew a thing or two about businesses and taxes.

On a warm summer day in 1971, Rafferty drove Erhard and Laurel Scheaf fifty miles or so down the San Francisco peninsula to the town of Saratoga, a charming little suburban village nestled against the rolling foothills of the Santa Cruz Mountains just outside of San Jose. Rafferty had set up an appointment there with Margolis, a gruff-mannered but somewhat elfin-looking man in his early fifties, whose law office was located next door to his ranch-style home. The group sat around Margolis's backyard swimming pool while the lawyer listened to Werner Erhard explain about the new organization he intended to start.

"I don't know what I want in legal terms because I'm not an attorney," Erhard told Margolis. "I don't have any experience at this. I'm relying on you, if you can do it, to put something together that enables me to accomplish the things I want to accomplish."

After Erhard finished talking about his plans for Erhard Seminars Training, Margolis said he'd be more than happy to help arrange Erhard's financial affairs. The lawyer explained a little bit about the kind of tax work he did for his clients, though the details sounded rather complicated and confusing to the others sitting around the pool. Margolis reassured them, however, that everything he did was perfectly legal so Erhard had absolutely nothing to worry about. Erhard seemed delighted with everything Margolis was telling him. Imagine running a profitable enterprise and paying little or no taxes. Werner Erhard was in a good mood on the drive back to San Francisco.

Harry Margolis had been practicing law since 1943, starting with a small firm in San Francisco's downtown financial district. After an illness forced him to give up his practice a few years later, Margolis operated a couple of liquor stores in the city, but he began putting his legal training back to work by helping some local beer distributors sort out some thorny tax problems. The sharp-minded Margolis discovered a knack for wading through the thick web of tax laws, and soon after he gave up the liquor stores to resume full-time work as an attorney. To speed along his recovery from the illness, Margolis moved from cool and foggy San Francisco to the drier, warmer climate of Saratoga.

Over the years his reputation in the tax area brought him clients who ranged from well-known entertainers such as the singer Nat King Cole to more obscure, though typically wealthy, business figures. Ironically, Margolis thought of himself as a radical leftist, whose Marxist political ideology meshed with his avowed antagonism toward the tax laws. In reality, he turned his law practice into an assembly-line factory that churned out elaborate tax shelters for his well-heeled clients. Margolis once engineered a complex tax deal that enabled the writer Dalton Trumbo to finance the movie version of his book *Johnny Got His Gun* while offering enticing tax savings to numerous investors in the film project. Years after Margolis met Erhard, the U.S. Tax Court ruled against Margolis's movie-related scheme, which he had set up as a financial version of a Rube Goldberg contraption. Margolis's clients, like others who fell for the lawyer's just-trust-me assurances, were forced to pay back the taxes that Margolis had illegitimately tried to avoid.

Jack Rafferty, Erhard's enthusiastic promoter, had known Margolis for years, ever since the lawyer had taken on as a client Rafferty's then-wife, a popular singer named Barbara McNair. Although McNair's financial affairs later soured because of the tax work performed by Margolis, Rafferty at the time was confident that an ambitious guy like Werner Erhard would do well in the hands of an effective attorney like Harry Margolis.

Sure enough, there was a feeling of jubilant excitement in Erhard's cramped offices on Kearny Street as he prepared to launch Erhard Seminars Training. For weeks he had been telling his staff that their job was to make him famous. Now it appeared as if he had just met the man who was going to help make him rich as well.

Margolis had his plan ready to go by the time Erhard made his break from Mind Dynamics in the fall and began offering his own self-awareness course called est. All it took was a rapidly prepared series of official-sounding documents designed to create a shiny new corporate identity for Werner Erhard. Over the next two decades, however, Margolis's handiwork would place Erhard and his corporate empire at loggerheads with the Internal Revenue Service.

The tax-shelter world of Harry Margolis hinged on an endless circle of dummy corporations and curious offshore bank accounts, all created and controlled within his Saratoga law offices or through a network of associates scattered around the world, from Panama City to the Isle of Jersey. For Erhard and est, the convoluted financial journey began in October 1971 when Margolis shuffled some legal documents that instantly turned one of his dummy corporations, the Saratoga Restaurant Equipment Company, into Erhard Seminars Training Inc. The newly transformed corporation announced in one of its charter documents that it was "no longer functioning as a restaurant equipment company, but as an organization for the development of human consciousness."

The next step in the Margolis system was for Werner Erhard to "sell" his knowledge about human consciousness to yet another Margolis-created corporation called Presentaciones Musicales, conveniently headquartered in Panama, where it operated beyond the reach of American tax authorities. For $1 million, which Erhard never actually received, Erhard sold to the Panamanian company what he later described as est's "body of knowledge," which included the various methods, procedures, and mental exercises that he had stitched together from other courses he had studied.

As a result of Harry Margolis's tax-avoiding system, no more than modest amounts of income would appear in Erhard's name. To that end, Margolis drafted a series of documents that made Erhard appear as simply an employee (at an initial annual salary of $30,000) of the same Panamanian company that had just bough: his lucrative body of knowledge.

Margolis's complex paperwork succeeded in bestowing two valuable gifts on Erhard. First, it paved the way for Erhard to begin operating an immensely profitable business that would soon provide him with the amenities and comforts of a king. Equally important, the Margolis system also allowed Erhard to answer all inquiries into est's shadowy financial affairs by pointing to his modest salary. As Erhard's own est-derived fortunes grew, the financial underpinnings of his empire for years proved too complicated and obscure for anyone to accuse him of unscrupulous behavior.

Beyond paying his modest "salary," Erhard's employment contract also provided him with a generous entertainment and travel budget, a wardrobe allowance of $5,000 followed by a monthly clothing allotment of $500, and a series of other perquisites. Tucked in among the benefits provided to Erhard was a $425,000 "loan" that he was free to use for anything he wanted. The blueprints were now almost completely in place for Werner Erhard to savor the financial rewards that est was about to offer.

First, however, Margolis had to put into place the final piece of another one of his circular tax-shelter puzzles. On December 4, 1971—several weeks after Erhard began est training sessions in San Francisco—Erhard's Panamanian "employer" officially authorized Erhard Seminars Training Inc. to carry out the business of est in the United States. Margolis's Panamanian company officially charged Erhard Seminars Training $1.2 million for an "exclusive" ten-year license to market the new est training course in the United States. Included in the license agreement was a provision offering Erhard's "personal services" in delivering the est course. In addition, the new agreement transferred Erhard's personal employment contract from Presentaciones Musicales to the corporate entity that bore his name and marketed his course.

The circle was complete, and Werner Erhard no longer would have to worry about explaining his curious relationship with an offshore company located in a well-known tax haven. Now Erhard had a much more plausible cover story for anyone who asked. He simply worked for a company called Erhard Seminars Training. And he had the documents to prove that he neither owned nor controlled the new company.

But where was Erhard Seminars Training supposed to come up with $1.2 million to pay for the est licensing agreement? Margolis easily solved that problem by simply arranging for the new company to "borrow" the funds from other dummy corporations included in the Margolis system. By the end of December, Margolis had directed another one of his circular money movements that were performed regularly to create the appearance of loans and other financial transactions necessary to claim a fresh round of tax deductions for his clients. Erhard Seminars Training suddenly found itself the recipient of a $1 million loan from a Nevada corporation controlled by Margolis. One day later Erhard's new company transferred $1.2 million into a Caribbean bank account held in the name of Presentaciones Musicales. For Werner Erhard, the Margolis shuffle was now fully under way.

While customers began trickling in to learn what his curious new course was all about, Erhard quickly learned how valuable Harry Margolis was to the new enterprise. When the lawyer filled out est's first corporate tax return in 1972, Margolis indicated that the company had collected gross receipts in the amount of $250,162. After Margolis had finished with the tax return, however, Erhard Seminars Training Inc. wound up its first year with a "loss" of nearly $39,000. For Erhard and est, the Margolis system was now fully up and running, with its complex financial transactions, licensing agreements, loan payments, and a host of other tax-reducing schemes.

As est's popularity and profits rose dramatically over the next few years, the Margolis system responded just the way the crafty lawyer had planned. In 1972 and 1973, Erhard's wardrobe expenses jumped to more than $25,000 while more than $242,000 was spent on travel and entertainment. Three years after his entry into the business of "human consciousness," Werner Erhard had sold nearly $3.4 million worth of est training sessions. He was on the verge of becoming one of the most famous pop gurus of all time, and the money that was pouring in was now providing him with an increasingly opulent life-style that a car salesman or door-to-door purveyor of books could only have dreamed about.

Six

SHADOWS FROM THE PAST

I am the source

of est. . . . A source creates

something from nothing.

—WERNER ERHARD

W erner Erhard always had to worry about his past, never knowing if or when it might catch up to him. By the time he started est in the fall of 1971, only a handful of those around him knew even the vaguest details about his days as a Philadelphia car salesman. Fewer still had any idea that his past included a wife and four small children who had survived on welfare and the largess of family and friends in the years since Jack Rosenberg had vanished without a trace.

Of course, Pat Rosenberg, Erhard's first wife, knew all about her husband's past. But she knew nothing about either his current identity or his whereabouts. Unable to track him down, at first all she could do was wait and hope patiently for the charming high school boy who had swept her off her feet to return to his rightful place as husband and father. Keeping her children fed and clothed, however, took more than hope, forcing Pat to rely on public assistance and the generosity of family and friends to get by. The children were told little about the absence of their father and sometimes assumed simply that he was dead. How else could they account for their mother's sadness and the lack of any other explanation for their father's strange disappearance? The couple's youngest daughter was barely six months old when Jack Rosenberg fled from his family. To her, there were not even any memories of a father's touch or smile to balance against the lonely feeling of abandonment.

Eventually Pat Rosenberg lost even the hope that her husband would return. In 1965 she obtained a divorce on the grounds of desertion. Lacking any skills for a decent-paying job, she went to work as a housekeeper for a plumber who lived near her family in Norristown. The two eventually got married, a situation that at least provided Pat with the security of knowing that her children's basic needs would be met. She tried to forget about the man who had disappeared from her life one spring morning years before. In truth, however, she never got over him, and she certainly never stopped loving him.

As est continued to grow, Erhard knew that sooner or later the time would come when he'd have to reestablish contact with his family in Philadelphia. As an obscure book salesman in San Francisco, it had been relatively easy for Werner Erhard to conceal his whereabouts from relatives living nearly three thousand miles away. As a self-awareness promoter whose business already had begun to take him around the country, it was not going to be nearly as easy for Erhard to maintain the secrets of his past life.

At the same time, Erhard knew his emerging image as the enlightened creator of est required him to be circumspect when it came to acknowledging his flight out of Philadelphia in 1960 and the long, unexplained abandonment of his family. He decided to play it cautiously, at first making public only those facts about his background that he did not think would tarnish excessively his carefully groomed reputation as a master of human transformation. Erhard shrewdly calculated that he might even derive some benefit from discreet admissions of past transgressions by casting his mistakes as evidence of the successful application of est's underlying theory of personal responsibility. Soon after starting est, Erhard began dropping hints in training sessions and guest seminars about leaving behind parents and siblings years earlier in Philadelphia. For the moment, however, he made no mention of walking out on a wife and children, perhaps assuming that his growing legion of followers might not tolerate a transformational flaw of that magnitude.

In late October 1972 Erhard hid behind selective revelations of his past during an est lecture he gave at San Francisco's Masonic Auditorium in which he discussed his long absence from his hometown. Nearly thirteen years after walking out on his wife and four children, Erhard now announced that he had finally returned to see his family. But the only family member he specifically mentioned seeing was his sister—nothing was said about his wife or kids. Erhard, indeed, had traveled back east a few weeks earlier as part of a carefully crafted plan to reconnect with his family and reveal his new identity to them. He had flown to New York to present the first est training there. Afterward, he traveled to Philadelphia to see his parents and his two younger brothers, Harry and Nathan, and his younger sister, Joan. Harry and Joan Rosenberg still lived in Philadelphia, but Nathan was attending the Air Force Academy in Colorado at the time.

For Erhard, the long-delayed reunion with the Rosenbergs succeeded in establishing himself in their eyes as a returning hero of sorts. At the time, the family certainly knew nothing about est or why Jack Rosenberg had turned himself into the exotic-sounding Werner Erhard. All that mattered to them was that Jack had returned. To Erhard, what mattered more was that he had gone back to Philadelphia on his own terms, as a master of his own fate, and free of the annoying entanglements that had kept him down at the time he left years before. Harry and Joan were seemingly thrilled to learn of their older brother's burgeoning fame.

But Erhard still wasn't completely ready to confront his past. While he basked in the attention showered upon him by his parents and siblings, Erhard kept his visit a secret from his first wife and four children. It would be another two months before Erhard's long-abandoned son and three daughters realized finally that their father was alive and thriving under a strange new name.

Likewise, the audience who listened to Erhard's San Francisco speech in October 1972 were left in the dark about the full facts of his past. Though he had decided to speak that evening about "love," and the relationship between parents and children, Erhard deliberately created the impression that his only responsibilities as a husband and parent were right there in the Bay Area.

> "All parents know that you must love your children. I have
> three children of my own," Erhard said, "and . . . it takes
> an enormous amount of perseverance to love children."

In Erhard's case, perseverance had little to do with his behavior toward his children in Philadelphia. Instead, he simply ignored their very existence.

Only as his own popularity continued to escalate did Erhard gradually come to acknowledge the full story of his having walked out on his first wife and children years earlier. At the same time, he began incorporating them into his sales pitches for est, eagerly announcing that everyone in his family had taken the training while insisting that no one bore any animosity toward him for his long absence from their lives. In the jargon of est, he explained how he had successfully "completed" his past by resolving his long years away from his family.

In reality, most members of Erhard's family—particularly his children—had little say about their role in the world of est. Although some of the children were seemingly enthusiastic about their father's work, they were also used as props to bolster his own enlightened image. Shortly after he reappeared in the lives of his children in Philadelphia, he made the startling announcement that he had little interest in being their father. Instead, he said, his role would be that of a "teacher."

Not long after Erhard's reconnection with his Philadelphia relatives, his twenty-three-year-old brother, Harry Rosenberg, moved to San Francisco to begin working for est. Joan Rosenberg, Erhard's sister, eventually followed him into a job at est. The youngest brother, Nathan, graduated from the Air Force Academy in 1974 and then spent four years in the navy. Eventually he moved to Southern California, where he worked in real estate investment and management consulting while playing a prominent volunteer role in est.

For Erhard, his past was turning—as far as his public image was concerned—into a confirmation of the transformational power of est. By the mid-1970s Erhard had moved his long-forgotten Philadelphia family to San Francisco. Pat's second marriage had broken up shortly after Erhard's reappearance in her life, and she now managed to store away years of resentment while building a new friendship with the man who deserted her. Erhard reacted to Pat's almost inexplicable devotion by putting her to work as an assistant in his personal office at est. As his children grew older, they appeared frequently at est events, as part of a well-orchestrated plan to present Erhard's family life as a powerful embodiment of est's principles. A magazine article on Erhard once published an old photo of Erhard romping through a game of touch football with some of his children. But the game was nothing but a staged event, set up years earlier to boost Erhard's image as a devoted father. The children were little more than props, and the frivolity of the game vanished as soon as the photographer finished taking pictures.

Privately, Erhard had trouble remembering his children's ages and spent little time with either his once-abandoned Philadelphia family or his second family being raised by Ellen Erhard in Marin County. When one of his daughters graduated from high school in the late 1970s, Erhard was absent from the ceremony. His aides had "mistakenly" scheduled him to be out of the country at the time.

In 1975, during a large est event at the Masonic Auditorium in San Francisco, Erhard grandly called to the stage his entire family— Ellen, Pat, both sets of children, and his parents—where they received a standing ovation from an adoring audience of several thousand est graduates. The loud and sustained applause that rang through the auditorium surely provided all the evidence anyone needed to confirm Erhard's crowning transformation as a man devoted to everyone in his family. Surely the evening symbolized the powerful and positive influence of est, with its miraculous ability to "create a space" that had allowed a man who once had walked out on his family now to share a stage with them, to profess his love for them, to "complete" his relationship with them.

But the illusory image of Werner Erhard as a transformed human being who joyfully embraced his once-abandoned family was only part of the façade he needed to project. Even before his reconciliation with his Philadelphia family, Erhard had been tiring of his role as a husband to Ellen and father to their three children. All during his days working for *Parents* and Grolier, Erhard kept up a steady stream of sexual affairs while spending little time at home with Ellen and the children. The pattern persisted once he started est. He began spending more frequent nights in San Francisco, sleeping in one of the apartments that some of his employees had rented in a fading three-story Victorian on Franklin Street in Pacific Heights, not far from the est office in North Beach. Gradually he began using part of the house as his own private office, leaving the rest of the staff to carry out the business of making him famous back on Kearny Street.

By the end of 1972, after est had completed its first year of business, Erhard told Margolis he wanted to convert the house on Franklin Street into his private domain. The owner of the house, who by then had been leasing office space to est, agreed to sell the property to Erhard Seminars Training for $142,500. On January 31, 1973, EST Inc. obtained a real estate loan commitment from Barclays Bank of California in the amount of $98,000 to finance the purchase of the house. When escrow closed two months later, Werner Erhard was the proud new occupant of a piece of San Francisco real estate that he soon began to refer to regally as the "Franklin House."

To Harry Margolis, the house was more than a prestigious new address for Werner Erhard; it was also the source of lucrative new tax benefits. By obscuring the true ownership of the house and grossly inflating its value as a place of business, Margolis converted the Victorian town house into a profitable tax haven for Werner Erhard. As he had done in the corporate structuring of Erhard's new "mind business" eighteen months earlier, Margolis in March 1973 created a paper trail of documents that would fully enmesh the house into his system.

First, Margolis drafted a document instructing the title company holding the property to do so "for the benefit" of a Margolis entity called the Maryelle Corporation, whose president was Michael Chatzky, one of Margolis's legal associates. At that point, Erhard Seminars Training Inc. signed a ten-year lease in which it would pay Maryelle $3,750 in monthly rent for the home. A year later the house was signed over to a third Margolis entity called Associated Convalescent Enterprises. Suddenly Erhard's "rent" was increased to $5,000 per month—all of it deductible as a business expense and all of it part of Margolis's patented circular movement of money from one pocket to another.

By the time Erhard moved into the Franklin House, which would perform service as est's social center while providing him with an office and private residence for the next several years, he had begun to assemble a staff that reflected est's rising popularity and his own solidifying status as an important human potential guru.

In early 1972, within months of his first est training courses, Erhard hired for $75 a week a former Mind Dynamics student named Charles Ingrasci and told him he was to become a "communicator," a position in which he was to serve as a liaison between Erhard and the rest of the est staff. A graduate of the University of California at Berkeley and a former traveling salesman for a line of Danish gift products, Ingrasci—who went by the nickname "Raz"—soon found himself constantly at Erhard's side, traveling with him to and from airports, attending est's recruitment lectures, sometimes conferring with him at midnight at the Franklin House at the end of a long day of promoting est.

Around the same time, the Australian Stewart Emery was becoming more disillusioned with Mind Dynamics. He decided the time had come to cash in the raincheck that Erhard had given him seven months earlier. Emery had kept a casual eye on the new est organization during that time. Although he had not taken Erhard's training course, he knew through Mind Dynamics circles that Erhard had been enjoying a fair amount of success, reflecting the same aggressive approach that he had taken when marketing the Mind Dynamics courses he had offered the year before. Erhard, he heard, was filling his monthly est training sessions with at least a hundred paying customers. No one came close to doing that with Mind Dynamics. Besides, Emery needed a green card to remain in the United States legally. Going to work for Werner Erhard could solve all his problems.

The two men agreed to meet for lunch at a restaurant in Sausalito. After arriving there first, Emery noticed that Erhard had been driven to the restaurant by one of his staff members, who also paid the bill at the end of the lunch.

After they were seated, Erhard wasted no time reminding Emery that he was being offered a golden opportunity that should not be passed up a second time. He repeated what he had told Emery the previous September: "There's enough money here for all of us to become millionaires." Erhard also mentioned something vague about figuring out a way to minimize taxes on est's generous profits.

But Erhard's bold talk of becoming tax-free millionaires ended abruptly when Emery insisted on a starting salary of $2,000 a month. Erhard, who was paying other members of his staff no more than a few hundred dollars a month, balked.

"We don't pay anybody that kind of money," replied Erhard.

"Well, I don't work for anything less than that," Emery insisted.

Erhard did not like ultimatums. But he knew he needed Emery on his staff, perhaps more than anyone else he had yet hired. Leading an est training was demanding work, and Erhard had already decided by the spring of 1972 that he would soon have to train others to lead some of the growing number of sessions. Emery had more than proven himself in the weekend-long "encounter session" he had led for Erhard's staff at the Canterbury Hotel. Now that's the kind of person I need to be up at the front of the room during est sessions, Erhard thought to himself. Ultimatum or not, Erhard knew that Stewart Emery was too valuable to let get away a second time. He agreed to pay Emery the higher salary.

There was one additional matter to discuss over lunch that day in Sausalito. Even if he was about to become Erhard's highest-paid employee, Emery still had to know that coming to work for Werner Erhard carried some special obligations. "Everyone who works for me serves me," Erhard told his prospective new employee. "How do I know you'll do what I say?"

Emery had already braced himself for the question since he seen for himself the manner in which Erhard demanded, and apparently received, total obedience and subservience from his staff. Of course, the incident at the Canterbury Hotel demonstrated to Emery that Erhard was prepared to dish out physical punishment and verbal abuse to anyone who hesitated to surrender to his authority.

"Werner," Emery told Erhard with a serious look on his face, "I haven't done the est training, and I have no idea whether it's valuable. The whole thing could be a bunch of bullshit. But whether or not it is, I'm clear that you've found some way to make it valuable, so people believe that it's valuable. And if I'm going to work for you, the only way I can learn from you whatever it is that you have that is valuable is to do it the way you tell me to."

Erhard looked intently at the silver-haired Australian. "Now I know I can trust you," he replied. Emery had passed the test. He went to work for est in April 1972.

At about the same time, a 1967 Harvard Business School graduate named Charles Landon Carter was meditating in India, teaching at a college near Bangalore, and studying with spiritual gurus. Carter had taken his business degree into the Peace Corps for two years, where he taught at a branch of Stanford's business school in Lima, Peru. Upon returning to the United States, the tall and ruggedly handsome Carter found a job perfectly suited to his outdoor tastes: working in Aspen, Colorado, as a vice president in a company that was developing the Snowmass ski area. Part of his job involved putting together real estate deals and other projects for the ski resort company. He enjoyed the work and the surroundings, but he longed for a spiritual force in his life that he couldn't find on the Aspen slopes. In November 1971 Carter bought a plane ticket to India, where he spent the next several months in study and quiet contemplation. It did not take long for him to hear about Werner Erhard and est after he returned to Aspen the following June; one of Erhard's early enthusiasts happened to live there and agreed to promote est trainings in the area. Carter was delighted to learn that he could enroll in a training course right there in Aspen. Erhard himself led the course, which included among the two hundred or so participants a local folk singer with round wire-rimmed spectacles named John Denver.

Although Carter was impressed with both Erhard and est, he left Aspen soon after for Los Angeles, where he continued his studies to become a yoga teacher while helping to run an Indian-flavored spiritual center there. But the powerful est experience—and the personal charisma of Erhard—was still fresh in Carter's mind. By September, still living in Los Angeles, he joined a program begun by Erhard to train those who had completed the est training to become volunteer leaders of est seminars. Carter's enthusiasm for est showed up in his zeal for leading the seminars, which focused largely on encouraging seminar participants to enroll others they knew in the est training. On January 1, 1973, Landon Carter accepted Erhard's offer to join the est staff. For a while he worked around Erhard in the Franklin House, but soon it became clear to Erhard that Carter, with his boundless energy, charisma, and good looks, would make an ideal est trainer.

In Carter's eyes, Erhard came across as a masterful teacher, someone who has sifted through the collected books of wisdom and studied an assortment of disciplines before weaving it all into the powerful est training. In fact, for Carter the training had almost seemed like a spiritual experience, with its power to turn people on, to instill in them a strange new sense of aliveness, of self-expression. "I was trying to find the fastest way to God," Carter told a writer years later. "Meditation was slow. Werner put things together in a way that went bing, bing, bing." After his months in India, Carter was thrilled that he had come across, in Werner Erhard, nothing less than a "direct path to the experience of enlightenment."

If Stewart Emery had a green card on his mind and Landon Carter a quick jaunt toward enlightenment in the spring of 1972, a smooth-talking attorney in his mid-thirties named Ted Long was pre-occupied with politics at the time. A year earlier Long had been re-called from a seat on the city council in the San Francisco suburb of San Bruno. Along with two other allies on the council, Long had raised some eyebrows with their selection of a replacement for San Bruno's retiring city manager. A group of civic leaders accused Long and his pals of short-circuiting official procedures for filling the vacant post and launched the successful recall campaign. Thirteen months later Long was trying to engineer a political comeback by running for a vacant seat in the state legislature.

To boost his campaign, Long turned to Werner Erhard and the young est organization for volunteers. In Erhard, Long discovered someone who shared his own love of self-promotion.

The attorney enrolled in one of the early est training sessions and began peppering his campaign speeches with est jargon. After insisting that his campaign manager and others helping him take the training, Long by election day ended up recruiting more than two hundred est graduates to work on his behalf. But voters in the district apparently were not quite ready for a political candidate who talked in such funny phrases. They elected Long's Democratic opponent in November. Long, however, remained fascinated by Erhard and est.

Erhard was always eager to take advantage of anyone enthusiastic enough about est to work for free. Long agreed to lead introductory est lectures, called "guest events," that Erhard had begun to organize in Los Angeles. For a few months Long took late-afternoon commuter flights to L.A., where he would catch a cab to the est event, and return on the midnight flight back to San Francisco. After proving his commitment both to Erhard and est, Long was asked to join the staff and was placed in charge of the "graduate division," a lofty way of describing his job of corraling est graduates into the post-training est seminars, which concentrated primarily on getting everyone there to enroll others in est.

Long lasted in the job only about a week before Erhard came to him with another assignment—working directly with him at the Franklin House. Soon Long found himself acting as a sort of cultural tutor, schooling Erhard in the fineries of food, wine, art, and other social matters Erhard intended to master as part of his plan to convert his Victorian home into a refined and early New Age salon.

It did not take long for Erhard to offer a tantalizing glimpse of the high life he envisioned for himself as the creator of est. Toward the end of 1972, Erhard and Stewart Emery flew to Honolulu, where Erhard was going to lead one of the first est trainings in Hawaii. After the weekend course, at which Emery had assisted as part of his own training to be an est trainer, the two sunned themselves on the beach at the Kahala Hilton, where they were staying. As they basked in the warm tropical sun, Erhard outlined an appealing plan. Erhard, Emery, and a third trainer, he explained, would rotate the monthly trainings in San Francisco and Los Angeles. In between, they'd lead a few sessions in such places as New York, Hawaii, and Aspen. What could be more idyllic? Emery thought as he lay there in the warm sun and dreamed, along with Erhard, of the millions of dollars that Erhard had once promised would be theirs as a result of est's success. Erhard even suggested that he and Emery move their families to Hawaii, leaving the others to run the est organization back in foggy San Francisco.

By the time of that sun-soaked weekend, Erhard had yet to allow Emery or anyone else to lead a complete est training by himself. Instead, he had begun a "training" program in which Emery and other staff members led parts of the sessions while spending hours and hours studying Erhard's every move, every word, every inflection as he conducted his course. The idea was not only to master the material that went into the est training but also to copy, nearly verbatim, the manner in which Erhard himself delivered the training. The team of would-be trainers began dressing like Erhard, showing up at est sessions in casual shirts, their wide collars flared outside cardigan sweaters. When Erhard spoke at est events, he would keep a beaker of tea nearby, and he liked to sit on high-legged stools with notes arranged on a metal music stand. His disciples followed suit, making sure that no little detail that went into Erhard's mastery of transformation escaped their own attention.

Erhard only a year or so earlier had mastered Alexander Everett's course in Mind Dynamics and succeeded, when creating est, in adapting much of Everett's structure and substance. He had no intention of allowing anyone else the same wide degree of latitude in adapting est for their own purposes. Instead, Erhard decreed, est and Werner Erhard were to remain inseparable.

Emery's big moment finally arrived in January 1973. A chiropractic school in Davenport, Iowa, had invited Erhard to present an est training there, which attracted only thirty people on a cold winter weekend. Erhard decided Emery was ready to lead the training. From Iowa, Emery traveled to Aspen, where est's popularity was growing, largely due to John Denver's glowing praise of Erhard and the training, and the fact that the singer encouraged everyone he knew to enroll. With est's word-of-mouth appeal rising as well in Los Angeles and Honolulu, Erhard had no choice but to allow Emery and three or four other disciples to lead their own sessions.

Emery enjoyed his new responsibilities, though he annoyed Erhard slightly with flashes of his dry and irreverent wit. Once he chortled to Erhard that est was more thrilling than a "ride at Disneyland," hardly the kind of comparison that Erhard wanted to hear. There were other opinions, however, that Emery kept to himself, mindful of Erhard's demands for absolute loyalty among the staff toward both est and himself. As a student of Mind Dynamics, Emery understood quite well many of the origins of the training. He also recognized how Erhard had adapted significant elements of Scientology and Dale Carnegie into the est training. While Emery saw value in some of those courses, he also dismissed much of the est training as complete nonsense, with its theatrical flourishes, loud berating of participants, and constant attempts by the trainers to tear down any resistance among est trainees to the course's sometimes tortured logic. Privately Emery began joking to his fellow Erhard disciples that the training course really was little more than a gimmicky brand of "entertainment."

Erhard, from est's earlier days, was looking for ways to monitor such irreverent attitudes among his staff while maintaining a rigid control over an organization that rapidly was turning into a phenomenon. He turned to some of the bizarre Scientology practices that he had used in his bookselling days to motivate performance. Now, however, he sought to use them to ensure and enforce unquestioned staff loyalty to himself.

Just as est was beginning, Erhard hired Clarence Boncher, a former trade unionist and ex–Mind Dynamics instructor, to be his staff's new "ethics officer," a position similar to the one played earlier by one of Erhard's Scientology buddies. Boncher himself was steeped in Scientology, and was eager to apply its detailed rules about conduct and behavior to the est staff. Erhard, who once had agreed to wear a dirty rag around his arm after "violating" Scientology ethics, told Boncher that he himself might get out of line from time to time and so would also be looking to Boncher to provide "ethical" directions.

Over the next several months, Boncher and his e-meter spent much time at est conducting personal auditing sessions with Erhard and his staff. But Erhard wanted more than an ongoing series of auditing sessions. He continually pressed Boncher for more details about Scientology "data," which he wanted to incorporate into est. When Boncher balked, Erhard dismissed him and hired two other Scientologists who provided some of the material he wanted.

After he left, Boncher realized he had never taken the est training himself, even after knowing and working with Erhard for months. He signed up for the next training session, after which Laurel Scheaf asked him what he thought of est. Had he learned anything? she wanted to know.

"Yep," Boncher shot back, his voice dripping with sarcasm. "I learned to stand in front of 250 people and say you're nothing but a bunch of fucking assholes. That's what I learned from the est training."

Erhard, meanwhile, was taking other steps to exert rigid control over his staff. In the fall of 1972 he hired Robert Larzelere, a Berkeley medical doctor who had become interested in the mind-control theories that Erhard had incorporated into est. Larzelere, a soft-spoken man with a gentle, reassuring smile, had taken one of Erhard's first Mind Dynamics courses and was instantly impressed with both the program and the instructor. He soon began suggesting to some of his patients that they consider exploring alternative ways of resolving various medical problems. Holistic medicine had not yet become as accepted as it would in later years, so the gentle-mannered Larzelere had to be careful about dispensing his new metaphysical advice to patients, lest any of them confuse him with some kind of New Age witch doctor.

Erhard seized the opportunity to add a medical doctor to his staff, realizing the boost in credibility that est would gain from having a trained professional among its ranks. But Erhard had other duties in mind for Larzelere besides his medical acumen. He steered Larzelere toward Scientology and had him trained to use the knobs and dials of the e-meter. Erhard also referred him to various Scientology books written by L. Ron Hubbard, explaining to Larzelere that it's "always good to go to the source."

Erhard figured out a perfect spot for Larzelere, a position that combined his medical background with his freshly minted Scientology training. Larzelere was introduced to the staff as the director of est's new "well being department." It was now Larzelere's job to monitor the physical and emotional health of Erhard's growing staff. Before long Larzelere would be given many more intrusive assignments by Erhard. Starting at a weekly salary of $75, Larzelere quit his medical practice and sold his Berkeley home, subsidizing his low pay by moving into a much smaller house in San Francisco.

Within a week Larzelere had his first lesson in Erhard's authoritarian regime. The doctor decided to listen to Erhard speak at a guest event held to sign up new enrollments. He brought with him a friend from Berkeley named Helen who had already taken the training. At one point during the evening, Larzelere turned to Helen and commented that Erhard did not seem his usual effective self that night. The next day an angry Laurel Scheaf pulled him aside at the office on Kearny Street. Helen had confided to her what Larzelere had said about Erhard.

"Bob, you know that you're on staff now," Scheaf reminded Larzelere.

"I realize that," he replied.

Scheaf gave him a stern look. "Do you know that no staff person ever says anything negative to any human being about Werner?"

"What did I say that was negative?" Larzelere wondered.

"You told Helen that you thought Werner was less than he could've been."

"That's right, I did," Larzelere admitted.

"Don't ever let that happen again," Scheaf snapped.

Werner Erhard had been the recipient of absolute loyalty from members of his sales staff when he sold books door to door in San

Francisco. He received the same unquestioning obedience when he shifted his selling talents as a Mind Dynamics instructor in the early months of 1971. Now that he had launched his own mind-enhancing seminar business, he required that his employees yield completely to his authority. For the core of his staff at est, bending to Erhard's authority posed no problems; those staff members largely consisted of the same group that had worked in his shadow earlier.

Others who had joined up with Erhard received their own lessons in surrendering authority to the imposing figure who, from the time that est started, always presented himself as the source of the material he was now selling to the public. For some, such as Robert Larzelere, the first lesson in the demands of Werner worship occurred only days after joining the staff. Others simply learned to accept as a condition of employment that they follow unquestionably his dictates and whims. One of Erhard's early part-time staff members, who had followed him from Mind Dynamics to est, got his first taste of the rigid rules in early 1972 when he was abruptly fired by Laurel Scheaf, only to be hired back a short time later. Over the years Erhard was to routinely fire and rehire other staff members, as if to tell them their standing in the organization depended entirely on how he judged their devotion to him along with the results they achieved for est.

Seven

ENLIGHTENMENT IN TWO WEEKENDS

In this training,

you're going to find out you've been

acting like assholes.

—EST TRAINER STEWART EMERY

Two hundred fifty people sat in straight-backed chairs in the flock-wallpapered ballroom at San Francisco's Jack Tar Hotel, waiting for the est training to begin. A few minutes earlier, on the mezzanine level of the hotel, a small army of cheerfully smiling est volunteers saw to it that everyone entering the ballroom had paid their $250 enrollment fee and had affixed a name tag with their first name spelled out in bold black print. Inside the ballroom, the seats were set up in three neatly arranged sections, each row of chairs facing toward the dais in ruler-straight lines. Another group of est volunteers patrolled the perimeter of the room, making sure everyone was silent and in his or her seat. A moment later a dour-faced man of medium build and short brown hair, wearing a sweater over an open-collar shirt and a name tag that said "Ron," walked to the front of the room and stepped onto the stage. Around the room, dozens of people exchanged nervous smiles and some throat-clearing coughs as they turned their attention to the man who seemed almost to be scowling at them. The est training was about to begin.

For the next two hours, Ron, using his best drill-sergeant voice, worked his way through a thirty-page recitation of the rules everyone had to agree to follow during the training. No one could move from his or her seat unless told to do so. There was to be no smoking, eating, or drinking at any time in the room. There would be one meal break during the course of the day, and the session, which began promptly at nine in the morning, might end anywhere between midnight and four o'clock the next morning. No one could leave to go to the bathroom except during short breaks announced by the trainer. Note-taking was strictly prohibited, and anyone wearing a watch had to remove it immediately and hand it over to one of the volunteer assistants stationed around the room. There was to be no talking except when the est trainer called on someone to talk, after which the person would wait until one of the assistants came over with a microphone. Ron spent several minutes showing everyone, in precise detail, how to hold the microphone, how to speak into it, and how to wait until one of the assistants retrieved it before sitting down again.

Someone in the room raised a hand and asked, after he was recognized by Ron and handed one of the microphones, what was the reason for all the rigid rules.

Training assistants were always prepared with a standard response to such questions. Anything used in the training was put there "because Werner found out that's what works," Ron and other assistants would say.

Most of Werner Erhard's customers had sat on the sidelines during the heady, mind-expanding years of the 1960s. They had not, for the most part, considered themselves part of the nation's counterculture during those tumultuous years, but rather had spent the time finishing school and beginning careers and raising families—and mainly becoming "responsible" adults. Attracting an overwhelmingly white and middle-class audience (made up of slightly more women than men), est provided hundreds of thousands of its participants with their first real adventurous taste of the exotic-sounding human potential movement. Of course, there were others who had come to est after dabbling in a variety of self-awareness programs, from Esalen and gestalt therapy to transcendental meditation and incense-tinged chanting. But they were the exceptions; the training sessions filled up mostly with newcomers to this business of transformation.

Some came to the hotel ballrooms because they wanted to find meaning in their lives. Most came because they were simply curious—because they had wives or husbands, boyfriends or girlfriends, bosses or employees, neighbors or relatives, who had already taken the training and couldn't stop gushing about this fantastic thing they had just experienced. They came because everywhere they turned, it seemed, all they kept hearing about was a handsome, smooth-talking, charismatic guy named Werner Erhard who had figured it all out and was willing to share his secrets. All it took was a credit card and the willingness to sit in a hotel ballroom chair for hours on end over the course of two weekends.

At the end of it, Werner Erhard held out the tantalizing promise of transformation, a word and a concept never precisely defined in the fuzzy syntax-twisted jargon of est. As a master salesman, he knew he didn't have to bother with simple explanations because his customers never demanded it. "I don't understand anything that's happened and I can't remember concepts at the [est] seminars or training," one est graduate remarked in the late 1970s. "But I'm able to do and handle and create so much now." Erhard never peddled logic and understanding, both of which were anathema to the est training itself. In concocting est out of a myriad of self-help, self-awareness, motivational, and psychological theories he had mastered over the years, he was interested only in convincing people they could "experience" transformation just by suspending logic and understanding, which he scornfully derided as the "booby prize" in life. Time and again he and other est trainers insulted and yelled and jeered at any est participant who insisted on "understanding" the methods and objectives of the est training.

But what was "it"? people still wanted to know before they put their money down. From est's earliest days, Erhard had come up with a pithy description of his new self-awareness course that soon was adopted as est's official mantra. In true Erhard fashion, the mantra provided no answer at all, succeeding only in drawing ever-increasing numbers of curious souls into the ballroom chairs. "The purpose of the est training," Erhard and his followers chanted over and over again, "is to transform your ability to experience living so that the situations you have been trying to change or have been putting up with clear up just in the process of life itself."

In the ballroom of the Jack Tar Hotel (and in similar ballrooms in hotels across the country), the est trainer finally emerged from the back of the room after the boot-camp rules had been read and digested by everyone. Bounding onto the stage with a burst of energy, microphone in hand, he turned to the 250 men and women sitting silently in the ballroom and shouted at them with all the fervor of a profane Sunday morning preacher.

"IN THIS TRAINING, YOU'RE GOING TO FIND OUT YOU'VE BEEN ACTING LIKE ASSHOLES. ALL YOUR FUCKING CLEVERNESS AND SELF-DECEPTION HAVE GOTTEN YOU NOWHERE!"

During the first year or so of est, Erhard himself led all the est trainings, since he was the only one who had yet mastered the hours of materials he had stitched together from Scientology and Mind Dynamics and Dale Carnegie and Maxwell Maltz and a variety of other sources. After a while others bounded onto the stages to repeat the same lines and deliver the same material. Always they conducted the est training exactly the way Erhard had done, for they trained countless hours to do it the way he told them to.

For the first several hours of the training, Erhard and his other trainers kept up a nonstop barrage of verbal insults, taunting the participants in the straight-backed chairs, insisting they were all worthless human beings who clung to beliefs about themselves and their own lives that were rooted in ridiculous notions about reason, logic, and understanding.

"Don't give me your goddamn belief system, you dumb motherfucker!" one of Erhard's est trainers once thundered at a man who had raised his hand on the first day with a question about the need to believe in something, in anything. The trainer stormed off the dais and perched himself within inches of the man's face. "Get rid of all that shit!" screamed the trainer.

The man sat down in his seat, only to be greeted with a loud burst of applause from everyone else in the room. It was part of the rules, part of the "agreement" for being in the training. Anytime someone got up to "share" something during the training, everyone else was instructed to acknowledge him or her with applause. It never took very long for est training sessions to take on the surreal dimensions of confusing logic. A stream of abusive epithets hurled at a skeptical participant always ended in a cheerful smile from the trainer and an enthusiastic round of applause from everyone else.

By the late afternoon of the first day, the est trainers always launched into another several hours' worth of lectures revolving around one of est's fundamental tenets. Taking responsibility for your life, in the world according to Werner Erhard, required people to accept the idea that they were equally responsible for everything that happened in their lives. From illness and disease to auto accidents and street muggings, Erhard and his trainers drummed into the heads of est participants that they alone caused all the incidents and episodes in their lives to occur. The est philosophy included no room for victims or excuses. Only when his customers accepted that, only when they realized that all people "create their own reality," were they in a position to resolve problems plaguing their lives.

Nobody believed that more fervently than Werner Erhard himself. More than ten years before he created est, Jack Rosenberg had already created a new reality by shedding his past and pretending for years it had never even existed. Driven by an overpowering ambition for fame (and its accompanying riches), Erhard discovered in the myriad self-help, get-rich, human motivation textbooks and courses a formula that seemed to accommodate so conveniently his own personal psychodrama. It had worked for him. Surely it was something that could work for others.

Ultimately, the product that Erhard sold, at first to a few hundred people but later to tens and hundreds of thousands, was a confusing sense of innocence born of a hybrid philosophy in which the past mattered little, if at all. With his charismatic skills of a salesman-showman, Erhard packaged his program of innocence lost in a way that no one had ever done before. He, quite literally, had claimed to invent, with the est training, a new "technology" offering nothing less than transformation. Happily for Erhard, a significant slice of the American population was ready for such a product in the early years of the 1970s, having emerged from a turbulent decade that tore at the fabric of social institutions, organized religion, and the nation's general spirit of community. The human potential movement, through upstart offshoots such as Esalen, promised—whether realistically or not—a degree of psychic and spiritual comfort in the wake of an increasingly alienated culture. Erhard, the salesman, wrapped up the promise of transformation in a nifty two-weekend package.

Better yet, he offered his customers some pretty easy answers that explained the sordid state of the world around them. "When I look at what we're doing in the world, it makes me feel helpless," an est participant said in the 1970s. "There's nothing I can do about it, except accept it. Est has shown me that's okay. At least after taking the training, I felt a big burden of guilt removed toward people who were having problems, whatever they were, because I got that they were responsible in a way." What Erhard left out of the training was any sense of human compassion and emotion. He and his est trainers angrily rejected such trivialities in the training sessions. Compassion, after all, was something reserved for life's "victims." In the world of est, as in the world of Werner Erhard, there were no victims.

During est's early years, Erhard sometimes went so far as to assert that 6 million Jews had been "responsible" for their own deaths during the Holocaust of World War II. One woman participating in the training had herself been imprisoned in one of the Nazi death camps, where other members of her family perished. At first, she was outraged at Erhard's audacity in arguing that Jews were responsible for their own horrific fate.

Eventually Erhard insisted the woman had seen his point of view and had then been able to find real value in the message of the est training. As a result of the training, the woman was able to finally free herself from the concentration camp, Erhard later recounted. "She took responsibility for putting herself in. It's that goddamn simple."

Someone asked Erhard how the woman could have avoided being in the camp in the first place.

Erhard deflected the question with a mystifying and brusque response. "How could the light be off when it's turned on? The question is completely stupid."

Toward the end of the first long day of the est training, Erhard plugged in the first of what he described as "processes," a series of directed meditation exercises conducted by the trainer and used, according to Erhard, to enable people to "create their own experience." Ordered to shut their eyes, everyone in the ballroom followed their monotone repetitions aimed at inducing a state of collective relaxation around the room.

Beginning with the left foot and continuing upward throughout the body, the trainer gently directed everyone to "create a space" in each part of their anatomy. With each direction repeated three times, the effect of the long trance-inducing exercise, coupled with the trainer's soothing homilies about the heightening powers of est, resulted in a roomful of dazed and fatigued trainees. At the end of it, they wandered off into the post-midnight darkness after finishing est's first fifteen-hour day, some of them certainly wondering what they had gotten themselves into.

Day two of the est training reflected even heavier doses of Erhard's training in Scientology and Mind Dynamics. Much of the day was spent carrying out another mental exercise known as the Truth Process, which more than anything else during the est training often resembled a mass psychotherapy session. After the neatly arranged rows of ballroom chairs had been pushed to the side of the room, participants were instructed to lie down on the floor, after which the trainer ordered them to shut their eyes again and choose a significant "item" or problem in their lives that they wanted to solve.

Over the next several hours, the est trainer—after leading everyone through another round of directed meditation—coached the lying bodies on how to search through their memories for all of the emotions, reactions, and consequences of the problem each person was trying to resolve. For many lying on the ballroom floors, the intensely introspective nature of the est Truth Process wreaked havoc on their emotional systems. People writhed and thrashed about with their bodies, the sounds of crying and screaming and groaning echoing around the ballroom. Erhard and his trainers were ready for every reaction, even stocking a supply of silver-colored "barf bags" for the poor retching souls who sometimes lost the contents of their stomachs during the process of resolving their long-festering problem. The goal of the Truth Process was to discover the ultimate cause of each person's self-chosen affliction, after which the problem itself was supposed to disappear.

Erhard, of course, had discovered no new miracle cure. Similar versions of the Truth Process already had surfaced in other self-wareness methods, including gestalt therapy, primal scream therapy, and the auditing practice in Scientology. Even earlier, a British psychiatrist named William Sargant had studied various techniques involved in indoctrination and thought control, only to discover a long-standing strain of the very same method used in Erhard's est training. In his 1957 book, *Battle for the Mind*, Sargant described the technique as a "time-worn physiological trick which has been used, for better or worse, by generations of preachers and demagogues to soften up their listeners' minds and help them take on desired patterns of belief and behavior."

The long second day of the est training ended with yet another process that was remarkably similar to Scientology exercises known as "bullbaiting" and "confronting." In the Scientology version, used in the introductory communications course that Erhard and his book-sales staff had once taken with his Scientologist friend Peter Monk, people paired off and took turns trying to goad the other into a response. In est, Erhard adapted the strange exercise for a large group and called it the "danger process." Row by row, est participants were directed to the stage and ordered to stand ramrod straight, leaving others in the room to stare back at them. On cue, a special team of est volunteers serving as "confronters" marched to the stage where they stood toe to toe and nose to nose in front of the trainees, not saying anything but only staring with blazing eyes at the nervous person standing only inches away. At the same time, the est trainer paced back and forth, playing the role of the "bullbaiter," shouting insults and epithets at those standing on the stage. Usually at least a few people broke down into sobbing fits or had their legs give way beneath them, traumatized by the fear of standing in front of a large crowd or being stared at by the menacing-looking est volunteer. A separate team of volunteers served as "body catchers," trained in the est-art of catching people who often fell to the ground during the process.

Before the second day ended, the trainer led the latest group of est inductees through one more process. Lying on the floor again, with closed eyes, participants were told to imagine they were deathly afraid of the person lying next to them. A few moments later the trainer asked them to experience the fear of everyone else in the room. From there he expanded the boundaries of fear so that eventually he had every person in the room convinced they were afraid of everyone else in the world. Again, the room often broke down into a cacophony of noise, with sobbing and screaming reverberating off the walls as people conjured up the emotion of absolute fear. Then the trainer reversed the process, asking participants to imagine that others now were afraid of them. By the end of the long night, a giddy sense of levity had managed to replace the wrenching emotions that had permeated the room earlier in the evening. Out into the dark and quiet streets spilled 250 exhausted souls, halfway home to becoming newly minted est graduates.

A week later the ballroom filled up again, and once more the est trainer bounded to the front of the room, this time to launch into a mind-numbing lecture lasting several hours, confusing participants about the differences between what was "real" and what was "unreal." As with other parts of the est training, the result of the lecture was to confuse trainees sitting obediently in the ruler-lined rows of chairs, to "blow their minds," as Erhard often explained.

The fourth and final day led up to the climactic moment of est. It began with another mind-numbing lecture, one that sometimes took the trainer at least ten hours to deliver. Erhard called the rambling discourse the "anatomy of the mind," and stuffed it with pseudoscientific analysis of how the brain always was functioning as a self-perpetuating machine, programmed to repeat over and over again the same mechanistic responses to similar situations facing people in their daily lives. Finally, after hours of droning on, the est trainer would stop the lecture and look out across the room, filled now with anxious faces. What was coming next? they wondered as they sat in silence in their seats. Was this what they had paid their money for?

"I'll tell you everything there is to know about life," the trainer gleefully announced. "What is, is, and what ain't, ain't." And that's about all there was. True enlightenment, the trainer concluded, "is knowing you are a machine." Finally, the magical revelation of est had been visited upon yet another group of curious transformation seekers. They were told that they were nothing but a collection of individual brain-powered machines. "Whether you accept this or not," the trainer instructed them, "it's so."

Around the room there were a few more nervous coughs and plenty of quizzical expressions. So they were machines, supposedly without emotions, without feelings, without the ability to understand. And for this they had paid a few hundred dollars while sitting in uncomfortable hotel chairs for dozens of hours. Just then, only moments after the trainer had plunged everyone into the depths of a depressing gray funk, he offered them a final redeeming ray of hope.

In a rising voice that signaled the training's climactic moment, the trainer exhorted everyone to accept the true nature of their own minds. Assume responsibility for creating everything in their lives, for being precisely who they were. And in doing so, the trainer summed up, each new est graduate now became what he or she always wanted to be. In a word, they were perfect. They were perfect just the way they were.

There were still plenty of puzzled expressions spread across the faces of those sitting in the uncomfortable hotel seats. But there was also a smattering of applause, of shrieks of laughter, even of gasps, as if four days of psychobabble had suddenly jelled into a glorious moment of epiphany. This, the trainer exultantly announced, was the miracle of est. You are what you are, and you are responsible for everything you do.

At the end of every training, the trainer always led the participants through an exercise that underscored, above all else, the ultimate logic-defying magic of Werner Erhard's sales technique. Going around the room, the trainer asked for a show of hands from everyone who had "gotten it," referring to the bottom-line message of the training. As dozens of hands were raised, the rest of the room burst into a round of applause. Next the trainer turned his attention to everyone else, whose hands had remained at their sides. One final dose of est's self-fulfilling logic was all that was needed to take care of them.

"I don't get it," one trainee once told trainer Stewart Emery during a New York est session.

"Good," Emery replied. "There's nothing to get so you got it."

"I get it," the trainee said, as a broad grin slid across her face. "So getting it is whatever you get."

"If that's what you got."

Got it?

Eight

A GURU
IS BORN

Californians have a

special constitutional weakness

for new messiahs.

—SAM KEEN
author and social observer

In September 1976, a Berkeley sociologist named Theodore Roszak
told *Newsweek* magazine that America in the mid-1970s was in the
middle of "the biggest introspective binge any society in history has
undergone." Nowhere was that binge more evident than on the streets
of San Francisco.

A walk down the city's Union Street a year or two earlier would surely have convinced a visitor that the city was obsessed with "self-awareness" programs of every stripe. Having outgrown the cramped office on Kearny Street, est had moved into new quarters at 1750 Union Street in 1974. On the same one-block stretch between Gough and Octavia streets could be found the Gestalt Institute, the Eductivism church of philosophy, the Unicorn Ashram (an astrology shop), and the San Francisco branch of the Esalen Institute. Even Scientology, though its main San Francisco headquarters was located a few miles away near City Hall, operated a smaller outpost on Union Street one block west of the human potential strip.

Farther up Union Street stood the headquarters of yet another self-awareness program called Lifespring, begun in 1974 and, like est, patterned after Mind Dynamics. Lifespring, in fact, owed its existence to Mind Dynamics, which had folded by the end of 1973 following a fiery plane crash that had claimed the life of William Penn Patrick earlier that year. An avid collector and flyer of small vintage military planes, Patrick crashed into a hillside on his 6,000-acre northern California ranch eighty miles north of San Francisco on the morning of June 9 and was killed instantly when his World War II–era P51 Mustang fighter plunged into a ridge, scattering pieces of the wreckage across more than two hundred yards of rugged foothills.

Two months after Patrick's death, his wife announced at a San Francisco press conference that Leadership Dynamics and Mind Dynamics—both targets of lawsuits by then—were closing down. A few months later five of Patrick's employees—including Charlene Afremow, Werner Erhard's Mind Dynamics instructor—set up Lifespring. Like est, Lifespring was aggressively marketed and copied many of the mental exercises at the core of Mind Dynamics. And like Werner Erhard, one of Lifespring's principal founders, John Hanley, had a checkered past that dogged him through the years. In 1969 the twenty-three-year-old Hanley was convicted in a federal court in Des Moines, Iowa, of fraud charges arising out of the sale of nonexistent territories for a toilet-cleaning service. He was fined $1,000 and placed on five years' probation. Soon after his conviction, Hanley went to work for Patrick's Holiday Magic cosmetic business and later joined the Mind Dynamics staff, where he became an instructor and later the company's national field director.*

It was est, however, that dominated the instant-fix therapy movement by the time of *Newsweek*'s eight-page report detailing the "consciousness revolution" around the country. By then Erhard was claiming nearly 100,000 est graduates, while another 1,000 signed up each week to take the training. Erhard, of course, was more successful than others in applying mass-marketing sales techniques to the human potential movement. Some 80 percent of all est graduates enrolled themselves into inexpensive posttraining seminars that covered topics such as sex, money, and relationships. But Erhard made sure a hefty portion of the weekly est seminars was devoted to pressing participants into bringing new people into the est training, a recruitment trick that he had picked up during his days at Mind Dynamics.

Est was hardly the only visible sign of the American "human potential" boom during the 1970s. Esalen continued to attract a steady stream of seekers to its Big Sur outpost, while other awareness groups and sensitivity therapies, such as Arica and primal scream, were attracting the likes of Jerry Rubin (who also was an est graduate) and John Lennon, whose wife, Yoko Ono, took the est training. In 1976 some 1,600 people had showed up for the annual conference of the Association of Humanistic Psychology in Atlantic City, New Jersey, which featured dozens of workshops and lectures on topics that ranged from adultery to Zen. The unofficial program for the conference also included nude pool parties at midnight and erotic film viewings.

The country's obsession with self-obsession seemed to show up everywhere, sometimes cast in a comically satirical light. In his 1977 movie *Annie Hall*, Woody Allen tossed in a zinger about est and took a sarcastic potshot at other kinds of self-awareness enthusiasts when he focused on a stressed-out Los Angeles partygoer complaining into the phone that "I forgot my mantra."** Allen's forgetful mantra-

---

*In the early 1970s the Wisconsin Justice Department sued Hanley and others over Holiday Magic's sales techniques. The civil case was settled in 1975 after Hanley agreed to pay $1,750 while denying any legal responsibility for the challenged actions.

**Erhard and est became satirical targets in other movies, notably the 1981 film *Semi-Tough*, which featured actor Burt Convy as an Erhard-like self-awareness leader named Friedrich Bismark.

chanter hardly was alone with his fear of some horrific spiritual mis-cue. By the mid-1970s there were an estimated 800,000 Americans practicing some kind of meditation, many of whom were trying to find inner peace through hypnotic hums and soothing ommmms.

Throughout the decade there was ample evidence that something quite strange and remarkable and disturbing was taking place throughout American society. Tom Wolfe acidly described the years as the "Me Decade" in a 1976 cover story for *New York* magazine that, not surprisingly, opened with a searing account of an est training, offered as a classic example of the self-obsessive nature of the times. Wolfe compared the new culture of "me-ism" to two earlier periods of religious awakening that had gripped the country, first in the middle of the eighteenth century and again in the early decades of the nine-teenth century. But in the Me Decade, worshipers sought to tap not some distant and unseen spiritual force but rather the more immediate and potent, self-absorbed power of the individual. Wolfe concluded his lengthy essay:

> Where the Third Great Awakening will lead—who can pre-sume to say? One only knows that the great religious waves have a momentum all their own. Neither arguments nor pol-icies nor acts of the legislature have been any match for them in the past. And this one has the mightiest, holiest roll of all, the beat that goes . . . Me . . . Me . . . Me . . . Me. . . .

Journalists such as Wolfe and others delighted in using Werner Erhard as an illuminating example of the narcissistic message so per-vasive during the 1970s. The central, underlying message that Erhard had planted in the est training—the same mantra that his cloned trainers drummed endlessly into the minds of those streaming into hotel ballrooms by the tens of thousands—was that reality centered in each individual sitting in each of those uncomfortable ballroom chairs. Each of you, Erhard and trainers repeated over and over again to every fresh set of customers, is ultimately and completely respon-sible for your own reality. Each of you is responsible for everything that happens in your life. Take charge, assume command, don't per-

mit yourself to become a victim when you control everything that life
throws at you.

Although Erhard hardly created single-handedly the phenomenon and culture that defined the Me Decade, Peter Marin, writing in
Harper's in 1975, castigated Erhard as a living embodiment of the
age's "new narcissism."

> Clearly Erhard has a genius—not only for the efficiency
> with which his program is organized and sold, but also for
> the accuracy with which he tells his audience what it wants
> to hear. It is the latter which binds them to him. The world
> is perfect, each of us is all-powerful, shame and guilt are
> merely arbitrary notions, truth is identical to belief, suffer-
> ing is merely the result of imperfect consciousness—how
> like manna all of this must seem to hungry souls. For if we
> are each totally responsible for our fate, then all the others
> in the world are responsible for their fate, and if that is so,
> why should we worry about them?

Werner Erhard could hardly be bothered by the musings of dis-
affected writers who obviously did not get the message of human
transformation. Anyway, what did he have to worry about? By the mid-
1970s est seemed poised on the brink of its own transformational
breakthrough.

Over the past few years, Erhard had watched—sometimes in
amazement and at other times with the confidence of a self-assured
salesman—est expand from the initial trickle of a few curious seekers
into a near flood that seemed ready to engulf the entire country. The
number of est graduates steadily climbed, from 1,000 in March 1972,
to 10,000 in August 1973, to 25,000 by October 1974. At the end of
1975, the number of est graduates had climbed to 65,000, with more
than 10,000 people already registered for trainings scheduled in the
first few months of 1976.

From his outpost in San Francisco, Erhard had moved aggressively to export the est training to other cities. Los Angeles was the
second city to boast its own est center, with the opening of a Southern
California branch in June 1972. Four months later est sprang up in

the Rocky Mountain playground of Aspen, where John Denver had first been enlightened. From there Erhard expanded to Honolulu in November 1973, followed a few months later with a center in New York. Plans were already in the works for other centers to open in the first half of 1975, in Denver, Washington, D.C., Boston, and Oakland. After serving as est's sole trainer in its early months, Erhard now had "designated" seven others to spread his message of enlightenment, all but one of them men who seemed to go out of their way to dress and sound and act like Werner Erhard. Besides the basic est training, Erhard was now conducting special training sessions for teenagers and children as young as six years old. Dogged by occasional criticism that the est phenomenon—like much of the human potential movement—was limited largely to well-educated whites, Erhard offered a special "black training" in Oakland and Watts, at a reduced cost to participants.

Werner Erhard's growing fame as America's premier pop guru also was beginning to spread to other parts of the world. Early est-sponsored journeys to Europe and India introduced Erhard and his rhetoric about transformation to enthusiastic audiences from Munich to Bombay, while setting the stage for est trainings in several foreign cities. Back in the United States, Erhard's rising prominence as the leader of the country's self-help movement also brought him lecture invitations from an impressive list of universities, medical schools, and psychotherapy groups fascinated by the est phenomenon and curious about the enigmatic man behind the movement. While many academics and professionals quickly dismissed Erhard as a smooth-talking quack, others who took the training zealously embraced both him and est and encouraged their colleagues to do likewise.

While his own popularity began to soar, Erhard's tightly controlled organization was evolving into a much more formal structure, though everything still revolved around "Werner." At the outset, est—from an organizational point of view—added up to little more than Erhard's sales pitches, with a half-dozen or so lowly paid staffers and volunteers handling all the follow-up work in the offices on Kearny Street. Although Laurel Scheaf was the nominal president of the organization, est during its first two years of operation had no management structure to speak of. That began to change in the summer of 1973 when Erhard conferred upon Stewart Emery the new title of chief executive officer, a position for which the Australian was little qualified, particularly given his main job of delivering est trainings around the country. By the spring of 1974 it was apparent to both Erhard and Emery that est's growth required a more experienced executive with solid business management skills.

A former Harvard Business School instructor named Donald Cox fit the bill perfectly. An est graduate himself, the portly Cox had been general manager of the Coca-Cola Bottling Company in San Francisco and was a former vice president for Coca-Cola USA at its corporate headquarters in Atlanta. Cox liked to hire other est graduates for openings there, and he quickly convinced Emery he was the right man to run est. Emery, in turn, persuaded Erhard that Cox was much more suited for the job than another leading candidate who had earned millions of dollars running a potato chip company. In April 1974 Don Cox became est's first genuine management expert.

Cox wasted no time in hiring other professional managers, signaling his attention to run est like any other corporation. He started with Gary Grace, a former mangement trainee at the Del Monte Corporation who later worked under Cox at Coca-Cola. Grace joined the staff two months after Cox arrived, with the title of chief financial officer. Other executives joined the est staff over the next several months, including Bob Curtis, a mechanical engineer and attorney who became est's first in-house legal counsel. In 1975 John Vincent Drucker joined the staff to head up a new marketing department and later replaced Grace as financial officer. Drucker, with a background in publishing and promotions, also was attractive to Erhard because of his well-known father, Peter Drucker, a prominent business management consultant who lived and worked in Southern California. Vincent Drucker introduced Erhard to his father, who advised the organization briefly in some management areas. Vincent Drucker, who later became one of Erhard's sharpest critics, received an early taste of Erhard's autocratic leanings almost immediately after joining the staff. After meeting Erhard, Drucker remarked how pleased he was to be working for Don Cox, the man who had hired him. Erhard quickly corrected his new employee.

"No, you're working for me," Erhard said abruptly. "You're hired by Don. You may be reporting to Don. But you work for me. Everybody in this organization works for me."

Erhard similarly dressed down other employees, offering them blunt reminders of where their loyalties must lie once they came to work for est. At the end of 1975, during a four-day staff meeting, a new staff member stood up to be introduced to the rest of the group.

"I'm happy to be joining the staff," said the new employee. "I'm happy that I will be able to bring my professional skills to bear."

Erhard cut him off sharply, yelling at the new employee, "Stop! I don't want your goddamn professional skills. I don't give a crap about your goddamn professional skills. You are not here because of your professional skills. You are here to re-create me." In Werner Erhard's world, est employees were there to imitate the boss, to reflect his image in everything they did.

By the mid-1970s Erhard had largely succeeded in building an enterprise that revolved, in almost every facet and detail, around the obligation to worship Werner. "I love you," he signed off constantly in est-promoting messages that appeared in a new monthly magazine distributed to est graduates around the country. Along with a litany of glowing testimonials about the power of est, the magazine usually included plenty of photographs of Erhard himself, always smiling, always showing off his handsome, almost boyish features. In person, as in his photographs, Erhard was always immaculately groomed and fashionably dressed. As he approached his fortieth birthday, Werner Erhard gave every appearance of a man completely in charge.

Around the country, a growing army of enthusiastic est volunteers (called "assistants" in est jargon) contributed free labor—sometimes up to forty hours per week—to the organization, filling every conceivable task from handling the phones in est centers around the country to cleaning out the toilets and scrubbing the pots and pans at the Franklin House. In 1977, as est approached the height of its popularity, thousands of assistants were contributing some 20,000 hours of free labor each week to the organization.

In their smiling eagerness to serve est and Werner, the volunteers hardly noticed the irony of the circumstances in which they found themselves. In the est training, they had triumphantly declared they had "gotten it," embracing Erhard's message of take-charge-of-your-life individualism and aggressive assertiveness. After streaming out of their training sessions, thousands of them were ready to do anything Erhard and other est employees asked of them, without stopping to question the motives and purposes of their free labor. Perhaps it never occurred to some of them just how ironic it was to "assist" as door guards at other est trainings, a job that required them—with all their newly acquired enlightenment—to do whatever they could to dissuade people inside from leaving the room.

Erhard always denied vehemently that est was growing into some kind of guru-centered personality cult. He insisted only that est graduates performed all the invaluable hours of free service not as a gesture of blind devotion to him but rather to carry out the principles of service to others that he maintained was a crucial part of the est culture. Undoubtedly that was true for many assistants who found themselves so caught up in the blinding light of est's appearance as a path toward human enlightenment. But Erhard and his staff also made sure that volunteers, just like the staff itself, faced constant reminders that service to est and to Erhard were synonymous. Volunteer receptionists at est's New York office were warned to "stay conscious" because "Werner might walk in at any minute."

Beginning in 1973, each new est graduate received a little booklet of aphorisms attributed to Erhard. ("The end is the end, or it isn't. The end justifies the means, or it doesn't," read one entry.) In est seminars, volunteer leaders—whose job was primarily to recruit new people into the training—were forever quoting "Werner" while singing the glorious praises of the life-changing value of "Werner's work."

While the level of Werner worship was rising, est's increasingly rigorous approach to spreading Erhard's vision of transformation was much in evidence within the est culture. It was no longer enough to sell est aggressively to increasing numbers of enthusiastic customers. No, Erhard also created an ongoing atmosphere of crisis and dire consequences in the wake of anything less than peak performance from his loyal minions. "The Germans are in Oakland," Erhard told his San Francisco staff, relying on a metaphor of approaching Nazi hordes to intimidate the staff into signing up more faithful est recruits. To the outside world, Erhard often appeared as a fuzzy-sounding though seemingly well-intentioned head of a popular self-awareness offshoot of the human potential movement. But inside the culture of est, he was becoming nothing less than the dictatorial general of a compliant army, whose sole job was to re-create the man in charge and carry out his every whim. "Provide Werner with as much certainty as possible," concluded an est secretary's note tacked above her typewriter.

An increasingly profitable enterprise that relied extensively on volunteers and low-paid staff members provided Erhard with the lavish material trappings of success as well. Thanks to the magic of the Margolis system, Erhard already had a perfect cover story to explain the steadily rising opulent life-style his growing fortunes from est were providing him by the mid-1970s. Whenever anyone asked about his profits from est, Erhard had only to point to his "employment contract" that made it clear he didn't own est at all, but rather that he took home only a modest salary from the company. At the same time, the business supplied Erhard with generous amenities befitting an increasingly popular guru.

During est's early years, Erhard continued his previous penchant for being driven around town; now the task fell to one of his ubiquitous "communicators" or other staff members. At first, a modest Audi was sufficient for the job of transporting Erhard. In September 1973 Erhard announced to the est staff that his "wealthy grandmother" Bessie Clauson had decided, as a birthday present, to bestow on him a shiny new black Mercedes sedan. Although Erhard did have a grandmother by that name, she had nothing to do with buying the luxurious car. Instead, it had been bought from a San Francisco car dealer with money from Associated Convalescent Enterprises, one of Margolis's shell companies. The personalized license plate on Erhard's new car read SO WUT.

With a generous clothing allowance—outlined in Erhard's "employment contract"—Erhard outfitted himself with expensive apparel from the posh Wilkes Bashford men's salon in San Francisco. Often one of Erhard's aides dropped by the exclusive shop on Sutter Street, walking out with an armful of suits and other clothes, from which Erhard later picked out new items for his wardrobe in the privacy of the Franklin House. To assist him in sartorial matters, Erhard called on a well-known local decorator and designer named Ron Mann, who had been hired as well to help redecorate the Franklin House, a project that began in 1973 and eventually cost hundreds of thousands of dollars. Erhard demanded nothing less than perfection, even when nobody else had questions about the quality of the work. During the remodeling of the house, Erhard ordered a soundproof room to be built at the back of the third floor. When it was done, he came by to inspect the work, only to start screaming that he heard a noise coming from somewhere in the room. Although no one else detected a sound, Erhard ordered the workers to tear out the whole side of a wall to find the mysterious tick that had so infuriated him. The cause of the offending sound was never discovered.

Elsewhere around the house, Erhard saw to it that the decorating and accoutrements matched his character and tastes. He ordered the installation of an elaborate security system, complete with a space-age set of controls permitting him to lock doors and handle other functions from his second-floor living quarters. He had his bedroom walls painted black, and he matched the dark, foreboding decor by coating the outside of the house in a dark shade of green that set off the building dramatically from others in the neighborhood.

The expensive remodeling of the Franklin House reflected Erhard's fervent desire, as his est fame grew, to transform himself into the proprietor and host of San Francisco's most dazzling salon, while converting his est-built home into a center of intellectual gatherings in the city. With a formal education that ended in high school, Erhard was determined to overcome his own intellectual shortcomings by surrounding himself with those whose very presence in his home would help to confirm his reputation as an enlightened source of big ideas.

With a guest list that ranged from world-class opera singers and astronauts to Nobel Prize–winning physicists and Hollywood producers, Erhard succeeded in turning the Franklin House, at least for a few years, into an important social gathering spot in San Francisco. Always a charming and genial host, Erhard treated his guests to sumptuous meals and fine wines, with aromatic cigars and expensive brandy lubricating the heady conversation that might touch on any-thing from world politics to the vagaries of quantum physics. In one year alone Erhard spent more than $12,000 stocking the Franklin House's cellar and humidors with wines and cigars. Attended to by a bevy of carefully trained volunteer est assistants, Erhard delighted in sitting back in one of his comfortable wing chairs, puffing away on one of his favored Monte Cristos, and sipping from his glass of wine. Occasionally he even joined in the conversation, though at other times he was satisfied to listen to the dizzying banter of thoughts around the room.

In his entertaining, Erhard made a particular point of courting the likes of Michael Murphy and other well-respected leaders of the human potential movement, hosting a series of Franklin House din-ners for them during the mid-1970s. Having been told of Murphy's affinity for Indian spiritual figures, Erhard once proudly pointed out to Esalen's founder a shelf in his own library containing the complete works of Sri Aurobindo, one of Murphy's spiritual mentors. It was doubtful, however, that Erhard had ever done more than glance at the titles along the shelves. Although insistent that his walls be adorned with books, he rarely read any himself. "I gave up reading about ten years ago," he told an interviewer, almost pridefully, in 1974. "I have really gotten over having to read them. I love tables of contents. I can truly read a book from the table of contents, most of the time."

To Murphy and his Esalen colleagues, Erhard was a curious enigma. Obviously, est was not something to be ignored, since it had clearly established itself as a potent sideshow in the human potential movement. Yet Murphy was greatly disturbed by the increasing signs of a personality cult he saw forming all around Erhard. Nowhere was that more evident than at the Franklin House itself, with all those smiling est assistants ready at a moment's notice to scrub bathrooms, pour wine, or do anything else Erhard instructed them to. Murphy was troubled as well by Erhard's hard-sell approach to personal enlight-enment along with his reluctance to acknowledge the true sources and

A GURU IS BORN

origins of the est training. Eventually Murphy distanced himself from Erhard, although est continued to attract the support of others in the human potential movement who applauded some of its underlying messages.

Always Erhard looked for ways to promote est, sometimes by linking it in the public eye with other leading cultural personalities. In 1976 Erhard began an enigmatic pairing with Buckminster Fuller, the famed designer, inventor, and philosopher, after the two had been introduced through Fuller's twenty-one-year-old grandson, who had taken the est training while living in Berkeley.

Erhard wasted no time in turning his blossoming friendship with the eighty-year-old Fuller into a profitable public relations coup for est. In September 1976 Erhard and Fuller walked onto the stage at a sold-out Town Hall in New York, where tickets had gone for $30 each to listen to "conversations with Buckminster Fuller." A second sold-out event followed in January at San Francisco's Masonic Auditorium, where thousands of est enthusiasts paid $35 each for another day-long "conversation" between Erhard and Fuller. The proceeds, a Fuller aide explained at the time, were split between est and Fuller.

"I've never been to an est class. I don't really know what it teaches," said Fuller, when asked during the est events about his connections to Erhard. But Fuller clearly relished the financial spoils of his friendship with est's creator. Two years after his initial outings with Erhard, Fuller learned that four Pennsylvania universities had decided to eliminate an $80,000 annual contribution they had been making to support his research projects in the Philadelphia area. Fuller hardly seemed worried by the news, saying he expected to receive about $160,000 from three seminars he was scheduled to do in 1979 with Erhard. Nor was he worried about the criticism he received for his odd association with est and Erhard. "I have quite a few million people who listen to me," Fuller told the *New York Times* in February 1979. "And I say Werner Erhard is honest. He may prove untrustworthy, and if he does then I'll say so."

Erhard, for his part, used his appearances with Fuller to lend credible validation to some of the principles of the est training. What are people going to be able to do when they leave this event? Erhard was asked at a press conference during the Werner and Bucky show at the Berkeley Community Theater in early 1979. "They're going out," Erhard replied, "being really in touch with being able to think for themselves."

Erhard, however, was a little embarrassed a few days later when an eight-page memo entitled "what Werner needs to know" wound up in the hands of a columnist for the *San Francisco Examiner* who promptly reported its contents in the newspaper. The memo had been prepared as a briefing tool for Erhard prior to his event with Fuller and the press conference that took place in the middle of the day. Erhard was advised in the memo not to place his hand on Fuller's shoulder because "it looks like Werner has Bucky in his hip pocket," read part of the memo. The memo also included a list of questions likely to be asked during the press conference along with suggestions for Erhard's replies.

In his persona as the guru of est, Erhard constantly sought ways to expand his own considerable sphere of New Age influence. In November 1974 California elected a new governor named Jerry Brown, a thirty-six-year-old former Jesuit seminarian who practiced meditation and enjoyed occasional visits to the San Francisco Zen Center. Happily for Erhard, the new Brown administration was stocked with a good supply of est graduates.

One of those est graduates was a public interest lawyer in San Francisco named Robert Gnaizda whom Brown had asked in early 1975 to come to Sacramento as deputy secretary for the state department of health and welfare. Impressed with the kind of enthusiasm that est graduates seemed to attach to their work in government agencies, Gnaizda arranged for Erhard to come to Sacramento and meet a few Brown officials, including the state's prison director and Gnaizda's immediate boss, Secretary of Health and Welfare Mario Obledo. For weeks after Erhard's visit in February 1975, Gnaizda was overwhelmed by the number of people around the agency who told him how eager they were to help him set things straight there. Shortly after, Gnaizda introduced Erhard to Brown himself, who was known for his intense curiosity about new philosophical disciplines and other facets of New Age culture. But Brown maintained a cautious distance from Erhard, part of his chronic nervousness about negative publicity he might receive from the curious company he enjoyed keeping from time to time.

In late 1976 Brown's chief of staff, Gray Davis, acknowledged that the governor had met on two occasions with Erhard and that the state had paid $2,500 the year before for forty Department of Corrections officials to attend a private training session with Erhard. Davis, however, maintained Brown's detachment from est. "I've never heard him express a position privately or publicly on Mr. Erhard's course, and to my knowledge he has never participated in his course," Davis told a reporter.

Not that Erhard had to worry much about increasing the number of high friends in influential positions. The est organization by the mid-1970s already had a name and a program in place for ensuring Erhard's increasing influence on the world. It was called SOIP, which stood for Sphere of Influence People—and it included those who needed to be courted and cajoled, wined and dined, treated to VIP est training sessions where they could "get it" without having to mingle with more ordinary people flocking into est trainings around the country.

An internal est memo drafted in 1975 discussed a covert plan to enhance est's public image. The memo explained Erhard's goal for courting the growing number of influential est graduates, urging staffers to "open space" for the SOIPs to "want to share est." Sure enough, as the word spread, the SOIPs flocked to Erhard's course: John Denver, Valerie Harper, Diana Ross, Cloris Leachman, Harvey Korman, Peter Guber, comedians Jerry Stiller and Ann Meara, Roy Scheider, Raul Julia, Joanne Woodward, astronaut Buzz Aldrin, Watergate figure John Dean, Olympic skier Suzy Chaffee. The est staff even had its own former Hollywood celebrity among its ranks by the end of 1974. Ten years earlier a teenage actress named Pat Woodell starred as a hillbilly country girl on a cornball situation comedy called "Petticoat Junction." After taking the est training years later, she joined the staff in Los Angeles, where she became the enrollment manager in the L.A. office. Later in 1975 Woodell moved to San

Francisco where she became est's national enrollment manager and head of the guest seminar leaders program.

By the middle of 1975, Erhard and est had taken Hollywood by storm. Warner Brothers executive Ted Ashley, an early est convert, was so enthusiastic about the training that he quickly insisted other executives at the studio take it. In keeping with the est spirit of assisting, Ashley began showing up in est's Los Angeles office, working the phones and getting people to attend posttraining seminars. Ashley's enthusiasm for est reached the point where some Hollywood wags began referring to the studio he led as "Werner Brothers."

Other entertainment celebrities were equally eager to sing the praises of est and Werner Erhard. In May 1975 actress Valerie Harper smiled in front of millions of television viewers as she accepted an Emmy award for best comedy actress, stemming from her title role in a situation comedy called "Rhoda." At the podium of the Shrine Auditorium in Los Angeles, Harper, who had gone through the est training only two months earlier, ended her acceptance speech with personal thanks to "Werner Erhard, who changed my life."

Erhard's first celebrity convert, John Denver, continued to stump for est as his own popularity as a golly-gee country singer soared in the mid-1970s with hits like "Rocky Mountain High." He dedicated one of his albums, *Back Home Again,* to est and wrote a song, "Looking for Space," that was inspired by the est training. "The absolute best that we can give est is to say 'This is who I am, and yes, I'm an est graduate,' " Denver once told fellow est enthusiasts. But Denver's close identification with est created some problems of its own. Eventually Denver found it necessary to make an announcement in an issue of the est *Graduate Review* aimed at gently discouraging the growing number of est graduates who tried to get backstage to meet him at his concerts.

Erhard found loyal and influential followers in other areas as well. One of est's most enthusiastic customers in the early 1970s was Bill Millard, a hustling salesman who soon was applying some of est's principles and methods at an upstart computer company he had formed in San Leandro, California, not far from Oakland. While he nurtured a friendship with Erhard and a growing devotion to est, Millard was laying the groundwork for what eventually turned into ComputerLand, one of the country's most successful and profitable personal computer franchise companies, and one that made Millard a billionaire.*

Intent on expanding est's credibility and his own stature as an emerging New Age guru, Erhard as early as 1973 created a prestigious "est advisory board" that included dozens of members from the fields of medicine, academia, the media, entertainment, religion, and business. Although the board never played much of a role in determining the policies or direction taken by est, Erhard made sure the names of its members were widely distributed. Its first chairman was Dr. Phillip Lee, who had been the chancellor of the medical school at the University of California's San Francisco branch from 1969 to 1972 and later a professor of social medicine and health policy. Lee, an early est graduate, headed the est board for four years and turned out to be an important image-enhancer for Erhard.**

At an advisory board meeting in December 1977, members carved out an ambitious plan to spread the news about est by forming thirteen separate committees that covered a broad range of fields, from women and older people to sports and government. "The committees' purpose," announced the *Graduate Review* magazine, "will be to establish ways for graduates with common interests to participate as a group to create a condition for transformation to be in the world by sharing their experience of transformation." Translated into English, the members of the new committees had promised to try to recruit more people into est.

Several times each year Erhard flew around the country to whip up continued support for est among graduates and guests. Usually appearing in large concert arenas or lecture halls, Erhard would use these "special events" to rally his troops, telling est graduates about

*For a revealing look at the tight est connection between Werner Erhard and Computer-Land, see Jonathan Littman's book, *Once Upon a Time in ComputerLand* (Simon & Schuster/ Touchstone: New York, 1987).

**Lee himself was something of an est skeptic. Although he once described having a "fairly dramatic" experience during one part of the est training, he later told a writer for *Psychology Today* that he had his doubts about what had caused the experience. "I think it's easy to be conned. I think we're fairly gullible. I'm skeptical constantly about whether it [the training] had all these profound effects."

a recent trip to Japan or plans to end hunger or some other message he wanted to impart to the faithful followers around the country. Always, though, the bottom-line message was the same. Erhard was selling est wherever he went—and those who filled the halls and auditoriums and concert arenas inevitably left with a new charge to take up Erhard's offer to sell est to even more people.

Every time he went out on the road, Erhard came up with a new est-flavored topic for the speeches that he would give to est graduates. Always they were rooted in the voluminous catalog of est expressions that said little, if anything, about the speech itself. "Getting Off It and Getting On with It" was one of the lecture tours. In August 1975 Erhard filled more than 25,000 seats around the country (at an admission price of $4.50) with an address he called "Something About Nothing." In New York that summer, Erhard walked onstage at the Felt Forum at Madison Square Garden to the thunderous applause and standing ovation from 5,000 Werner worshipers. What did he have to tell them that night?

> My real purpose in being here is not for me to be but for you and me to be. I'm here to create the space for you to be and I'm here to be in the space that you create for me to be. And that's the whole purpose. That's the whole point. And as you'll notice, we've already achieved that so the night's a success as far as I'm concerned.

A few months later est offices around the country were put on notice again to sell tickets for another series of "experiences of Werner"—a five-city tour he was planning in January 1976 in Los Angeles, Oakland, Honolulu, Boston, and New York. This time more than 30,000 people gobbled up the tickets in a two-week period. By December, a month or so before Erhard's tour, est seminar leaders around the country were reminded that there were other ways as well to sell est during the slow holiday period. Est graduates were told during weekly seminar sessions in early December 1975 to invite a friend to that month's guest seminar. If they hadn't, they were told to buy tickets and bring someone with them. In the mass-marketing approach to transformation, Werner Erhard never left anything to chance. The name of the game was selling, and the time for selling was always at hand.

Werner Erhard "looks like someone I should keep my eye on," San Francisco writer Leo Litwak wrote in an article about est that appeared in the Sunday magazine of the *New York Times* in 1976. "He goes all out for what he wants. My inclination was to close my heart and guard my pockets."

Esalen founder Michael Murphy, in the same article, noticed two sides to the curious persona of Werner Erhard. "[There is the] rough cut, self-taught philosopher with a dazzling gift for philosophy," said Murphy. "Where did he get it? He hasn't read the texts. He has no academic background. And then there's the super-salesman, the founder of an autocratic organization held in reverence by staff and graduates. The mixture is disconcerting."

Even more troubling was the darkest side of Werner Erhard that neither Murphy nor most other est outsiders ever managed to glimpse at all. In public, Erhard was almost always the picture of charm and good manners, able to use his warm and energizing smile and penetrating pale-blue eyes to create an unnerving sense of charisma that helped, in large part, to explain the enthusiastic devotion of so many est adherents. Meeting him for the first time, many insisted they had been in the presence of no less than a holy man. Some were dazzled by what they insisted was an aura of light surrounding him and overwhelmed by his seeming sincerity. One of his aides, a woman deeply imbued with a sense of spiritualism, attributed the Erhard mystique to a "sense of grace" that seemed at times to pervade the premises of the Franklin House where he lived and worked.

But there were uglier incidents, moments of a flashing temper and vulgar behavior, that defined Werner Erhard and the est culture he created around him. Behind the scenes at some of his Franklin House feasts, Erhard turned into a raving tyrant, provoked by the slightest miscue or oversight. One evening the resident chef accidentally turned off the oven while cooking a rack of lamb, which was unwittingly served to Erhard and his dinner guests. Normally Erhard insisted that one of his aides taste everything before it came out of the kitchen, though for some reason the lamb had escaped such careful scrutiny. After Erhard bit into the meat and discovered it was under-cooked, he stormed into the kitchen, his plate in hand, and yelled at the chef, "This is raw! You eat it!" He flung the plate across the room, splattering its contents against the kitchen wall, while the chef and other assistants in the kitchen watched in stunned silence. On another occasion, in 1976, an angry Erhard lit into one of his aides, Jack Rafferty, for not following Erhard's precise orders to clean up a closet where he kept some of his clothes. Yelling at Rafferty while he angrily tore the closet apart, flinging its contents around the room, Erhard did not let up even though he knew Rafferty's mother was seriously ill at the time. "I don't give a shit if your mother dies!" Erhard screamed.

Werner Erhard seemed to reserve his fiercest hostility for some of the women who were part of the est culture. Though the feminist movement in the United States roughly paralleled the rise of est, Er-hard rarely hesitated to make demeaning remarks about women who worked for him. He would deride women as "snakes," and insist that men were the source of power, leaving women to fill subservient roles. Once, when one of his aides walked into a meeting to let him know his next appointment was scheduled to begin in a few minutes, Erhard glanced at the busty woman and then chortled to others in the room, "Pretty good, a clock with tits." At other times he tossed around crude remarks, telling one employee, for example, how nice she looked in the "fuck-me shoes" she wore to work that day.

But his demeaning attitudes toward women did not stop with his verbal insults. Though he was insulated by a layer of protective per-sonal aides, there have been persistent reports that Erhard allowed his quick and sometimes violent temper to spill over into physical abuse of women. Though he could be seductively charming, Erhard also possessed a deep-seated resentment of women, the origins of which were likely to be found in his unsatisfying relations with the most prominent women in his life, including his mother and each of his two wives. Perhaps fearing personal intimacy in long-term rela-tions, he resorted instead to a long-standing series of affairs. He also preferred to hire for his various sales staffs attractive women, some of whom he seduced into utter obedience and total loyalty. Now, as the mystique of est conferred upon Erhard still more power over the lives of his most faithful followers, he carried his behavior and attitudes toward women to even more disturbing depths. On more than one occasion, it became the task of one of his closest aides and confidants inside the Franklin House to be ready with an ice pack and some soothing words to treat a blackened eye and comfort another victim of Erhard's demons. Werner Erhard's seductive charm sometimes had a habit of giving way to the back of his hand.

TROUBLE IN PARADISE

As you can see,

this universe is perfect.

Don't lie about it.

—WERNER ERHARD

During its first few years, est relied almost solely on word of mouth to attract new adherents. Eventually, of course, the word started to get picked up by journalists, particularly those who were fascinated with cultural fads of the day. Werner Erhard certainly saw nothing wrong in boosting est further with the help of friendly writers. One of them was a Los Angeles freelancer named Marcia Seligson, who had been hearing enthusiastic bits and pieces about est from some of her friends and contacts in the Hollywood entertainment industry.

By early 1974 Seligson agreed to see what the fuss was all about and attended a guest seminar that Erhard led at a crowded Los Angeles hotel ballroom. Her initial reaction to Erhard was one of complete horror, watching in drop-jaw amazement at the fawning crowd that lavished its praise on the slick-looking guru who came across to her as a "slightly oily salesman-type." As Seligson would later write in *New Times* magazine. "All my buttons were being pressed furiously: Hitler and the *jugen*, mass hypnosis, the Messiah, mystical cultism, Elmer Gantry, Charles Manson and his army of idolizing murder machines. It didn't seem just cuckoo, it seemed goddamned dangerous."

Seligson left the hotel that evening determined to write a damaging exposé of Erhard and his menacing est machine. After lining up an assignment from *New Times*, Seligson enrolled in an est training in Los Angeles. By the end of the second weekend, however, she had dropped all notions of damning Erhard in print. After her training, she continued to research her article by spending a considerable amount of time with Erhard and assisting in the Los Angeles office. Excited by the new shape that her article was taking, she lobbied her editors at the magazine for a cover piece that would herald nothing less than the birth of a new religion. To her disappointment, Seligson's article didn't make the cover, greeted as it was by a fair amount of skepticism from the editors. That hardly mattered to Erhard and his followers once they saw the published version of her article in October 1974.

"I think that est has been one of the truly powerful experiences of my life," gushed Seligson in the opening paragraphs of her piece. "And I love Werner Erhard."

Over the next eight magazine pages, Seligson spun out a glowing tale of Erhard and the miracles that est seemed to be providing those who were signing up by the thousands for the $200 course. She described how her trainer, Ted Long, demonstrated how to cure headaches and took away one man's eyeglasses, waiting there until the man "gets" that he has created his own myopia throughout his life. She told about a friend of hers who had taken est in Aspen a year before, leaping up at the end of the third day and screaming: "This is the biggest ripoff horseshit I've ever seen in my life." Seligson explained how the trainer patiently asked him to stay until the end, which he did. Of course, he then promptly "got it" and went on to work for the organization.

In her article, Seligson dutifully recounted Erhard's official version of his shadowy past—acknowledging that he had grown up as Jack Rosenberg though without knowing the sordid details of his bigamy and his flight out of Philadelphia. Seligson talked to early Erhard employees such as Jack Rafferty and Locke McCorkle, a former building contractor who became the chief house manager at Franklin House and whose main goal in life, she wrote solemnly, was "to create more space for Werner." She revealed that John Denver had once wanted to give up his career to become an est trainer "but Werner wouldn't allow the sacrifice."

Throughout the article, Seligson dispelled negative rumors about est. Mentioning the "public assumption . . . that est is raking in the money," the journalist dismissed such idle speculation by pointing to Erhard's $30,000-a-year employment contract and noting that the organization itself was set up "so that its cash flow is used to expand the services." More important, Seligson declared, was how effective and successful est was as an organization. "There are no corporate politics here, no manipulating for power, wheeler-dealing, climbing over bodies or into bed in order to rise on the ladder. No stealing of pencils, or calling in sick. Even Werner, who produced it, doesn't fully understand it." She likened the process of getting onto the est staff to "an ordeal of service and sacrifice, not unlike the path toward priesthood or becoming a Zen master."

Seligson concluded her piece with anecdotal testimonials from several people who had taken the est course and left with rave reviews of the training. From an executive at Columbia Pictures to a school guidance counselor in New York, everyone she quoted sang to the heavens the praises of est. Seligson even described a show business manager in Los Angeles who began writing into his contracts that actor-clients must take est "if things aren't working for them." She closed out her lengthy article with a general homage to est: "Clearly, est is not a panacea, a penicillin, nor a replacement for any of the other functioning implements in the salvation tool chest. est isn't the Answer. Even Werner would agree to that—but for sure it's one of the better games in town."

The glee that Seligson's glowing article created around est's San Francisco headquarters was mitigated only by the unfortunate fact that *New Times* magazine—a trendy, antiestablishment-oriented publication—had a tiny circulation. A few months later, however, the much larger *Cosmopolitan* magazine reprinted a version of Seligson's original article, touching off a flood of letters to the magazine inquiring about where readers could go to enroll in est trainings. Until then the est phenomenon had remained a fairly isolated one, catching on in places like San Francisco and Los Angeles and Aspen, but otherwise not penetrating heavy population centers elsewhere around the country. Now the floodgates had opened, and the est staff could hardly keep up with the rapidly expanding demand for trainings. By the middle of 1975, est had to begin a waiting list for all those eager souls anxious to transform themselves over the course of two weekends.

Suddenly the organization couldn't open new est centers fast enough. Volunteers continued to provide the bulk of the manpower in est circles, but the paid staff—though still working for low wages—grew from 160 in the spring of 1975 to 230 by the fall. Once again est's San Francisco headquarters outgrew its office space; soon it relocated to several floors of a building on California Street in downtown San Francisco. The growth curve was spiraling upward at a dizzying pace, and no one—not even Werner Erhard—seemed to be able to imagine just how high and far est might go. Once he had dreamed, almost wistfully, of "transforming" 40 million people around the planet. Now, in the heady days of mid-1975, perhaps those dreams were not as unreachable as he once thought.

By the end of the year, nearly two hundred articles had been written about the cultural phenomenon that was est. Many of them contained the same kind of superlatives and accolades that Seligson had heaped upon est and Erhard in her earlier magazine piece. In the fall of 1975, the *New Age Journal* reprinted over the course of two issues a four-hour radio interview that Erhard had done on a public radio station in San Francisco the previous January. In addition to reprinting the interview transcript, the *New Age* staffers attended their own est training session in New York and wrote short essays about the experience, virtually all of which were immensely positive. Erhard, however, wasn't taking any chances on negative publicity, and insisted—in exchange for providing "scholarships" that would cover the costs of the staff's training—that est have right of final approval of the stories that *New Age Journal* would eventually publish about est. The magazine's editor reluctantly agreed to est's condition, even allowing the organization to influence the artwork that accompanied the articles.

But if Seligson and the editors at the *New Age Journal* had been transformed into committed est followers, others emerged with a more skeptical view of the world according to Werner. In February 1975 a San Francisco freelance writer, Mark Brewer, wrote one of the first critical articles about the organization in the *San Francisco Bay Guardian*. Brewer's report made a much bigger splash when he published a lengthier version in *Psychology Today* six months later. Like other writers before him, Brewer traced the substantive origins of the est course to Zen, Scientology, gestalt therapy, and Dale Carnegie, while also describing the program's content as "a good double dose of common sense psychology from which almost anyone could profit." But Brewer went far beyond previous writers in detailing the rigorous training and reaching the ominous conclusion that Werner Erhard, above all else, was selling a beguiling form of brainwashing and thought control. "What the training is more than anything else—and far more than any wide-eyed description that est graduates or staff give—is a brave new application of classic techniques in indoctrination and mental conditioning worthy of Pavlov himself," wrote Brewer.

Brewer dug considerably deeper than other writers in chronicling Erhard's past as a book salesman and promoter of Mind Dynamics. Other journalists who had interviewed Erhard often accepted without question his descriptions of his past employment. In one magazine interview published in the fall of 1974, Erhard embellished the true nature of his thirteen years as a book sales manager, telling the writer he had worked in the lofty-sounding field of "executive development and motivation" where his job was to increase people's "leadership" and "executive ability."

The est office misled inquiring journalists by distributing a copy of Erhard's past "professional activities" that omitted details of his earlier jobs. One résumé left out entirely his two years at the Grolier Society while also failing to mention his affiliation with Mind Dynamics. Perhaps, as Brewer speculated in his article, shedding light on Erhard's earlier mind-control days "would also dull his claim that he is solely responsible for the techniques used in est, for much of est is patterned after Mind Dynamics. Some of the processes are almost perfect copies."

Erhard was outraged by the *Psychology Today* article, particularly because he had talked at length with Brewer and had never foreseen how critical the article might turn out to be. But his anger was directed as much toward his own organization as it was toward the author of the piece. After all, Erhard concluded, est was ultimately responsible for providing journalists with information, access, and other help in crafting pieces about the organization and its work. Although it was never stated so explicitly, by 1975 the organization had adopted a media policy that assumed Erhard would not be understood by journalists and would invariably get bad press despite efforts to cooperate with reporters. Seligson's piece in *New Times* and *Cosmopolitan* had given everyone a false sense of comfort about the media's kid-glove treatment of Erhard and positive attitude toward est. Brewer had brought everyone back to reality. Now it was time to take control.

As more journalists began to search out their own stories about Erhard and est, the organization, on orders from Erhard and Don Cox, took steps to prevent staff members from making any critical comments, whether deliberately or inadvertently, that might find their way to the ear of inquiring writers. A confidential "staff responsibilities" memo prepared in late 1975 laid out explicit instructions on handling journalistic inquiries about est. The memo instructed staff people to refer all inquiries to the est public relations department and then to call est's main headquarters in San Francisco. It was essential, said the memo, "that all media information be divulged immediately."

Within the organization, Erhard demanded that any staff members who felt the need to air complaints—or "upsets," in est jargon—must do so only in a way that would prevent the information from ever reaching the outside world. Staff members experiencing upsets were instructed to write a report about their problems without making any copies of the document. They were then told to seal the information in an envelope, mark it "confidential" and address it to "est attorney, Command Division." By doing so, staffers were told the information would then become "privileged communication" falling within attorney-client confidentiality. Erhard's point was clear. No dissenting views about est were to be tolerated. Any breaches would be considered an act of extreme disloyalty both to est and to Erhard personally.

At the Union Street headquarters, est staff members learned quickly that the organization's public commitment to "full self-expression" did not include anyone who worked for Werner Erhard. Instead, the staff was instructed to behave in public in ways that would support est's goals. Their job at est always was "to represent Werner" and to not interfere with "the purpose of est." To make sure that happened, no staff members were to "play trainer" in public places, nor were they permitted to complain about anything, from their jobs to their family. Proper public behavior included the avoidance of words that convey "power and attention." Among the words that were to be stricken from a staff member's public vocabulary were "fuck," "est," and "Werner."

The role of suppressing negative comments about est extended to staff members whose responsibilities included the identification of anyone who might be inclined to criticize est publicly. Cox once received a memo from in-house attorney Bob Curtis who had listed various doctors and patients who might have critical things to say about est. Curtis and another est staffer were given the job of contacting these people and "closing them off as a source of rumors about est." Ultimately, however, even the powers of Werner Erhard were not sufficient to stifle all dissenting opinions.

By the fall of 1975 Erhard faced another, even more serious problem that, unless managed correctly, threatened to undermine everything he had built for himself during the first four years of est's existence. Erhard's financial angel and tax magician, Harry Margolis, was about to be indicted on federal criminal tax fraud charges.

Federal agents from the U.S. Justice Department and Internal Revenue Service had been after Margolis for years, as part of ongoing efforts to crack down on illegal tax shelters relying on the mazes of offshore banks and dummy foreign corporations favored by Werner Erhard's lawyer. On December 23, 1975, a federal grand jury in San Francisco handed down an indictment against Margolis, charging him with conspiracy and the preparation of false tax returns for his clients. One of the counts in the indictment alleged that Margolis had filed a fraudulent tax return in 1972 for Erhard Seminars Training Inc.

Publicly, Erhard reacted calmly to his lawyer's indictment, reminding anyone who asked that est itself had not been charged with any improper acts. Privately, on the other hand, Erhard and other est officials worried that the criminal charges against Margolis might easily blow up in their faces and leave them with a public relations disaster. At the time, few if any details of est's curious financial structure were known among more than a small group of people inside the organization. The upcoming trial threatened to expose in greater detail Erhard's ties to the controversial attorney.

Margolis himself did his best to reassure Erhard and other clients they had no reason to be worried about his indictment. After all, he told them, the pesky federal government had been after him for years and so far had never managed to crack his tax shelters. He calmly insisted it was business as usual in his Saratoga law offices.

In fact, before his indictment Margolis already had taken steps to transform est's corporate structure and, in doing so, polish Werner Erhard's image as a dedicated humanitarian. Margolis also knew he had to find a few different ways to shelter est's increasing flood of cash from the tax collector. With Erhard's ready endorsement, Margolis now put into place a structure that, for the first time, gave est the appearance of being controlled by a nonprofit foundation. In reality, however, nothing had really changed at all.*

*An earlier attempt to organize est's operations in Hawaii as a tax-exempt, nonprofit organization failed when the Internal Revenue Service refused to grant "est of Hawaii" its exemption on the grounds that it was linked directly to a profit-making business. In 1979 the U.S. Tax Court upheld the IRS's decision, which also was confirmed by the Ninth Circuit Court of Appeals two years later.

In the wake of a new series of corporate documents drafted by Margolis, the company called Erhard Seminars Training Inc. passed out of existence and was replaced by a new entity known as est, An Educational Corporation. Next, Margolis transferred "ownership" of the est body of knowledge from a Panamanian company to a new entity that listed its headquarters in the Netherlands. The new company was called Welbehagen (Dutch for "well-being," a popular est phrase). Now it was the Dutch company's turn to authorize est, An Educational Corporation to offer Erhard's est training sessions. Margolis, however, made sure to pump up the price of that licensing agreement in order to create a more lucrative tax shelter for est's profits.

After Margolis had finished his latest handiwork, Erhard officially found himself working as an employee of the new est company, though his salary had jumped from $30,000 a year to $48,000. More important, a separate "profit participation" agreement entitled Erhard to a percentage of est's gross revenue for the next several years.

The latest transformation of est achieved one more important public relations objective for Werner Erhard. Margolis had placed the entire new operation under the supposed control of charitable organizations. The Werner Erhard Charitable Settlement, a magnanimous-sounding entity set up in the British Isle of Jersey, technically owned est, An Educational Corporation. To complete the bewildering maze of companies, Margolis set up a Swiss organization named the Werner Erhard Foundation for est, placing the Dutch company in the hands of the Swiss "charity."

Erhard offered lofty explanations for est's corporate makeover, insisting that its Swiss connections, for example, would lead to est ties to "major international nonprofit organizations" already headquartered in Switzerland. Margolis, of course, had more practical reasons for choosing the new foreign locales in which est's apparent owners were situated. Both provided ideal places in which to shelter money from American tax collectors.

Werner Erhard once described Harry Margolis as the "one person who always gave me the space to discover myself." He surely was not exaggerating, for Margolis alone had been instrumental in defining Erhard's financial self. Now Erhard had only to hope that such a pivotal person in his life would not end up in prison.

Ten

Erhard and the Private Eye

I'm very clear about lies.

Lies persist, and the

truth doesn't.

—Werner Erhard

Take responsibility for your own life" was the message that Werner Erhard and his est trainers pounded into the heads of their paying customers. But Erhard himself had little interest in that lofty piece of self-assertive advice. And when he began to face the sharpest criticism yet leveled against both est and him personally, he simply absolved himself of all responsibility. The fault, he insisted instead, always rested with others.

By the summer of 1975, yet another freelance magazine writer had taken the est training with the intention of writing an article about his experience. But the writer, a New York–based journalist named Jesse Kornbluth, also began to pick up various tidbits and tantalizing rumors about Erhard and his organization and decided that his article should cover more ground than simply another rehash of the est training itself. After lining up an assignment to write the story for *Esquire* magazine, Kornbluth wrote to Erhard in late August requesting an interview. A couple of weeks later an aide wrote back saying that Erhard had just left for Europe and would not be able to speak to the journalist for the next several weeks.

Determined to meet personally with Erhard, Kornbluth exchanged several letters and phone calls with est president Don Cox over the next several weeks in an effort to arrange an interview. Kornbluth stressed that he had discovered critical information about Erhard's past and est's financial dealings that deserved direct responses from Erhard. He also made it clear that he felt he was being "jerked around" by est as part of an effort to dissuade him from publishing his piece. Kornbluth knew Marcia Seligson and had learned in early October that est's media advisory board, of which she was a member, was advising Erhard not to talk to journalists in the wake of *Psychology Today*'s critical article. Seligson dutifully did her part for est by trying to talk Kornbluth out of writing his version of the Werner Erhard story.

After hours of delicate negotiating, Kornbluth finally hammered out an agreement with Cox to interview Erhard. But Cox included several restrictions on Kornbluth's ability to use any of Erhard's statements. First, Kornbluth would have to submit beforehand an "agenda of questions" that would be put to Erhard. In the interview itself, Cox would not permit Kornbluth to use a tape recorder. Instead, est would tape the meeting and prepare a transcript. After that, Kornbluth could circle the quotes he wanted to use, which would then have to be approved by Erhard. Finally Cox insisted that if the journalist violated any part of the interview agreement, he would have to pay $10,000 "to a charitable foundation" chosen by Erhard. Kornbluth chafed at the restrictions but knew he needed Erhard's comments for his story.

He told Cox the conditions were acceptable to him and flew to San Francisco from Los Angeles, where he had been doing other est research, to see Erhard in late October.

At midnight on the night before the scheduled interview, an est staff member called Kornbluth at his hotel and accused him of violating the interview agreement by "not submitting a complete agenda" for the next day's meeting with Erhard. Kornbluth was told that est did not feel he would honor the agreement that had been painstakingly hammered out with Cox.

An angry and frustrated Kornbluth got Cox on the phone the next day, but to no avail. Cox said Erhard remained willing to talk to Kornbluth, but now it was the journalist's turn to beg off. He realized what Cox and Erhard were doing, spelling out conditions restrictive enough so that Kornbluth's refusal to abide by them could be interpreted as his own decision not to talk to Erhard. From Kornbluth's point of view, est itself had deliberately engineered his refusal to speak to Erhard.

Erhard, however, still wanted to know what damaging information Kornbluth might have on him and est. For help, he turned to Harry Margolis, whose creative ideas often extended well beyond the narrower confines of taxes and money. Over the years Margolis occasionally had used the services of Hal Lipset, one of San Francisco's most famous private investigators. In 1965 Lipset had stunned a Senate subcommittee investigating electronic snooping by demonstrating how to place a powerful listening device in a martini olive. He later put his eavesdropping prowess to work for Hollywood by serving as a technical consultant on Francis Ford Coppola's movie *The Conversation*. Lipset also played a role in Richard Nixon's Watergate scandal, serving for a time as head of the investigative staff of the Senate Watergate Committee that looked into the affair in 1973. In San Francisco Lipset built a solid reputation as an ace private eye who often worked for attorneys representing an assortment of clients associated with radical political causes. By the mid-1970s Lipset's clientele also included various cult leaders who sometimes needed the discreet services of a trusted private investigator. Among his clients were Jim Jones, the People's Temple leader who in 1978 ordered nine hundred of his followers to commit suicide in Guyana, the Reverend Sun Myung

Moon of the controversial Unification Church, and Charles Dederich, the founder of Synanon, a one-time drug rehabilitation program that later turned into a dangerous cult.

Erhard liked the idea of working with Lipset. After turning over a $40,000 retainer, he sat down toward the end of 1975 for a long, candid discussion with the investigator. With Don Cox and another staff member sitting at his side, Erhard answered dozens of questions about his past and other matters that a muckraking journalist might be able to uncover.

For Lipset, the assignment didn't seem particularly difficult. He assigned one of his associates to the case, instructing him to learn everything he could about Erhard's past. To aid in the investigation, Lipset hired other operatives who, among other things, tracked down details involving Erhard's first wife, Pat, such as her divorce from him and her subsequent marriage and divorce from her second husband. Erhard wanted to take no chances on family members or anyone else who might be inclined to spread critical information about himself. While Lipset carried out his investigation, Margolis sent a letter to several of Erhard's relatives around the country warning them not to talk to journalists.

In San Francisco, Lipset planted operatives in the est headquarters on California Street, where they snatched up memos and other materials that might shed light on est's inner workings. At night Lipset's minions would haul trash out of the est offices and carry it back to his Pacific Heights office, where they spent the next several hours sifting through the purloined garbage. It wasn't long before est officials installed paper shredders around the office to guard against any embarrassing leaks.

By the time Lipset began his Erhard investigation, one of his staff operatives was Fred Gardner, a freelance investigative journalist with a radical bent who a few months earlier had written about Margolis in the *San Francisco Bay Guardian*. Gardner accepted Lipset's job offer on the condition that he could turn down any case if he thought the client was "too reprehensible."

Not long after Gardner started, Lipset told him he had a case that was "just up your alley." Lipset explained that the firm had been hired by a "wealthy Nevada businessman" interested in digging up dirt on Werner Erhard in an effort to pry his daughter away from est. Lipset asked Gardner to look into the est organization and, as Lipset explained to him, "see what a good muckraker could get on this guy." A week later Lipset came to Gardner again, this time with an unusual request.

"Fred, I understand you have some contacts with the New York media. Our client has heard about an article that's in the works for *Esquire* by a guy named Jesse Kornbluth. Do you think there might possibly be a way for the client to see a copy of the article before it's published?"

It wasn't long before Gardner discovered the true identity of Lipset's client. As part of his investigative duties, Gardner had talked to the Sausalito security officer who had been involved in the 1967 incident at the Cote d'Azur apartments that had led to criminal charges against Erhard. Later, back at Lipset's office, Gardner happened to see a note sitting atop one of the desks that mentioned the apartment incident in connection with Kornbluth's pending article. It began to dawn on Gardner that Lipset had lied to him, that there was no wealthy Nevada businessman out to damage Werner Erhard and est. Erhard himself was the client. Gardner quickly confirmed his suspicion when he casually asked one of the secretaries in the office to get the "Erhard file." The whole arrangement was spelled out in the file, the contents of which Gardner photocopied before returning it to its rightful place.

For the moment, Gardner kept his discovery to himself, carrying out his investigative duties as if nothing unusual had happened. By then Gardner thought he had turned up plenty of damaging information about Erhard's involvement with Harry Margolis. But the anger he felt toward Werner Erhard paled in comparison to the outrage he felt toward Hal Lipset, whose phony story about a Nevada client had tricked him in the first place. By early January 1976 he had gathered enough information to write a confidential report detailing his part of the investigation.

Gardner, who already knew a great deal about Margolis, said Erhard probably risked nothing more serious than "guilt by association" because of his ties to the controversial attorney. But Gardner warned that Erhard might face more serious problems if est turned out to be directly involved in the maze of disputed companies that stood at the core of Margolis's ongoing legal problems. In his report, Gardner wondered rhetorically whether est was involved in the Margolis system currently under investigation. It would be several more years before the prescient question would be answered in the most damaging way for Werner Erhard.

A few days later Jesse Kornbluth received a phone call from Fred Gardner.

"You don't know who I am, but I know who you are," Gardner said. He told Kornbluth about the role that Lipset's firm had played in investigating what the journalist was writing and what Lipset's operatives had uncovered during their covert glimpse into Erhard's organization. Gardner was offering to turn over what he knew to Kornbluth.

By then Kornbluth had learned of *Esquire*'s decision not to run the Erhard story. He submitted it instead to *New Times* magazine, the same publication that earlier had printed Marcia Seligson's glowing testimonial to Erhard and est. The editors there decided it was time to take a more critical look at Werner Erhard, particularly given the information that Kornbluth had provided. Kornbluth rewrote part of his article to reflect the information he had received from Gardner. Not only had Erhard been foiled in his attempt to preempt an inquisitive journalist, but the scheme of using a private investigator to carry out his covert plan had backfired. Around the est offices, staff members were warned that a damaging article was in the works and that it would contain a string of lies, all motivated by a scornful journalist's attempt to discredit Werner Erhard. Anyone truly loyal to est and Erhard would have no choice but to dismiss the article as an utter fabrication.

"The Fuhrer over est" appeared in *New Times* in March 1976 and painted Erhard as a despotic leader who exercised God-like control over his expansive est empire. From his car-selling days in Philadelphia to his mind-control techniques in San Francisco, Kornbluth cast Erhard as a master schemer seemingly intent on capturing the minds and souls of millions around the world in the name of transformation and enlightenment. While Kornbluth acknowledged some positive attributes of the training, he wrote of an organization that, beneath its happy-face exterior, stood for blind devotion to a dubious cause. "However much the est training may be about spontaneous joy and the reclamation of the self, the est organization increasingly looks like Werner Erhard's private army," he wrote toward the end of the article.

It was an army, wrote Kornbluth, that employed sophisticated weapons that included an efficient propaganda machine, a hostile attitude toward critical journalists, and a sales apparatus in which its "lowest-level operatives sell an ideology to their friends for an abstract reward." And it was an army that measured its victories with the est-praising songs of John Denver and with each new Hollywood celebrity who toasted Erhard's path toward enlightenment.

On the evening of March 19, 1976, a few weeks after Kornbluth's article appeared, Erhard—accompanied by Don Cox and another aide—walked into a ballroom in New York's Waldorf-Astoria hotel and faced more than two hundred est graduates connected in some way with the media. The est organization had sponsored a similar "media seminar" in Los Angeles the previous month, but the New York session took on a much different, and harsher, tone, coming as it did in the aftermath of the *New Times* article. Several participants, including est-trained journalists, were anxious to ask about the charges raised by Kornbluth. First, however, they sat and watched a videotape that had been produced by the est staff—a parody of a television news program called "est-witness news." One the skits portrayed an interview taking place in the future between a reporter and an est trainer who was out of work because est had succeeded so well there was no one left to train. The skit had obviously been designed to poke fun at the harsh criticism that est had been receiving in the media in recent months.

"Do you remember back to the time when est was getting all that attention from the media?" the "reporter" asked at one point in the skit.

"Oh, yes," replied the trainer. "All those articles and stories about how est was fascistic, neo-Nazi brainwashing, and how est was dangerous and wanted to control everything."

"How was all that handled?" asked the mock interviewer.

"Well," said the trainer, "we gave them space, expanded to include them in our purpose, took total responsibility for them, and then we beat the shit out of them."

Many in the audience laughed wildly as they watched the videotape. But others in the room were both offended and horrified at the frivolous tone used to address serious allegations about both Erhard and est. After Erhard arrived in the room, several participants flung questions at him. One man jumped to his feet, shouting: "Why don't you just say you're in it for the money? I don't give a shit if you are. Just say so, for Christ's sake! Admit it!"

Erhard responded in a typically evasive manner. "Look, if I was really in it for the money, I wouldn't tell you. And if I'm not in it for the money, then I won't tell you either."

Several people asked Erhard about est's finances, and particularly the unusual manner in which Margolis had organized est's corporate structure. But Erhard brushed aside such questions, insisting that est paid all its taxes appropriate to its income. "I dare say there is not a person in this room—there might be one or two exceptions— who does not pay as little taxes as he can possibly pay."

During most of the evening, Erhard characteristically maintained his cool and unflappable composure, refusing to let either the tone or the substance of the sharp questioning jar him. Only for a moment did his demeanor change, when someone wondered whether Erhard might be guilty of improper conduct because of his association with an attorney, Margolis, who now faced criminal charges of tax fraud. "How dare you attack my integrity with guilt by association," he shot back. "Look, if you're willing to make me wrong, I know how to make me wrong much better than you could ever hope to do it . . . I have done evil things. Leaving a wife and four children is one hell of a lot more evil than any of the bullshit that comes up in any of the articles. There is not one fact that is in any way generally considered by people to be evil that I have not shared publicly. Not one."

Over the next few months, with Erhard and est increasingly finding themselves under the microscope, Erhard knew he had to look for ways to defuse the situation, to regain the offensive, and to devise a strategy to dull the sharp edge of the allegations made against him and the est organization. The new public relations campaign began in June, when est released a fourteen-page report, "The Legal and Financial Structure of est," that spelled out in considerable detail (but with the usual display of confusing est jargon) the Margolis-structured organization.

In a letter introducing the report, Erhard assured everyone that all the facts "support graduates who have continued to come from their experience in the face of opportunities to be invalidated." In other words, he told them simply to believe everything he was telling them, while ignoring anyone else who might insist otherwise. Erhard then explained that he had "chosen to 'own' est by giving it away." Although he said that, legally speaking, he neither owned nor controlled est, "I experience being completely responsible for est in all its aspects and dimensions."

Over the next several pages, the report spelled out in intricate detail est's original corporate structure, including Erhard's "employment agreement" with a Panamanian company. The report further described est's restructured look in 1975, after Erhard decided that he wanted est to be owned by "non-profit foundations and trusts that would be solely devoted to supporting est and the transformation of the quality of people's lives." As for his own financial stake in est, Erhard offered a coyly phrased but ultimately revealing comment: "Even though the bulk of my financial worth has not come directly from est, the truth is that est is the source of everything that I have."

By midsummer 1976 est's public relations department continued to field calls and letters from journalists, as well as est graduates themselves, about many of the charges that had surfaced in Jesse Kornbluth's article. To deal with the persistent complaints, Erhard decided to go out on the road, where he would "communicate" something about the organization to est graduates around the country. In a tour that brought him to eight cities and had him speaking to more than 20,000 est graduates, Erhard crafted a long, winding talk that not only was aimed at defusing the serious charges brought against the organization, but pointed an accusing finger at the real source of est's problems. In his speeches he blamed staff members, volunteer assistants, and est graduates themselves who had the nerve to question the integrity of Erhard and est in the first place. An "evil had begun to crystallize" within est, Erhard told his rapt audiences that August. What was this evil? Where was it coming from?

Erhard first ripped into former staff members for doing "the most incredibly treacherous things that you could imagine." Though he named no names in his speeches, Erhard railed against turncoat staff members who, in his opinion, had violated "the privilege of intimacy," presumably by speaking to journalists about some of the excesses they had observed both in Erhard and est. With equal fervor, Erhard blamed est graduates for the "evil" that was lurking inside the organization. "You were out there mumbling and grumbling, 'The training is terrific, but the organization stinks.' Remember? That's another way of avoiding responsibility for the evil." As the mesmerized masses sat riveted to their seats in auditoriums stretching from New York to San Francisco, Erhard told them they themselves were to blame for the mysterious "evil" that had befallen est.

Eleven

NIGHTMARE ON
FRANKLIN STREET

I'm sure I will be accused of everything

from being the father of someone's illegitimate

child to being a child molester, to being a

tax evader, to being a CIA agent.

—WERNER ERHARD

It had all the trappings of a visit by the president of the United States. Entrances and exits had been staked out. Security forces were in place. The lighting and sound systems inside the auditorium had been checked and rechecked. A professional television producer from Hollywood was on hand to oversee the production. Local police officers were called in to control the traffic overflow. VIP receptions had been planned to take place afterward.

On January 5, 1976, Werner Erhard was traveling across the bay from his home on Franklin Street to the Oakland Coliseum. That night he was to begin a five-city speaking tour aimed at rallying the growing masses of est graduates around the country by treating them to an "experience with Werner." For weeks teams of est staff members and assistants had been scurrying around the Coliseum Arena, normally the site of basketball games and rock concerts. For most commuters, the trip from San Francisco to Oakland was no special deal, requiring a short jaunt across the Bay Bridge and onto the southbound Nimitz Freeway. The sports complex was a few miles south of downtown Oakland, across the freeway from the airport. For most Bay Area commuters, just another normal freeway drive.

There was nothing ordinary when Werner Erhard drove across the bay. During the afternoon, two est staff members and two assistants met with five Coliseum security people for a security sweep through the entire backstage area. Before they completed their check, they made sure that all the entrances to the area had been sealed. From there, the staff members coordinated the evening's plans with fifteen more est assistants, all of whom were dedicated solely to making things work for Werner.

In San Francisco, Erhard was readying himself for the evening. A thirty-page briefing report, written by a staff member two days earlier, filled him in on every minute detail about the night's event, along with the others that would follow elsewhere around the country. The report told him that the paid attendance ($4.50 per person) that evening was a capacity crowd of 11,649. The report told him that est's preferred marquee announcement, "Thank you for your support, Werner Erhard," had been turned down by the Coliseum's management office because of a policy that precluded personal rather than promotional messages. Instead, the message would read only "est Tonight 8 pm."

The logistics for transporting Erhard across the bay sounded like something out of a Secret Service logbook. An internal memo spelling out the schedule for the evening discussed command posts and code words for the Mercedes sedan in which Erhard would be chauffeured to the est event. Once he arrived at the sports arena, Erhard waited in the wings, where he was reminded about the timed cues he would receive during the course of his speech. Afterward, one of his personal aides stood ready to drive him to a VIP reception; along the way another assistant briefed Erhard on some of the people attending the special event.

When he traveled or when he worked at home, Werner Erhard demanded, and received, ever-increasing levels of detailed care and devotion from his followers. Inside the Franklin House, from which Erhard directed his minions, nothing escaped the attention and demands of the master. Erhard's "communicators" and aides were constantly handing out a stream of memos to beleaguered assistants, outlining precisely how things were to be placed, cleaned, arranged, folded, and laid out in keeping with Werner's wishes. While Erhard showered in the morning, three or four aides would huddle in the bathroom, scribbling notes as Erhard barked out commands. Sometimes Erhard screamed about hair on the shower door or that "some asshole" had placed the wrong kind of soap in the shower.

The smallest details of his surroundings rarely failed to attract his demanding attention. Once, Erhard insisted on getting a "status report" on a leather chair used at the Franklin House. On another occasion, Erhard arrived home late one night only to angrily discover a burned out light bulb near the front porch. "I don't believe it!" shouted Erhard, leaving a poor assistant to attribute the egregious oversight to "a lack of consciousness." Faithful service to Erhard extended as well to his dog Rogue, a terrier who enjoyed the rare privilege of having eager est assistants wait on him as well as his master. Franklin House aides were given detailed instructions on caring for the animal, including directions for patting the dog on the head after he would relieve himself in his kennel. It fell to one of Erhard's personal aides to make sure that all those "who may be around Werner and Rogue" were fully briefed on proper canine procedures.

While Erhard was on the road in early January, one of his top aides distributed a two-page memo to every member of the est staff. The memo outlined the precise manner in which staff members were to write "Notes to Werner" every other month. The memo spelled out some of the details involved in writing the notes. The second page of the memo that came directly from Erhard's office—staff members were trained to recognize the source of any material typed in Erhard's distinctive style of IBM Selectric upper-case letters—spelled out several items that had to be included in every staff member's notes. Not only were est staffers instructed to tell Erhard everything on their mind, they were also required to report "anything you don't want to say." Finally, Erhard made it clear that the notes were to let him know that he could count on them to do their jobs.

Erhard's increasing cultlike grip on his staff reflected his astonishing ability to erase any distinctions between est's own powerful promises of human transformation and his role in creating those promises. From his corps of est trainers to the swelling legions of happy-face est volunteers, Erhard positioned himself as the wellspring from which est's persuasive message of enlightenment flowed. He was surrounded by acolytes, whose zealous fealty to Erhard seemed to them only a logical extension of their joyous embracing of est's dazzling principles of individual empowerment and heightened consciousness. Few if any of est's most fervent admirers realized that their increasing devotion to Werner Erhard corresponded to a diminishing loss of their own self-determination. Erhard had transformed himself into something more than the creator of a mishmash concoction of self-help theories, commonsense psychology, and dime-store ideas about motivation. He was becoming Source, and he expected his followers to treat him accordingly.

Under policies that more closely resembled religious confessionals, staff members were expected to lay out in great detail virtually all events going on in their lives, both personal and est-related. Staff members were regularly called on to divulge information about their personal relationships, their sex lives, their family problems, and a host of other personal matters that extended far beyond their est responsibilities.

Given the intimacy of these matters, staff members assumed that the information they disclosed would be treated confidentially. Erhard, however, had another purpose in mind in requiring his staff to divulge such information. Still enamored of the Scientology practice of auditing, Erhard had incorporated Scientology's confessional practice into est's "consulting services group" that had been patterned after Hubbard's teams of auditors and organized as a separate branch of est. Under the overall supervision of Bob Larzelere, all est consultants had received extensive training in the Scientology practice of confessional auditing sessions in which the consultant (or auditor, in the case of Scientology) asked a series of questions designed to elicit frank responses on topics ranging from personal matters and job satisfaction to loyalty to Erhard.

Officially, no est staff members were ever required to undergo consulting as part of their jobs. But Erhard made it attractive for them to do so by offering consulting as a perk, yet another method of hastening and maintaining personal transformation. As a result, most staff members who went to see consultants had already convinced themselves they truly wanted to be there. They also went with trusting attitudes toward the consultants, based on an assumption of confidentiality. It was as if they were going to see a priest for confession. What was said between the staff member and a consultant, they naturally assumed, went no further than the two of them.

But Erhard had no intention of permitting such valuable information to remain a secret between staff members and their confessors. Without telling staff members, he initiated a second form of consulting that became known as "integrity checks." These consulting sessions were reserved for staff members who were exhibiting problems on the job, "upsets" toward the organization, or, perhaps most important, critical thoughts about Erhard. The same staff member who might have been unfortunate enough to raise a suspicion about loyalty in Erhard's mind after writing a "note to Werner" might suddenly find himself or herself with an unexpected appointment with a consultant. Erhard's use of consulting services mirrored Scientology's practice of "security checking." In both cases, the purpose was to identify people inside the organization who were critical of either the group or its leader.

Well into the mid-1970s, Erhard's corps of est consultants relied on the flickering needles of Scientology's e-meters to discover which staff members did or did not accept Erhard as Source. For hours at a time, they fired questions at staff members who would clutch the tin cans attached by wire to the machine, all the while keeping a nervous eye on the quivering needles that supposedly revealed whether they were telling the truth.

"Do you really think you have to ask me that question?" a mischievous Stewart Emery sometimes replied to one of the consultants, who demanded to know of Erhard's first est trainer whether he had finally surrendered to Source. Emery, after undergoing a couple hundred hours of e-meter auditing, had long ago figured out how to trick the telltale needle into remaining still against the meter. The hapless consultant would write up his report, and a few days later a bemused Erhard would shoot a frustrated glance at the sly-grinning Australian. "Well," Erhard would tell Emery, "I see you stonewalled them again."

Emery soon learned there was a price to pay for resisting Erhard's demands for obedient devotion from his staff. In the spring of 1975, Emery heard from a friend outside of est about an intriguing idea for an "entertrainment" stage production that would combine Hollywood glitz with a psychobabble script concocted from est, Scientology, and other self-awareness programs. Emery's friend wanted to know if the est trainer might be interested in getting involved. The Australian said he'd certainly consider it and wanted to learn more about the idea.

But first Emery had to fly to Washington, D.C., for the beginning of a training session scheduled for the first weekend in April. From there he was supposed to travel to New York for a guest seminar, followed by another event in Boston and then back to Washington to complete the second weekend of the training.

Ten minutes before he was due onstage at the packed event in Washington, Emery was called to the phone. On the other end of the line, he heard the icy and abrupt voice of est executive Don Cox, who had gotten wind of the "entertrainment" project. Cox demanded to know of Emery whether he had submitted a memo either to Erhard or to Cox informing either of them of his conversation about the project. Emery tersely replied that he saw no reason to write a memo about a casual conversation with a personal friend.

Cox was not satisfied, and wondered out loud whether Emery could still be trusted to lead est events. "I would only be willing for you to be at est if I were absolutely certain that you had given up all your own intentions, purposes and desires in life and only had those that Werner agreed for you to have," said Cox. "I'd like to know where you are about that."

Emery was stunned and shaken by Cox's ultimatum. "Don," he finally replied into the telephone, "where I'm at with that is that I don't have time to be anywhere with that. I've got 250 people waiting downstairs for me. But if I did have time to be somewhere about it, right now where I'm at about it is that what you just did represents to me everything that sucks about est. And I don't have time to talk to you now."

Emery hung up the phone and walked into the est event, regaining his composure to make it seem as if nothing unusual had happened. The next morning Cox called again to let Emery know the rest of his trip had been canceled. Furthermore, Cox wanted it understood that he considered Emery a "traitor to est" who could not be trusted again "until you have unquestionably demonstrated your loyalty to Werner."

Cox, as it turned out, was willing to keep Emery on the staff but at a stiff price. First, Emery would have to accept a salary cut and for a period of time would no longer be permitted to lead large est events or special guest seminars. Instead, his duties would be confined to leading weekly training sessions. Emery told Cox that he had no intention of accepting the conditions. On April 1, 1975, exactly three years after Emery began working for est, he left the staff, one of the first victims of Erhard's blind loyalty pledge. At a staff meeting held shortly after, Cox said that Emery had been asked to leave est because he had improperly looked at "data" outside the organization, an act interpreted as a sign of unforgiven disloyalty to Werner Erhard.

Stewart Emery was dumbfounded by his abrupt ousting from est's inner circle. He was equally outraged when Erhard not only refused to offer him any severance pay but also demanded the return of an Audi automobile that he had earlier been told was a gift. Emery's sudden departure also left him in a precarious position with the Internal Revenue Service; he had paid no income taxes since joining the est staff as a result of the creative "tax planning" advice he had received from Harry Margolis. Now it was Emery's turn to play hardball with Werner Erhard. He asked an attorney friend (himself an est graduate) to meet with Erhard in order to work out a satisfactory severance settlement. If Erhard refused to cooperate, Emery threatened to tell the media what he knew about the est founder—everything from Erhard's curious dealings with Margolis to the periodic verbal abuse he heaped upon his wife Ellen and others around est. When the lawyer went to see Erhard at the Franklin House, he dropped a few hints about filing a lawsuit in Emery's behalf. Though the attorney was largely bluffing about the lawsuit, Erhard backed down and offered Emery the car along with several thousand dollars to settle his tax problems.

For the next several months Stewart Emery remained quiet whenever he was asked about the reasons why he had disappeared from est. He moved to Los Angeles and launched his own self-awareness program that lacked many of est's harsher edges. Finally he spelled out the details of his abrupt break with Erhard in an interview he gave to *East-West Journal* at the end of 1975.

"I'm somewhat overwhelmed," the interviewer told Emery after hearing what had happened the previous spring. "The impression I've gotten from reading things and talking to people is that part of the drive behind est, the purpose of est, is to help people get in touch with their own power."

"Ah, yes," Emery replied. "The purpose of est is to serve people. The purpose of the [est] staff is to serve Werner."

The flap over Emery's departure from est bolstered Erhard's determination to surround himself only with staff members willing to acknowledge his complete authority over their est-related lives. Though Erhard's reliance on the supposed truth-telling powers of the Scientology e-meters gradually disappeared, his faith in the powers of confessional auditing remained reflected in the est culture. Staff members involved in the consulting side of the organization spent hours poring through pages of Scientology source materials, translating the words into est jargon in order to mask the true origins of the "data." Erhard, as enamored as he was of the science fiction theories of L. Ron Hubbard and as eager as he was to subject his own staff to the same tyrannical methods that Hubbard inflicted on his, had no interest in divulging just where he was getting his ideas and theories.

Having a "bad thought about Werner" was more than sufficient grounds to be called in for an integrity check with one of the consultants. Trained to elicit confessions out of the "guilty" party, the consultant would work with the staff member for as long as it took to "flatten" the bad thought, to make it disappear so that the needles would no longer flicker on the e-meter when certain questions were asked. After staff members confessed their "crimes" to the consultant, they had to follow up by asking in writing for Erhard's forgiveness, admitting they had been "living in disloyalty" to him and to est—one of the most egregious sins within the organization's culture. Usually a staff member's confession to some transgression or another brought a sympathetic response from Erhard, or more likely from one of his "communicators," whose job was to dispatch Erhard's absolutions. "Werner loves you one hundred percent," staff members would be told. And though Erhard "acknowledged" the staff member's transgression, he was willing now to accept a request for forgiveness along with the staff member's renewed declaration of commitment to him and to est.

Erhard's reliance on the powers of est consulting methods often was mirrored by staff members who sometimes entrusted life-and-death matters to them. One of the est trainers turned to Bob Larzelere—Erhard's in-house medical doctor who headed est's "well being" department—for help after discovering his teenage son had fallen seriously ill with cancer. After discussing the matter with the soft-spoken Larzelere, the trainer decided that a series of consulting sessions with his son might help to "disappear" the cancer. Larzelere assigned to the case one of his consultants, who flew to Texas where the boy lived. After visiting with him, the consultant learned the boy hardly ever saw his father, the est trainer, anymore and that he thought the whole idea of est and its consulting theories were "complete bullshit." Sympathetic to the boy's plight, Larzelere's emissary returned to California without subjecting him to the full brunt of est consulting.

Erhard spared no one from the anxious ordeal of est consulting, even members of his family. Sometimes he summoned his wife, Ellen, or one of the children from Marin County to meet with Larzelere or one of the other staff consultants. With or without the help of the e-meters, they were tested whenever Erhard suspected any of them of lying about something or being guilty of a "withhold," another word out of the est dictionary that meant a refusal to confess a personal secret. At one point Erhard sent one of his daughters to an est consultant after learning she had been experimenting with marijuana and other drugs. The consultant realized right away the girl had no interest in going through with the sessions and had shown up only because her demanding father had insisted she do so. Torn between his concern for the girl and the consequences of a disloyal gesture toward Erhard, the consultant found himself in a difficult dilemma. In the end, he only pretended to carry out the sessions with Erhard's daughter, while telling Larzelere the situation was "being handled." He never heard back from Erhard or the daughter.

At est events around the country, Erhard continued to use his family as convenient props, offering them as shining examples of est's power to transform human relationships. At an est training in 1975, a beaming Erhard quoted his wife, saying, "Werner, I have got everything in the world I want. I am totally satisfied." Likewise, Erhard insisted that his kids no longer needed him. "So when I tell you my life works, I'm not talking about symbols."

His self-assuring words about a contented family life masked a much different family portrait that was well hidden from public view. Long before est came into existence, Ellen Erhard had grown accustomed to playing the role of a dutiful wife, putting up with his absences from home and his womanizing habits. She compensated by devoting herself to maintaining a clean and comfortable home for herself and her children, realizing that her husband—with his expansive ego-driven ambitions—had little interest in sharing in that life with her. She contemplated divorce from time to time, but always backed away because of the anxious fear that leaving Werner Erhard might jeopardize her own ability to provide a secure home for herself and the children. Once est began, Ellen Erhard found herself trapped further in her curious relationship with her husband. Though she largely remained in the background, Ellen appeared reluctantly from time to time at est events or social functions at the Franklin House, where she played the role of a gracious, though reserved, hostess. Privately, she cared little about est and even less about all the fawning attention her husband attracted. She was happiest when she was left alone with her children in the privacy of her own home.

Erhard settled into his own est-influenced pattern of dealing with his family. On occasion, he summoned the children to his book-lined private study on the second floor of the Franklin House, where they dutifully reported to him on their progress in school and on other matters in their lives. Before each meeting, one of Erhard's aides always prepared a detailed agenda that outlined the topics to be discussed with the children. Each one had separate written "agreements" with Erhard, which he used in his meetings with them to evaluate their results. He imposed on his own children the same rigid demands placed on his staff about making commitments and achieving results. Once he had used the same method to squeeze more sales out of his teams of booksellers. Now it had become the est way to take more responsibility for your life.

Living inside the est culture, the young offspring of Werner Erhard hardly could escape the same strict demands and angry temper that often marked their father's dealings toward his staff. During one social gathering at the Franklin House, Erhard stood in the corner of the elegant dining room talking to some of his children while others milled around waiting for dinner to be served. Suddenly, and without any provocation, Erhard launched into a bombastic tirade aimed at his nine-year-old son, St. John, berating the frightened boy over a poor grade he had received in school. As others in the room watched in muted embarrassment or pretended not to notice, Erhard grabbed St. John by the shoulders and shook him harshly, forcing the boy to fall to the ground.

"If you ever get grades like this again, I'll break your leg with a baseball bat, and don't think I'm kidding!" Erhard screamed, as he towered over the boy who could only look up at his father with terror in his eyes. The episode ended in a matter of seconds, and the rest of the evening proceeded without further incident. But for some of his guests that night, Erhard's threatening behavior toward his son provided a chilling glimpse into a side of his character that, until then, had only been the subject of whispered rumors. The wife of one of Erhard's aides, after witnessing the scene with St. John, later turned to her husband and said under her breath, "I'm never coming back to this house again. Never."*

Through the years of est's existence, Erhard periodically had subjected members of his staff to grueling interrogations aimed at confirming their loyalty to himself and est. He patterned them after the weekend "sensitivity" session that Stewart Emery had led for Erhard and his staff shortly before est had begun. The sessions had since come to be known as "fishbowls" because of the way individual staff members were subjected to intense scrutiny. For hours, the hapless person in the fishbowl was subjected to a barrage of taunts and insults and screaming by Erhard or other staff members, the purpose of which was to produce in the individual an enlightened "breakthrough."

In the fall of 1977, Werner Erhard decided it was time for his wife, Ellen, to be placed in the fishbowl. After all, he thought, if he had managed by then to win the blind devotion of his est staff, he had every reason to expect the same from his own family, including his wife. He paved the way for his wife's upcoming ordeal by telling Larzelere that he suspected she was either having an affair or had been thinking about having one, either of which he was not going to tolerate. He decided that Ellen should undergo est consulting sessions with Larzelere.

Though she thought of est consulting as one of the sillier aspects of her husband's self-help business, Ellen agreed to meet with Larzelere, if only to keep Werner quiet. After a few sessions Larzelere was convinced that Erhard was mistaken about his wife's supposed affair. But Erhard did not let up, prodding Larzelere to dig out more details about Ellen's "deceitful ways."

Further sessions with Larzelere failed to satisfy Erhard, who now settled on other ways to force a confession out of his wife. It was time,

*Erhard has repeatedly denied ever hitting St. John.

he decided, for Ellen to "get off it," just as thousands of est graduates did whenever they were accused of acting inappropriately. For the setting, Erhard chose one of his occasional "family" dinners at the Franklin House, this one scheduled for October 1977. The periodic social gatherings, besides including Erhard's own family, were usually attended by other close staff members whom Erhard had designated as part of his larger est family. All seven of Erhard's children from both of his marriages also attended. So did Erhard's first wife, Pat.

After dinner, everyone gathered on the third floor of the house, an attic area that had been converted into a large meeting room. After everyone was seated in a circle of chairs, Erhard turned to Ellen and began angrily accusing her of having an affair and of concealing secrets from him. "What are you withholding?" he demanded, while she remained quiet. Besides her supposed affair, Erhard also accused Ellen of trying to "undermine" him by gathering her own loyal "allies" among est's inner circle who had agreed to support her against her husband's accusations. As the mood in the room grew increasingly tense, Erhard refused to let up on his wife, treating her the same way he treated est employees during their occasional fishbowl sessions. Now it was Ellen's turn to endure the abuse of the fishbowl.

While Erhard continued his verbal abuse, someone else in the room (eyewitnesses differ in recalling who it was) stood up, walked over to Ellen, and kicked her lightly, almost as if he wanted to demonstrate what might happen if she refused to "get off it" by confessing her transgressions to her husband and the others gathered around the room. Now Ellen was lying on the floor, curled up in a ball in an effort to protect herself from any further blows. A few moments later she got to her feet and returned to the chair she had been sitting in.

The time had come for Erhard to complete his wife's transformation. He walked over to her chair and slapped her across the face, and then, with greater force, he knocked her to the floor. No one in the room came to her aid as Erhard began kicking her—not the kind of kick that earlier had been delivered, but sharper blows that hurt her and had her begging for him to stop. Finally Erhard's brother

Harry and another assistant got up from their chairs and pulled Erhard away.

There was silence in the room after that. Erhard, his blue eyes blazing while an angry scowl covered his face, retreated to his chair while Ellen, getting up from the floor, did her best to compose herself. After a few moments, one of Erhard's attractive female assistants walked up to him and whispered into his ear. "I've got an idea," she told him. "Let me go out with the kids to San Rafael. I can run a house. I've raised kids. I can handle things there and you can have Ellen stay in my apartment in the city."

By the time the family gathering finally ended near dawn, Erhard decided that his wife indeed needed to be taught a harsh lesson. Ellen was taken to a nearby motel and later moved to the apartment of Erhard's aide, around the corner from the Franklin House. A week later the family gathered again on the third floor of the house for the second installment of Ellen Erhard's nightmarish ordeal. A large table had been pushed to the side, with the chairs again formed in a circle. It was time for Werner Erhard to treat his family to another violent glimpse of life in a fishbowl.

Again, the subject was Ellen's supposed affair. Erhard remained adamant that she confess her transgression, that she "get off it." Pushed out of her chair, she was ordered by Erhard to her knees while he continued to yell loudly and repeatedly at her to stop "withholding" from him.

"You are having an affair!" Erhard screamed at his wife, who looked back at him with empty eyes but said nothing. "What do you think you're hiding?"

Ellen remained mute on the ground, hoping, as she had done in vain during the previous session, that someone would come to her aid. But no one did. And when Erhard asked for a volunteer to "handle" Ellen, Bob Larzelere suddenly felt the time had come to demonstrate his complete loyalty and obedience to him and est's principles of transformation. This was the moment, thought the former Berkeley doctor. This is when I can prove to Werner Erhard that he can count on me, fully and without any doubt, to serve him. Larzelere got to his feet and approached Ellen, who was lying prone on the floor. He put his hands around her neck and began to squeeze. He meant only to frighten her, since that is what he assumed Erhard wanted him to do. Applying enough pressure to bruise her neck without cutting off her supply of oxygen, Larzelere acted almost as if he were in a trance, a trance induced by his commitment, above all else, to win the love of Werner Erhard.

Erhard's children looked on in horror as they watched their mother's face turn pale, as a little saliva dribbled out of the side of her mouth. Celeste, fourteen years old at the time, grabbed hold of nine-year-old St. John and turned his head away so that he would not have to see his mother endure such physical abuse. Clare, Erhard's oldest daughter from his first marriage, also tried to shield some of the younger children from the ugly scene unfolding in front of them.

"Stop it!" Celeste finally shrieked at Larzelere, as she watched her mother slump on the floor. "You're going to kill her!"

Until then, Erhard had remained in his chair, calm and without emotion, as he watched Larzelere choke Ellen. Only when his daughter screamed for Larzelere to stop did he turn to her with a cold stare and an angry outburst. "Sit down!" he snapped at her. "Or you're going to get the same treatment."*

The night Ellen Erhard was choked in front of her children marked the beginning of a year-long "rehabilitation" program that Erhard decreed for his wife. He assigned the job of "managing" Ellen to Gonneke Spits, giving her authority to control Ellen's comings and goings while insisting as well that Spits supervise her every action,

---

*The precise details of what happened those two nights are hotly disputed. All eyewitnesses agree that the incidents occurred. Erhard would later admit that at the first "fishbowl" he grabbed Ellen by the shoulders and shook her, causing her to fall—either from his push or her attempt to avoid it—and that he may have slapped her. He explained that Ellen was in "an hysteria of lying, withholding" and that he was trying to "shake her out of the hysteria." There is disagreement among eyewitnesses over whether or not Erhard kicked his wife.

Several witnesses at the second fishbowl, including Larzelere, have said that Erhard asked for a volunteer to handle Ellen. Erhard's brother Harry, who was present on both nights, has denied that Erhard asked anyone to do anything to Ellen.

In March 1992 Erhard sued CBS for libel, alleging that, among other claims, a "60 Minutes" broadcast a year earlier "falsely publicized that Mr. Erhard launched into a jealous rage toward his ex-wife wherein he kicked her a number of times while she was on the floor" and "falsely publicized that Mr. Erhard assaulted her to such a degree that he was killing her by causing her to be hurt, choked, strangled, or punished and made to talk or confess." However, Erhard subsequently dropped the suit without any decision on the merits of his claims.

including forays to San Rafael to see the children. Confined to an apartment near the Franklin House, Ellen lived like a woman under house arrest, sadly and painfully aware by now of her husband's immense power. Erhard himself reminded others inside est just how far his influence extended over his wife. "If she doesn't get off it," he once boasted to a group of est trainers, "I'll have her thrown into an insane asylum. And I can do it." No one for a minute doubted Erhard's ability to make good on his threat.

For Ellen Erhard, at least for now, seeking a divorce was out of the question. More than anything else, she was frightened that Erhard would insist on custody of the children, tearing her away from the most precious part of her life and leaving him free to treat them as he always had. No, she would do whatever was necessary to prevent that from happening, even if it meant suffering the emotional abuse that he now was putting her through.

For months Ellen was not permitted to have money or to drive a car. She spent some of her time cleaning Erhard's second-floor living quarters at the Franklin House. Gonneke Spits, at Erhard's direction, gathered up Ellen's credit cards and distributed them to other members of the staff while offering no explanation for such a curious gift. Of course, there were rumors around the est offices that "something had happened between Werner and Ellen." But Erhard had long since seen to it that such rumors were dispelled by the philosophy of est itself. Whatever had happened, staff members came to believe, must have been for Ellen's own good. After all, there were no "victims" in the world according to Werner Erhard. Everyone was responsible for everything happening in their lives.

It wasn't until weeks after Ellen's ordeal first began that she was finally allowed to see her children again, though under painful conditions imposed by her husband. Ellen was driven to her home in Marin County, but only to clean the house without being allowed to talk to the children. Within the est culture, enthusiastic staff members and volunteers cheerfully spent hours scrubbing toilets and windows until they shined, convinced that such mundane service was part of a Zen-like philosophy offering Erhard's version of the path toward enlightenment. For Ellen Erhard, there was no Zen enlightenment in getting down on her hands and knees to scrub kitchen floors in her own home. There was only sorrow and bitterness in her heart as she looked up and, in silence, stared into the frightened eyes of her children.*

*Erhard has denied that he ever forced Ellen to work like a maid or prevented her from living with or talking to her children. Instead, he has said she chose not to live in her own home for a period of time after agreeing to "put herself in a program to regain herself" in the wake of the 1977 incident at the Franklin House.

Twelve

SURRENDER TO SOURCE

Our family was really

the roots from which I sprang.

It still is.

—WERNER ERHARD

Werner Erhard's ugly and abusive treatment of his family was always covered up with public displays of loving relationships between Erhard and his wife and children. The announcement in the May 1978 issue of est's *Graduate Review* magazine showed a smiling close-up picture of Werner and Ellen Erhard above an announcement for a new all-day course he was preparing to present to est graduates.

The latest in a four-part series of est-related programs called "Making Relationships Work," Erhard's upcoming course promised new "breakthroughs" in creating "brilliantly alive, magical relationships."

The first three installments of the est-promoting series had proven to be a great success for Erhard. At first he presented them live, conducting the twelve-hour seminars in a few cities across the country. After that, a videotaped version of the program would be repeated from time to time in a wider number of cities where est centers were located. "Relationships can be nurturing and magical," read the announcement for the latest $50 seminar, "when you come to them out of your wholeness and magnificence, with the intention of contributing your joy and satisfaction—rather than using the relationship to get something."

Inside the large arenas where Erhard conducted his seminars for thousands of est graduates, he presented himself as a self-taught master of human relations, spicing his rambling lectures with the poetry of e.e. cummings and passages from George Bernard Shaw and other writers. Though the programs, like all of Erhard's public appearances, were aimed principally at urging est graduates to keep recruiting others into the est training, Erhard also used his relationships lectures to perpetuate his image as a transformed human being who had figured out the secrets of creating "inspiring" relationships with others.

This public portrayal of Erhard was bolstered further in the fall of 1978 with a much balleyhooed publication of an authorized biography that purported to tell the amazing story of Erhard's life and the creation of est, complete with selected details of Erhard's family life. The book was written by a college philosophy professor and est enthusiast named William Bartley III, who had been paid more than $30,000 as a "philosophical consultant" to est during the two years he worked on the book. While the growing legions of est graduates snatched up copies of the book, not all readers shared Bartley's glowing opinions of either Erhard or est. Erhard "has no original ideas, but he is sharp enough and glib enough to impress a lot of folks," a reviewer wrote in the *Los Angeles Times*. As for Bartley, the *Times* said his "philosophical justification of est as a mishmash of totalitarianism, hucksterism and existentialism makes this book more a public relations product than an objective study." Illustrating the front-page Sunday review was a cartoon caricature of Erhard outfitted as a slick used-car salesman pitching his dubious wares.

Erhard's sales pitches for est depended heavily on his image as a strong-willed but compassionate father determined only to bring out the best in his children through the application of est principles. In 1978 he agreed to allow two of his children from his first marriage to be interviewed at the Franklin House for a book on the offspring of famous personalities written by the daughter of CBS newsman Walter Cronkite. Erhard's nineteen-year-old son Jack had curly hair, but otherwise closely resembled his father, inheriting his facial features and adopting some of his est-influenced mannerisms and speech. Deborah, a year younger, had the soft features of a girl turning into a young woman. Her blond hair brushed against her shoulders and her eyes twinkled brightly, even as she concealed from the interview the family's darkest secrets.

When Kathy Cronkite arrived for the interview, Erhard's public relations director steered her into the cozy second-floor den at the Franklin House and took a seat in the corner to monitor the children's comments. Not surprisingly, the interview provided the writer with a decidedly upbeat—and distorted—glimpse into the lives of Erhard's children. Only once, and even then in the most subtle of ways, did either child provide even a hint of the true nature of their relationship with their father. It came when Cronkite asked Deborah whether her father's public personality differed from the way he related to his family at home. Deborah, of course, had witnessed several months earlier the cruel treatment of Ellen Erhard one floor above the den where she now was talking so positively about life with her famous father.

"Dad's in the public eye a lot," Deborah said. "He's got his way of being in the world. None of it's a front or anything. It's just that he doesn't lay himself totally wide open. So when he's into the family, I think it takes awhile for that to disappear."

Toward the end of the interview, Deborah talked further about her own relationship with her father. "See, I just want to make sure that my experience of my dad came across," she said. "I know there's a lot of room in my relationship with him to expand. I think that our relationship could become something very positive and something very powerful in the world."

There was no way for any casual interviewer to read between the lines that Deborah uttered that day at the Franklin House. She was barely six months old when her father disappeared from home, and she grew up assuming he had long since died. By the time he came back into her life when she was almost a teenager, he crushed her a second time by announcing he had little interest in acting like a father. Still, she had shown at least some enthusiasm for the work that he did, enrolling in one of the teenage est training sessions when she was fourteen. Of all of Erhard's children, Deborah probably had the most genuine interest in the things her father seemed to stand for. But her comments to Kathy Cronkite hardly reflected the searing reality of her true relationship to her father. Instead, they represented everything she so desperately wanted in that relationship but had long since been denied.

The most serious allegations about Werner Erhard would not be found in publicity-minded interviews orchestrated by him and his aides. Instead, several years would pass before Deborah had the courage to state publicly that her father had sexually molested her when she was about sixteen years old, well before the pretty soft-faced girl first sat down to talk about her famous father. She said it had happened only once, after which she tried to tuck it into the background so that she might yet have a loving relationship with her father.

It was not to be. According to Deborah, Erhard, a few years later, coerced one of his older daughters—one of Deborah's sisters, in her twenties—into having sexual intercourse with him in a hotel room they were sharing during one of his frequent out-of-town trips. Again, according to Deborah, the sexual abuse happened only once, but Deborah's sister nonetheless was frightened and traumatized by the incident and she remained silent about it for years, afraid of what Erhard might do if she ever uttered a word to anyone. She recounted the ugly episode to Deborah only after Deborah told of her own abuse. Still, the two girls did not immediately say anything to others in the family, not even to their mother, for fear that they simply would not be believed. But, Deborah says, Erhard's older daughter made one solemn vow that she kept ever since. Never again, she swore to her sister, would she ever see her father alone.

According to Deborah, Werner Erhard's daughters finally confronted their father with their accounts of his sexual abuse at a stormy, twelve-hour family meeting on board his Sausalito houseboat in the mid-1980s. With most of his family present, Erhard vehemently denied that he had ever raped his older daughter, although, Deborah says, her father admitted having sexual intercourse with her sister. What's more, Erhard explained that the episode had been a "nurturing experience" for the young woman. Erhard has denied all allegations of sexual abuse.*

The man who sermonized at est meetings about the special bond between parents and children made a mockery out of his words with his own behavior toward his children. Even with his younger daughters, he sometimes talked suggestively about sex, sitting around the table as he reached, almost playfully, for their breasts. "Oh, I wish I could be the first to teach you guys," he would tell his teenage daughters Adair and Celeste. "Wouldn't that be great?"

Throughout est's existence, Erhard had treated sex as simply another form of human behavior to be controlled and manipulated in ways that enhanced his own overpowering control over the lives of others who inhabited the est culture. Long before he ever started est, Werner Erhard—even when he was still Jack Rosenberg—used his powerful sexual appeal and charismatic energy with women to intensify their own sense of loyalty and devotion to him. During his bookselling days, Erhard maintained the nucleus of a dedicated, and predominantly female, staff partly by showering his romantic attention

---

*Deborah's allegations of sexual abuse of herself and her sister were first publicly aired in early 1991 on the CBS program "60 Minutes." Prior to the broadcast, Erhard's attorney sent to CBS a polygraphist's report asserting that Erhard had truthfully denied raping or sexually molesting any of his children. On the program, CBS broadcast a blanket denial by Erhard: "It's just plain not true. Just plain not true. And anybody who would say something about it has got to be sick." Erhard's subsequent libel suit against CBS, which he later dropped, included an allegation that CBS had falsely reported that he had "sexually abused his daughter Deborah Rosenberg," "forcibly raped and had sexual intercourse, committed incest with his daughter," and "admitted having sexual intercourse with his daughter and claimed it to be a 'nurturing experience' for her."

from time to time on some of the women who followed Erhard first into Mind Dynamics and later into est.

Inside the emerging est culture, Erhard continued to view sex as an integral part of his obsessive demand that others around him pledge their devotion. He required staff members to divulge the most intimate details of their personal lives as part of a series of policies aimed at controlling their thoughts and behavior. A staff policy imposed in the mid-1970s instructed est staffers to "stay in communication" with Erhard about their personal relationships, particularly those of a sexual nature.

Although the policy was designed to proscribe sexual relations between staff members, exceptions were possible in cases in which Erhard was informed about existing affairs. These relationships could continue to include "fucking," the staff was told, but only as long as the trysting staffers got their jobs done and showed no signs of "upsets." The policy made it clear to the staff that Erhard would attribute declining job performance to the fact that "you are fucking whoever you fuck" and would ask the offending party to leave est.

Erhard generously added a "family policy" to the est rules governing sexual conduct, mindful of the occasional desire among married staff members to enjoy dalliances with other partners besides their spouse. The policy, which otherwise prohibited extramarital affairs, allowed such liaisons as long as Don Cox received a letter from an est staffer's wife or husband allowing their spouse "to fuck someone else." The letter also had to include "guidelines" aimed at identifying those with whom the spouse could enjoy sexual intimacy.

In the early years of est, Erhard had a habit of announcing strict rules proscribing sexual liaisons among staff members, only to drop them at particularly opportune times and reinstate them at a later date. While treating the staff to a weeklong Mexican cruise in 1974, Erhard abruptly lifted the sexual ban, delighting many along for the trip. After the amorous week at sea, Erhard reimposed the no-sex rules back in San Francisco.

A few years later Bob Larzelere, Erhard's director of staff "well being," was given the dubious responsibility of enforcing est's sexual rules. Part of his duties gave Larzelere the role of permitting or rejecting sexual interludes among staff members who required permission, under est's sexual codes, to carry out such activities. One night Larzelere received an anxious phone call from one of Erhard's personal aides. From the breathy tone of the man's voice, Larzelere realized the man had made his call while on the verge of consummating a sexual act with his partner. Still, the dutiful disciple of Werner Erhard felt the need to get a green light from Larzelere before proceeding. "For Christ's sake," a stunned Larzelere whispered into the phone, "go ahead and fuck her."

No such self-reporting sexual rules applied to Erhard. Instead, he entrusted to his closest aides the confidential role of assisting in the steady, though usually clandestine, flow of women in and out of his private black-painted bedroom on the second floor of the Franklin House. Sometimes his partners came from the ranks of celebrity est enthusiasts, including actress Cloris Leachman, with whom Erhard maintained a relationship for a few years. Otherwise, Erhard helped himself to the sexual favors offered to him by an assortment of attractive staff members and est volunteers. A comely Franklin House assistant once confided to an est trainer that another Erhard aide "schedules Werner's cock" and that she planned "to get on the schedule."

For the most part, Erhard managed—with the help of his sworn-to-secrecy aides—to keep the details of his frequent trysts from other staff members. To them, as well as to the legions of Erhard followers around the country, he wanted to maintain the image of a devoted husband and father whose long hours away from his family represented a willing sacrifice to his passionate and consuming dedication to est's goals of human transformation. Only when occasional evidence of his other extracurricular activities surfaced did staff members see, firsthand, another side of Werner Erhard.

One of the est trainers, a former New York City accountant named Irving Bernstein, had been put in charge of overseeing est's six-day advanced program offered on the West and East coasts. A woman whom Bernstein supervised happened to confide to Bernstein's wife that she had been sleeping with Erhard. After noticing that the woman sometimes disappeared from the est office, Bernstein reminded her of est's admonition to be "honest and open" about any problems she might be having. The woman found herself in a terrible bind since she already had sworn to Erhard that she would not divulge their sexual relationship.

Erhard flew into a rage when he discovered that the Bernsteins knew about his affair with the woman. "It's none of your business who I'm fucking!" he yelled at Bernstein's wife. Later he warned that he would "squash her like a bug" if she dared to continue to "interfere" in his private life.

From est's earliest days, Erhard deliberately drew the connection between loyalty and service to him personally and commitment and allegiance to the personal enlightenment goals of est. In doing so, he found it amazingly easy to seduce staff members and volunteers into a giddy sense of blind faith in him as the source of est.

Though virtually everyone who inhabited the est culture fell prey to the cultlike aspects of Werner worship, Erhard exercised his greatest power over the elite corps of est trainers with whom he always professed a special bond. In turn, the small group of trainers—there were still fewer than ten well into the mid-1970s—looked to Erhard as a supreme master who had figured out the path toward enlightenment and had conferred upon them the rare privilege of pointing out the path to others through the est training. Est trainers were to "recreate" him, which had the effect of further blurring in their mesmerized minds any distinction between Werner Erhard and "Werner's work."

Following a trip he made to Japan in 1975, Erhard added a dramatic new twist to the bonds of loyalty he expected from the est trainers. He began conducting meetings dressed in a black kimono, playing the role of a Japanese warlord straight out of the pages of *Shogun*, James Clavell's epic novel of the warlord Toranaga and his faithful samurai warriors. Not long after, est executives Don Cox and Vincent Drucker met with Erhard to discuss some financial cutbacks needed to offset a temporary decline in enrollments. On their list of proposed budget cuts, Cox and Drucker included a decrease in the number of est trainers. Erhard cut them off immediately, angrily insisting he would never agree to such an action.

"You do not understand the relationship of the bond that these trainers have with me," said Erhard. "They have committed their lives to me, and I have committed myself. They are committed for life, and I have committed myself to take care of them for life."

Erhard's heightened sense of his own powers took on other-world dimensions at various times during the est phenomenon. "How do I know I'm not the reincarnation of Jesus Christ?" Erhard once wondered of a friend. A few years later he hinted to his est trainers about his own illusions of mystical powers. "When you get to a field of open snow," he told them, "on which you have never walked before, and on which no one has ever walked before, and on which you don't think it is possible to walk, look for my footprints."

Erhard's heavenly aspirations may have reached their climax in the fall of 1977 when he appeared at a meeting of est seminar leaders at a beachside retreat center near Monterey. Flushed with enthusiasm about the transforming power of doing Werner's work, some of the leaders asked Erhard where he placed himself on the spectrum of human transformation. Swept up in the fervor of the discussion, one of the seminar leaders got to his feet with a serious look on his face.

"The question in the room that nobody is asking," the man told Erhard solemnly, "is 'Are you the messiah?' "

The room grew silent as Erhard looked out to the curious faces of some of his most devoted disciples. After a few moments he replied, "No, I am who sent him." Undoubtedly, there were many in the room who were sure they had just witnessed the ultimate transformation of a man; Werner Erhard wanted them to believe he was on par with God.

In solidifying his position as Source, Erhard adopted an increasingly ritualistic approach toward his custom of "designating" new est trainers. Within a few years of est's creation, Erhard had largely stopped conducting est trainings himself, devoting much of his time instead to large est-promoting events around the country such as the "Making Relationships Work" seminars and other mass-audience speeches pivotal to est's recruitment of new adherents. But he was going to make sure that all those new customers experienced est only with the help of trainers who looked to Werner Erhard as the source of their own power and influence over the lives of others.

"Are you willing to create Werner being the source of your being a trainer?" one of the new est trainers was asked at the time of his designation by Erhard in the spring of 1977. Erhard was not satisfied merely in having the est trainers acknowledge him as the source of their exalted position. After all, Japanese warlords demanded and received much more from their faithful warriors. It was now Erhard's turn to demand the same from each new est trainer.

One by one, the would-be trainers were asked if they were willing to perform Erhard's work for the rest of their lives. For most of Erhard's disciples, the answer to those questions was an unequivocal and unquestioning yes.

One of those disciples was Charlene Afremow, Erhard's former Mind Dynamics instructor, who had eagerly switched from teacher to student after becoming convinced that Werner Erhard and est together represented a formula powerful enough to change the world. Another was Laurel Scheaf, whose history with Erhard stretched back to the days of selling books door to door, long before he ever decided to turn his considerable talents as a salesman into a scheme for mass-marketing a human potential course. From the start, the former schoolteacher had fallen under Erhard's hypnotic spell, carrying out any duty he assigned to her, and, ultimately, dedicating her life to serving him and his purposes.

In December 1978 the two women donned formal evening dresses and sat on either side of Erhard at an elegant dinner held at the Silverado Country Club in Napa Valley, an hour or so north of San Francisco. Each of them had trained for years for the moment about to unfold amid the sparkling crystal and polished silver that gleamed under the lights of the room's chandeliers. They had reached what was, for them, the pinnacle achievement of their lives. That night they were to be designated as the two newest members of Erhard's elite corps of est trainers.

"Each trainer I acknowledge is really an acknowledgment of myself," Erhard told the assembled est trainers that evening. "It's a reflection of my own magnificence and my own magnanimity and my own wonderfulness."

As he carried out the designation of his two newest trainers, Erhard spelled out the vows and promises expected of them, while reminding them of his own special role.

"Let's be clear between you and me that you have no rights," Erhard told Charlene Afremow and Laurel Scheaf, "that if you accept the job of trainer that you give up your rights . . . and that you've got nothing to lose."

As Afremow and Scheaf stood, a little nervously, to accept their exalted position, Erhard continued to outline the unique role of an est trainer. That role, he reminded them, meant that their commitment to his work would be paramount to their attachments to children, husbands, or other personal relationships. "Until I release you from that, my intentions will be more important than anything else in your life."

Several months later, est trainer Stewart Esposito distributed to the rest of the trainers a transcript of the ceremony designating Afremow and Scheaf as new trainers. He urged them to study the document, which he said had helped him to "re-create Werner" while reminding him of "Werner's experience" of what constituted an est trainer. Esposito, a former life insurance salesman who had joined Erhard's staff after losing several thousand dollars selling Mind Dynamics franchises on the East Coast, also asked his wife to read the transcript so that she would be "clear about what my life is about."

Some of Erhard's other est trainers, however, slowly began to realize that their lives were turning into degrading and subservient roles in a tyrannical drama that was turning sour.

For a time, the wife of one of Erhard's original trainers, Landon Carter, shared her husband's faithful devotion to Werner Erhard and est. The couple, in fact, had met at an est seminar in Honolulu not long after Landon had joined the est staff in 1973, following his spiritual studies in India a couple of years earlier. Like her husband, Beky Carter viewed Erhard with awe and adoration, finding him to be filled with intense charisma, powerful energy, and seductive charm. Indeed, Erhard's beguiling ways once had induced Beky to write him a private note confessing that she had behaved at one point like a "manipulative snake." Erhard later sent her a birthday cake in the shape of a snake, but with an amethyst in the serpent's mouth.

It wasn't long before Beky Carter saw other manipulative sides of Erhard that, more annoyingly, were reflected in her own husband. Around the house, in the increasingly rare moments he was at home with his wife and two small children, Landon Carter often smiled the same sly, cunning smile that flashed regularly across Erhard's face. He acted demanding and arrogant, rarely interested in talking to his wife about anything but the value and wonders of Erhard and est. If any problems arose at home, Landon Carter always insisted it was his wife's fault. "Just get off it!" he shouted at her, the same way he shouted in the est trainings he led almost every weekend. "My job is to do Werner's work," Carter often reminded his wife. "And your job is to support me."

Eventually Landon Carter himself began to entertain some doubts about the vows of lifelong service he had given to Erhard. He began to notice how drained, both physically and emotionally, he felt at the end of yet another est training weekend, walking through the airport like a "sucked-out orange" after standing all those hours in a hotel ballroom and now on his way to another city, another ballroom, another training. He was tired of haranguing each new roomful of est trainees, tired of calling them cunts and kikes and niggers and assholes and just about anything else that was necessary to break them down. He was tired of berating people for having ulcers or heart problems or any other kind of physical malady that, according to the transformational principles of est, existed only as part of their "racket," their excuse for their own sorry lives.

Carter had other reasons for questioning his commitment to Erhard. A physical fitness enthusiast and a marathon runner, Carter was the major force behind est's advanced six-day course, which combined elements of the est training with a rigorous regimen of physical exercise such as early-morning runs and rope-climbing adventures. Begun in the mid-1970s as an est program for teenagers, the six-day course had evolved into a highly profitable program for Erhard, with a steady schedule of sessions held at resort sites in New York and California. Although his $50,000 salary as an est trainer certainly made him one of the higher paid staff members, Carter thought he deserved some kind of a partnership in the profits that Erhard was earning from the six-day course. But Erhard, for all his talk about the special bond he had with his est trainers, had no interest in sharing the wealth he was earning from the est training and other courses. Instead, he ordered Carter to resume his fatiguing schedule of weekend est trainings.

At the end of each year, between Christmas and New Year's, Erhard usually gathered his est trainers together to review the year and prepare for the new one ahead. At a formal dinner meeting at the Franklin House in December 1979, Carter decided to announce his departure from the staff. The session, however, turned into a tense competition of wills after Erhard reminded the est trainer of his lifelong commitment to carry out Erhard's will.

"Are you willing to keep your word and do what I tell you to do?" Erhard demanded of Carter.

For Carter, the moment of truth had arrived. Oddly, even though he was resolved to make his break from Erhard, he still felt the man's power reverberating around the room. Looking at him from across the room, Carter suddenly felt as if he were standing at one end of a dark tunnel, barely able to see the small circle of dim light at the other end. He struggled to focus on Erhard's words, feeling faint and wondering if he had the courage to tell Erhard what he knew must be told.

Finally he forced a resolute "no" out of his mouth, as he continued to stare at Erhard. And then, with the liberating denial of Erhard's grip over him, a dazzling light shone into Carter's eyes and left him with a giddy sense of relief. At that moment one of the other est trainers stood up close to Carter and angrily spat at his face, calling him "Judas" for renouncing his sacred vows. Carter was stung by the epithet and even wondered for a fleeting moment whether he had just made an awful mistake by turning away from Werner Erhard. His decision, however, stood—after nearly seven years of surrendering to Source, Landon Carter never worked for Erhard again.

Carter's departure had little effect on Erhard's continued determination to demand and receive the utmost devotion of those who worked for him. In May 1980 a group of est trainers—known as the Trainer Candidate Development Committee—submitted a ten-page memo to Erhard reporting on a series of lengthy evaluations of a set of prospective new trainers.

The memo vividly illustrated the extent to which Erhard's est consultants were used to delve into the personal lives of other est staff members. One of the trainer candidates, the committee said, was trying to sort out some marital problems and had to figure out whether his "need" for his wife interfered with his "having to surrender completely into his relationship" with Erhard. To resolve the conflict, the trainer candidate and his wife attended a joint session with one of the est consultants. The purpose, the committee reported, was to address the issue of whether the candidate's wife would stay with her husband.

In an atmosphere in which Erhard's est trainers were expected to declare unlimited devotion to Erhard, some began to pressure est's management executives to follow suit. Surely, the trainers reasoned, if any of the executives balked at committing their own loyalties to Erhard, such an action could be seen as an unacceptable refusal to carry out his own vision for the organization.

In January 1980 a small group of trainers and executives gathered in a conference room at the est offices on California Street. While the executives talked about some of the problems facing the company, the trainers at the meeting were more interested in berating the managers for not "re-creating Werner." One of the executives, Vincent Drucker, found himself feeling more frustrated by the minute, thinking how little these fanatical est trainers knew about running a multimillion-dollar business. He had little patience for all this crazy talk about Source and re-creating Werner. After listening to the conversation for a few more minutes, Drucker decided to speak his mind.

Drucker acknowledged the importance of a personal commitment to Erhard. But he also mentioned problems stemming from high staff turnover and Erhard's lack of attention toward developing new programs.

To some of the trainers, Drucker's words sounded like nothing less than heresy. One of the trainers turned toward Drucker, his face reflecting his rage.

"It's thinking like this that got your daughter drowned!" said the trainer.

Drucker froze in his seat. He and his wife, Wendy, had had a baby girl who had fallen into a swimming pool and died the previous year. Drucker, as a longtime est employee, was aware of the prevailing belief inside the est culture that terrible things happened to those who were "not complete" or "out of integrity" with Erhard. The trainer's chilling words carried only one meaning. Drucker himself had been responsible for his daughter's tragic death because of his own unwillingness to accept Werner Erhard as Source in his life.

Drucker resigned from the staff the next day. Erhard, who had not attended the meeting between the trainers and the executives, sought out Drucker to learn what had happened. After Drucker explained the incident, Erhard replied, "Some things are unforgivable." But he offered no apologies or regrets for the turn of events.

After five years on the est staff, Vincent Drucker left without ever knowing whether Werner Erhard considered as unforgivable the est trainer's or Drucker's own choice of words that day.

153

Thirteen

ERHARD TAKES ON THE WORLD

I take responsibility

for ending starvation within

twenty years.

—WERNER ERHARD

O n a February evening in 1978, Werner Erhard sat in the private dining room on the top floor of the exclusive French restaurant 1789 in the tony Georgetown district of Washington, D.C. After the waiters cleared away the dinner plates from the gourmet multicourse meal and brought out coffee and dessert, Erhard returned to the topic that had brought him to the nation's capital. "You and I want our lives to matter. We want our lives to make a difference," he told the small group gathered at the restaurant. "We want to make the world work. We want to create a context and a process that will lead to the end of starvation within two decades."

For the past couple of hours, Erhard's dinner guests had listened with a mixture of curiosity and bemused bewilderment while their gracious host talked about a new program he had unveiled the previous fall called the Hunger Project. In September and October of 1977 Erhard had barnstormed the country, speaking to 40,000 est graduates in eleven cities (at an admission price of $6) to hear of a bold new plan to end worldwide hunger. As usual, standing ovations greeted him everywhere he appeared, after which the rapt audiences settled into their seats and listened to Erhard's noble pledge to rid the world of the ugly blight of famine and starvation. The est graduates quickly "got it" when Erhard told them that the Hunger Project really was little more than an extension of est's basic approach toward each individual's life. If everyone was responsible for his own life, Erhard explained to the cheering throngs, then everyone equally could take on responsibility for the fate of the planet itself. Take on responsibility for the end of worldwide hunger, Erhard solemnly urged the est enthusiasts, and within two decades hunger would vanish.

Now Erhard had come to Washington, where he spent a few days breezing through the city's corridors of power, meeting with members of Congress, with officials from Jimmy Carter's administration, with hunger experts like the small group he met with at the Georgetown restaurant. Unlike the beaming est graduates who had walked out of Erhard's Hunger Project speeches a few months earlier feeling as if they had just experienced an epiphany, his guests in Georgetown were a bit more skeptical about his grandiose plan.

"Is the project directed at anything to ease hunger?" wondered Dr. Lincoln Gordon, a former president of Johns Hopkins University who was by then attached to a Washington think tank, Resources for the Future, that studied issues concerning the environment, hunger, energy, and population. "Does the project have a philosophical approach?"

Erhard's answer hardly satisfied those sitting around the table, leading instead to more head-scratching in the room. "The key thing of the context of making a commitment," he replied to Gordon's question, "is that it really commits us to ending hunger."

Others at the dinner pressed Erhard on what kinds of prescriptions his Hunger Project would offer for ending hunger around the world. Again, Erhard's reply failed to offer much illumination. "If you let a tree be a tree, you get a tree, not a jackass. The truth is that you make choices within your own context. In a world of green and blue, you can't get yellow." Such logic-defying statements were a regular part of the vocabulary inside est trainings and seminars. But Erhard's guests in Georgetown spoke a blunter language that evening as they finished coffee and dessert.

"The trouble is the context doesn't get you anywhere," replied Martin McLaughlin, who had been a member of the American delegation to the 1974 World Hunger Conference. "It lets you do something or nothing."

Before leaving Washington, Erhard made a trip to Capitol Hill where he held several private meetings about the Hunger Project with senators and House members. Erhard was not without his followers and supporters within Congress. Senator Claiborne Pell, a patrician Democrat from Rhode Island, enlisted in Erhard's Hunger Project, later hosting a fund-raising party at his posh Georgetown home. A former member of Congress from Texas, Alan Steelman, volunteered to serve as a Hunger Project liaison between Erhard and sitting members of the House and Senate. For the most part, however, the reaction to Erhard's est-filled talk of ending hunger around the world was cordial though skeptical. "We're not sure what he's all about," one confused congressional official told a newspaper reporter covering Erhard's mission to Washington.

From the outset, Erhard was quick to insist there was no direct connection between est and the Hunger Project other than a $400,000 "interest-free loan" to begin the new endeavor, a $100,000 grant from a separate est foundation and the many hours that est staffers and volunteers contributed to the cause.

When he embarked on his tour to launch the new project in the fall of 1977, Erhard was supported by an enthusiastic corps of est staff members and volunteers who contributed some 40,000 hours of free labor. During the Hunger Project's first year, another 4,000 est volunteers donated a total of 60,000 hours to Erhard's newest crusade. To run the project, Erhard tapped a faithful disciple named Joan Holmes, a 1973 est graduate who had served in various est staff positions over the years. Within a year of its formal launching, the Hunger Project had taken over a four-story town house conveniently located only two blocks from Erhard's Franklin House.*

From the very outset of the Hunger Project, Holmes herself made it clear that the program had much more to do with spreading the transformational message of est than with actually doing anything to end hunger. Hunger, as Holmes candidly told readers of the *Graduate Review* in August 1977, had little to do with the overall goals of the project. "Of course, I'm not insensitive to the people who are hungry and starving," said Holmes. "But the truth is that it could be any issue. The process is the same."

Erhard, for his part, stressed that he had little interest in using Hunger Project money to feed hungry people. Nor, he insisted, did he want anyone to feel guilt or remorse over the hundreds of millions of people around the globe who lacked enough food. The Hunger Project, like est itself, depended on a flock of supporters unwilling to be bothered with such unpleasant emotions. Spelling out the "generating principles" of the Hunger Project in January 1978, Erhard made it perfectly clear where he stood: "It has nothing to do with guilt. If you want to feel guilty, fine. Keep it to yourself. It's not part of the project. The Hunger Project has nothing to do with feeling sorry for starving people. I consider feeling sorry for those people demeaning to their humanity. If you want to feel sorry, please don't get it on me."

Above all else, the introduction of the Hunger Project provided Werner Erhard with a lucrative new marketing tool for est. After all, anyone confused about the fuzzy-sounding objectives of the Hunger Project could easily get a much clearer picture simply by enrolling first in est. Sure enough, non-est graduates who showed any interest

*The Hunger Project sold its San Francisco town house for $850,000 in 1982, a year after the city planning commission ruled the group never had a permit to operate.

in volunteering for the project almost immediately found themselves under tremendous pressure to sign up for the next est training.

Erhard also used the Hunger Project to keep est graduates themselves fervently imbued with Erhardian spirit. Within months of the project's formation, est graduates found a new est post-training seminar in which they could enroll. Initially titled the "Hunger Project Seminar Series," the program attracted during its first few months some 4,200 est graduates who paid $30 each to attend the sessions, with the money flowing directly to est. Though the seminars had little to do with ending hunger, those who attended were pressured into making financial contributions to the Hunger Project and recruiting others to do the same.

In New York, 200 participants in one of the seminars once were given a quota of 3,000 people to sign up in the Hunger Project. Bearing in mind one of est's cardinal rules against breaking agreements, the zealous New Yorkers attacked their assignment with fanatical ferociousness and exceeded the quota by 1,000.

Only when the Hunger Project began to attract criticism for its close links to est did the name of the seminar change to the more ambiguous "Making a Difference." Still, the emphasis on signing up new supporters for the Hunger Project remained the prime objective of the seminar, while the vocabulary of the sessions themselves differed little from that of the est training.

By the time he made his bold proclamation for ending hunger in two decades, Erhard had plenty of reasons for wanting to portray himself as a social crusader and a zealous humanitarian. At the beginning of 1977, the number of est graduates around the country had passed the 100,000 mark, with new participants still streaming into an expanding number of est centers around the country. In February of that year, the Aspen center—one of the first out-of-town est outposts—closed its doors because of waning interest there. But enthusiasm was running high elsewhere, and that same month est opened new centers in Philadelphia and Houston. Two months later est went international with a training session in London, followed soon after by the opening of a full-time est center in the British capital.

But Erhard, despite the rising growth curve of the est phenomenon, knew he had to take a bold step to shore up his reputation outside the immediate est environment. To the tens of thousands of grinning est disciples, he still was simply "Werner," the man who had created est and who had bestowed, in that creation, all the seemingly miraculous and transforming changes in their lives. To them, he had remained a man who could do no wrong, make no mistake that could not be cleared up with a simple "acknowledgment," and who had shown them the way to enlightenment after only sixty hours in a hotel ballroom.

Werner Erhard always wanted more than that. He wanted his image and reputation to soar in the hearts and minds of those who lived outside the world of est. He wanted to be respected and admired by those he had wined and dined at the Franklin House. And he wanted to be taken seriously by the influential molders and shapers of public opinion from Hollywood to Washington, D.C. But Erhard also knew many of these same people had heard the stories that focused on his authoritarian ways, his lavish life-style, and the absolute loyalty he seemed to demand from his army of obedient followers. It was the Hunger Project, he decided, that would finally earn him the universal respect that he felt he so rightly deserved.

For a while, it seemed that Erhard's strategy paid off handsomely. The first batch of articles about the Hunger Project largely described the program as a worthy humanitarian endeavor. "est Hopes to End Hunger Before 1997," the *Los Angeles Times* announced in October 1977. Besides describing Erhard's cross-country tour then in progress, the *Times* provided a welcome platform for Erhard to explain, without much critical questioning from the newspaper reporter, the est-filled objectives of the Hunger Project.

To further boost the credibility of the Hunger Project, Erhard assembled a "hunger council" whose blue-chip members monitored the project. The roster included such people as Roger Sant, who had served in President Gerald Ford's administration and had earlier been a successful food industry executive; Gregory Votaw, a World Bank official; Jack Thayer, president of NBC Radio; Curtiss Porter, a professor of black studies at the University of Pittsburgh; and Kate Lloyd, a former *Vogue* editor who later became managing editor of *Working*

Woman magazine. (Lloyd was also the mother-in-law of Raz Ingrasci, Erhard's longtime personal aide.) For celebrity appeal, the hunger council included diehard Erhard supporters John Denver and Valerie Harper. Several members of the council had served on the est advisory board and were est graduates themselves, further cementing the already solid ties between est and the Hunger Project. To serve as the Hunger Project's president, Erhard tapped New York attorney Ellis Deull, an est graduate who regularly proselytized for Erhard among the secretaries, paralegals, and lawyers employed at his corporate law firm.

In 1978 Werner Erhard found an even more influential platform from which he could spread the est-filled message of the Hunger Project. President Jimmy Carter had been instructed by Congress to establish a blue-ribbon commission to study hunger and turned to one of his aides, Peter Bourne, to recommend panel members. Bourne already knew about the Hunger Project because he had been introduced to Erhard by one of the members of the hunger council.

On his list for Carter, Bourne included both John Denver and fellow singer Harry Chapin, who had been active on hunger issues and had spearheaded the lobbying campaign to create the new commission. Bourne assumed Carter would pick Chapin as a token celebrity member of the commission because of his activist stance against hunger. But Carter surprised him by appointing both Chapin and Denver, whom he had met previously through his son Chip. Denver had campaigned for Carter's election in 1976 and was eager to promote the Hunger Project in keeping with his own Erhard-inspired enthusiasm.*

The connecting tether between Werner Erhard and the White House appeared even stronger several months later when Chip Carter attended a three-day conference sponsored by the Hunger Project at a retreat center in Tarrytown, New York. "If my father can go from being almost unknown to being president in four years, we can certainly end hunger in twenty years," Carter told the conference

*Chapin, no fan of est or the Hunger Project, once told the *Washington Post*, "It is not enough to be conscious of hunger. The first rule of political organizing is to give people something specific to push for."

participants. Erhard gushed with delight when he heard Carter's words. What better way to silence his critics than to be stamped with the apparent approval of the president of the United States?

By the end of its first year, the Hunger Project had "enrolled" 180,000 people throughout the United States. (One could enroll simply by signing a card "committing" to end hunger.) More important, 30,000 people had made tax-deductible contributions to the Hunger Project amounting to just under $1 million. "The basic operating strategy for 1978 is to continue communicating the principles of the Hunger Project as widely as possible in order to generate the alignment necessary for transforming those conditions that perpetuate hunger," read part of the Hunger Project's 1977 financial report.

While the money began pouring in, Werner Erhard made good on his pledge to refrain from helping to feed people directly or feeling guilty about massive hunger and starvation. After raising more than $1 million during its first full year in business, the Hunger Project contributed the grand sum of $1,000 to a San Francisco church that operated a soup kitchen at Christmas. The previous year, the project gave $2,500 to OXFAM, a prominent hunger organization.

It wasn't long before the Hunger Project began attracting critical attention from some of Erhard's skeptics. "Werner Erhard is using the Hunger Project not only for self-aggrandizement but for promoting the for-profit corporation he funded, as well," concluded *Mother Jones* magazine in December 1978, following a six-month investigation. "I have serious doubts about the social value of the Hunger Project," one hunger expert in Washington told the magazine. "It's probably collected more money in the name of hunger and done the least about hunger than any group I can think of." After threatening a libel suit against *Mother Jones*, est responded instead with a call for seminar participants to devote two minutes of "negative energy" on the magazine's writers.*

---

*Six years after *Mother Jones*'s investigation of the Hunger Project, the magazine announced that a follow-up look had revealed several changes since the original article. For instance, the magazine found that the Hunger Project had severed all financial and legal ties with est while instructing its staff and volunteers not to recruit new customers into est, which was soon to be replaced anyway by a new Erhard program. *Mother Jones*, however, made it clear that it firmly stood by everything reported in its 1978 article.

While critical media articles hindered Erhard's attempts to use the Hunger Project to bolster his image outside the world of est, they did little to dampen the growing enthusiasm of est graduates themselves toward his latest gambit.

A legal secretary in New York named Carol Giambalvo was typical of these enthusiasts. She signed her enrollment card in the Hunger Project at the end of her est training session in February 1978. Privately she thought that Erhard's grandiose pledge to end hunger within two decades sounded like a bit of a reach, but she was flushed with enough enthusiasm about est to begin signing up others in the antihunger campaign. Along with another dozen est volunteers, Giambalvo scoured weekend flea markets, crowded summertime beaches, rock concert parking lots, and the lines of people waiting to enter New York Islander hockey games—armed with stacks of Hunger Project enrollment cards and always ready to ask for contributions to keep the project going. Most of those who reached into their pockets naturally assumed their money was going to a noble-sounding cause aimed at feeding hungry people. Little did they know that their money instead helped only to pay for a large organization devoted to spreading the message of Werner Erhard.

Carol Giambalvo and her fellow volunteers were careful about what they told new recruits and potential contributors. Although they never bothered to explain that none of the money would be used to feed anyone, they also were intentionally vague about the real purpose of the Hunger Project. That's the way they had been trained by other Hunger Project officials.

Undaunted by the occasional criticism he faced from the media, Erhard found other ways to promote the expanding Hunger Project. By 1980 the project had raised more than $6 million while attracting the attention of United Nations officials and other experts who knew little about Werner Erhard but applauded any efforts to promote an antihunger message. Erhard also trained his sights on Hollywood, where a host of est-graduate celebrities were ready to lend some glitter to his crusade.

In November popular television actress Valerie Harper traveled as a Hunger Project representative to the famine-ravaged country of

Somalia, where refugee camps were filled with the hungry and mal-nourished victims of a cruel five-year border war with Ethiopia. De-scribing the Hunger Project as a "free public-relations firm for the voiceless," the est-influenced Harper admitted that "we don't send one grain of rice but we support those who are."

A few months later movie actor and est graduate Roy Scheider (*Jaws*, *All That Jazz*) was the featured speaker at a gala Hunger Project benefit dinner in Washington, D.C., where three hundred guests dressed in formals and black tie dined on chicken stuffed with spin-ach and ricotta cheese, fish mousse, pasta salad, and a walnut tart dessert. "I always thought hunger and starvation were supposed to be always with us, like death and taxes," Scheider told the well-appointed crowd that included members of Congress and other in-fluential Washington figures. "The end of world hunger. What a cockamamie idea, right? Even the words feel strange in the mouth at first. So say it with me. Come on, say it with me. The end of world hunger. The end of world hunger. The end of world hunger."

One of the most vocal and earliest supporters of the Hunger Pro-ject was Raul Julia, a successful Broadway stage actor and est gradu-ate who was soon to become a major film star. Before the Hunger Project began, Julia and his wife, Merel, accompanied Erhard on a trip to India, where Erhard's exposure to blinding poverty, according to Erhard, had provided the impetus for the Hunger Project's launch-ing a year later. Julia, flushed with enthusiasm about est and Erhard's inspirational message, threw himself into the Hunger Project, always making sure to mention it in his *Playbill* listings on Broadway while raising funds around the country.*

With the zeal of aggressive sales managers, Erhard's Hunger Project officials constantly exhorted volunteers to sign up increasing numbers of new recruits, goading them on with est-filled lectures about producing higher results and achieving larger targets.

In 1980 Paul Gutfreund was a successful environmental engineer in Marin County who had been talked into taking the est training by

*Julia has continued his affiliation with the Hunger Project. During his 1991–92 nation-wide tour, in which he performed the lead role in a stage revival of *Man of La Mancha*, Julia was the featured guest at a fund-raising benefit in San Francisco for the project.

a friend. Although Gutfreund was not terribly impressed with the course, he instantly threw himself into the Hunger Project after learning about it from one of the post-training est seminars he attended. Soon Gutfreund was spending Saturdays as a volunteer receptionist at the Hunger Project's San Francisco headquarters, proud to be helping arrange conference calls that sometimes would link twenty Hunger Project officials from around the globe. Impressed and satisfied with the goals of the project, Gutfreund eagerly signed up for a five-hour "hunger briefing" held in a lecture hall at the University of California at Berkeley. In 1982 he attended his first Hunger Project "contribution meeting" where he pledged $1,500 to the goal of ending hunger by the turn of the century.

Over the next several months, Gutfreund stepped up his support of the Hunger Project, working as a volunteer proofreader for a splashy book that the project was preparing to publish. He agreed to contribute $10,000 to the book project. Increasingly drawn into the Erhard network through his Hunger Project companions, Gutfreund enrolled in some advanced est courses, one of which was called the Mastery of Empowerment. After the book was published in 1985, Gutfreund pledged to buy 2,000 copies at a cost of $36,000. He planned to distribute them to government leaders around the world.

But Gutfreund's zealous passion for the Hunger Project coincided with increasingly manic behavior that he later attributed to the Erhard courses he had taken throughout 1985. One suicide attempt was followed by two hospitalizations in Marin County, after which Gutfreund quit his job at the San Rafael environmental consulting firm where he had worked since 1979. Rather than accept an offer to become a partner in the firm, Gutfreund chose instead to work as an independent consultant so that he would have more time to devote to the Hunger Project. By 1986 he had depleted his savings, though that hardly stopped him from boldly declaring his intention to raise $1 billion for a UNICEF campaign to vaccinate children in poor countries around the globe. Gutfreund over the next several months lost his cars, his house, and his once-thriving career.

Sinking further and further into despondency, Paul Gutfreund in 1988 filed a massive lawsuit claiming that Werner Erhard and the

Hunger Project were responsible for his deteriorating mental condition as a result of fraud and the intentional infliction of emotional distress. By the time his lawsuit began, Gutfreund was living on a houseboat in Sausalito and surviving on a monthly income of $960 from Social Security disability.*

The increasing controversy surrounding the Hunger Project was not limited to Erhard's activities in the United States. In England the project skirted local licensing regulations against collecting contributions on the streets while instructing volunteers to play up the project's fuzzy goals. British volunteers in Erhard's campaign also were misled into believing that the Hunger Project was involved in a "partnership" with a hugely effective antihunger group begun by rock singer Bob Geldof. In Canada, the Hunger Project's links to Erhard and est resulted in a stringent denunciation from schools and reputable charity groups worried about the project's major push there.

Undaunted by the mountains of criticism, Erhard and other Hunger Project officials planned a promotional "relaunching" of the project in the fall of 1987, to celebrate its tenth anniversary. "Well, folks, I don't know about you," John Denver said at the time, "but when you listen to Werner articulate what it is that we're about, you truly have the sense that we're participating in something historic."

A UNICEF volunteer in Portland, Oregon, had a different reaction to the lavish celebration that marked the completion of the Hunger Project's first decade. "For what they spent on that production," he told a local newspaper reporter, "I could feed the nation of Ethiopia."

Erhard and his fellow Hunger Project enthusiasts had little patience for such complaints. Instead, they continued as they always had to spread a fuzzy message about "taking responsibility" for ending hunger while collecting millions of dollars in the process. Between 1977 and 1989 the Hunger Project collected more than $67 million

---

*By 1992 Gutfreund's mental condition had deteriorated to the point that he began accusing his attorney and others assisting in his case of waging a "conspiracy" against him. After Gutfreund failed to provide Erhard's lawyers with court-ordered responses to a series of questions about his case, the court dismissed Erhard from the suit in April 1992. The Hunger Project subsequently offered to settle the case, but by then Gutfreund no longer responded to calls or letters from his own lawyer, resulting in a dismissal of the case in October 1992.

from around the world while claiming to have "enrolled" some 6.5 million people into its ranks. During that time it gave less than $2 million to other organizations directly involved in antihunger efforts. The rest of the money remained inside the Erhard network, paying for glossy publications and other promotional campaigns to keep expanding the Hunger Project.

In the end, Werner Erhard himself turned out to be both an asset and a liability to the Hunger Project. His crucial role as its major promoter certainly was essential to bringing in thousands of est volunteers and raising tens of millions of dollars to keep it going through the years. But his own critical reputation always ensured that the Hunger Project would be viewed skeptically by other organizations involved in the worldwide struggle against famine. Though the project featured an international board of directors that included a few genuine hunger experts, Erhard typically controlled board meetings with his rambling lectures and twisting jargon that came straight out of est. Finally, as new storm clouds gathered over him in late 1990, Erhard formally broke all ties to the Hunger Project. But it continued to be managed by Joan Holmes, a longtime Erhard associate.

Years earlier Werner Erhard had had other ambitious plans to spread both his power and the mesmerizing message of est beyond the hotel ballrooms where est trainings were conducted. A confidential report prepared for him in the fall of 1978 outlined an expansive campaign to extend est's tentacles into everything from schools and religious groups to the media and government agencies. Its goal was to "transform social institutions," according to the secret report.

Ever since est's earliest years, Erhard devoted special attention to exposing children to his mind-control techniques. He encouraged teachers to enroll themselves in est trainings and claimed by 1975 that nearly 9 percent of all educators in the San Francisco school district were est graduates. Stocked with enthusiastic Erhard followers, the district offered merit credits (used by teachers to earn salary increases) for a special est course offered through the extension program of the University of California at Santa Cruz.

That same year a five-day est session was given to second- and third-grade students at a school in Castro Valley, California, at the instigation of est-trained teachers and with funding from the federal government's Department of Health, Education and Welfare. Erhard also offered regular est trainings for children as young as six years old, complete with many of the same rigid rules used in adult est trainings.

Erhard himself sometimes led portions of the children's trainings, and once caused a young girl, probably no older than six, to break down in tears by embarrassing her in front of others. The little girl had been fidgeting nervously while Erhard was talking one day to a group of children seated in a large circle of chairs.

"Stop that!" he told the girl brusquely as she wriggled uncomfortably in her seat. For a moment she obeyed his order, but then she began fidgeting again, this time laughing a little nervously when Erhard turned to her with a harsh look in his eyes.

"I said stop that!" he repeated in a rising voice. An angry Erhard grabbed a chair next to him and slammed it down in front of the children, ordering the now-frightened girl to sit on it.

"Okay," he told her. "Now start fidgeting."

The girl looked up at him with a puzzled expression on her face.

"I told you to fidget," Erhard said. Slowly she began to squirm in her seat. But Erhard was not through with her, demanding that she wriggle even more in front of everyone else. She began to cry, and soon the tears were streaming down her face. Erhard kept up his little demonstration for another moment before pulling her off the chair and ordering her to sit outside the circle of children in the room.

In addition to young children, Erhard looked to other parts of the population that might be receptive to the message of est. For a while he found a somewhat captive audience among prison inmates, dispatching his est trainers to conduct six trainings between 1974 and 1978 in state and federal prisons that included California's maximum-security San Quentin and federal penitentiaries in Lompoc, California, and Leavenworth, Kansas.

At least some prison officials eagerly welcomed Erhard's message of accepting personal responsibility since it seemed to fit perfectly with the need to maintain order among restless inmates. After all, what could have been more comforting to a nervous warden than watching inmates cheerfully accept their own unhappy life behind bars? Still, it probably was asking a lot to believe one inmate's reaction to the est training he received at San Quentin in 1976.

"I love San Quentin," the convict told a visitor, apparently with a straight face. "I don't hate San Quentin because I love myself. I'm happy right here. I'm not planning on staying here. But I'm happy while I'm here."

Other prisoners, however, were not willing to be so sanguine about est's philosophy toward their lot in life. At one of the trainings given at the federal prison in Lompoc, more than two-thirds of the inmates who signed up for the voluntary est session dropped out before the end of the first weekend. By the summer of 1978, Werner Erhard's initial effort to "transform" the lives of convicts around the country had come to a quiet close.

Next Erhard was ready to train his insights on businesses, armed with a blueprint for a new est division aimed at bringing "transformation" to corporate America. With his impressive marketing skills, Erhard had little trouble convincing his loyal staff that he could easily create a demand for est wherever he wanted to take it. In a January 1979 meeting with other est officials, Erhard laid out a plan to create "est in business." During the meeting, he bluntly reminded the others of his bottom-line objectives. "I don't give a fuck," said Erhard, "that there are a lot of people interested or not interested. . . ." Always the consummate salesman, he was supremely confident he could find a market.

But Erhard also knew he needed to act with some caution as he made plans to spread his influence beyond the adoring army of est graduates that now numbered more than 200,000. Already tarnished with an image of a cultlike leader whose methods smacked to some of brainwashing, Erhard knew it would be wise to play down the est connection. Although he wanted est to benefit from the plan, he suggested that the goals would most likely be achieved "by not using the name [of est] in it."

Indeed, Erhard was about to embark on one of the most bizarre episodes that reflected both his fanatical desire to spread the influence of est and further inflate his own ego. Erhard decided to become a race car driver, a project financed by est devotees who eventually contributed hundreds of thousands of dollars to the strange endeavor that Erhard called Breakthrough Racing. The goal, he solemnly explained in torrents of est jargon, was to research the way teams and organizations worked and apply that knowledge to other institutions. The same man who had barely driven an automobile at all for years now began his "research" by donning white flame-retardant racing suits and getting behind the wheel of $23,000 Super-Vee formula racing cars. To assist him in his latest project, Erhard assembled a crew of a dozen mechanics and personal aides who traveled with him from San Diego to Atlanta in an estian pursuit of glory and trophies.

Unfortunately for Erhard, a steady series of mishaps wreaked havoc on his quest for a transformational championship on the road-racing circuit. Faulty throttles, blistered tires, and brake failures marred his efforts and provoked him into angry temper tantrums against his crew. But there was still time for Erhard to enjoy other pleasurable indulgences along the way. He broke away from the circuit long enough to watch a series of yachting races in Seattle, explaining how he wanted to gain insights into the competitive traits of sailing champions such as Ted Turner. After a busy day at the races, Erhard hosted a lavish eight-course dinner for the yachting crews that lasted until two in the morning.

To preserve his racing endeavors for posterity, Erhard commissioned a Los Angeles filmmaker to direct a feature-length movie released in July 1980 under the title *Today Is for the Championship*. The cinematic effort, designed as a public relations vehicle for Erhard and est, turned into a disaster. The film amounted to little more than a jumbled and erratic montage of racing scenes, frequently interrupted by close-ups of Erhard mouthing an endless stream of est-speak.

Audiences and critics alike panned the movie. One reviewer, Sheila Benson of the *Los Angeles Times*, who saw the film as a glimpse into the world of est, found it to be comprised of "a rigid, humorless collection of Erhard clones surrounded by almost hysterical supporters."

The film . . . works on no level. Est persons, its only possible hope as an audience, won't understand the racing seg-
ments because they're never decently explained. And the
racing crowd who might be interested in the film . . . won't
sit still for the waves of est-speak.

Shrugging off his embarrassing foray into the movies, Erhard
announced plans for Breakthrough Racing to conduct seminars offering estlike tips on achieving "dramatic breakthroughs" in businesses
and organizations. By 1982, however, the newest addition to Erhard's
enterprise had changed again. Now it was called the Breakthrough
Foundation and had as its mission the creation of a program called
Youth at Risk that raised money to send troubled urban kids to est-
patterned summer camps around the country.

At first, the Youth at Risk program appeared to achieve some
positive results. In Oakland, California, dozens of est graduates from
around the Bay Area worked with hardened street gang members.
Another group of volunteers repainted the San Francisco offices of the
Guardian Angels, while an est contingent in San Jose sponsored a
surfing contest and helped out at a local youth club. In the summer
of 1982 some eighty teenagers from around the state attended a Youth
at Risk camp in the desert outside of San Diego. Some of the participants returned to their gritty urban neighborhoods filled with dreams
of ending violent gang wars and leading more productive lives.

The ambitious Oakland project foundered a year after it began
after volunteers were unable to raise enough money to build a new
teen center. By then the well-heeled est enthusiasts from the Bay
Area's more affluent communities had vanished. Still, loyal Erhard
supporters wondered what had gone wrong. "The hardest thing for me
personally was how people viewed Werner Erhard and est," a local est
volunteer told the *San Francisco Examiner*. "Here we were trying to
get something done in the world, and it amazed me how people viewed
us so suspiciously."

Despite the setback in Oakland, the Youth at Risk program continued to expand elsewhere, increasing to thirty-four chapters around
the country by the summer of 1992. But even as it promised "dramatic

results" for those who participated in the program, Youth at Risk continued to be dogged by its long-standing ties to Werner Erhard and est.

In June 1992 an investigation by the *Austin American-Statesman* revealed a series of troubling questions about the local Youth at Risk program, including unverified claims about success rates, funding sources, and relations with other youth agencies. Youth at Risk officials in Texas promised significant reductions in crimes, drug use, and school truancy among those participating in the program. Other studies, however, indicated no such results from those attending the programs in other cities.

Ultimately, Werner Erhard fell far short in his quest to achieve the level of global est-flavored influence he had doggedly pursued for years. From a fuzzy crusade against hunger to persistent efforts to reach the impressionable minds of young children, he waged a never-ending campaign to carve out for himself an image of achievement and respectability. He failed every time.

Fourteen

THE PROBLEMS
WITH HARRY

None of my associates or I

have ever operated in the work with

the notion of making money.

—WERNER ERHARD

Twice during est's first ten years, attorney Harry Margolis had performed his tax-avoiding magic for Werner Erhard. In 1971, when
Erhard first began marketing est, his lawyer had concocted an elaborate financial scheme to shield est's profits from taxes by placing the
company in the hands of a dummy Panamanian corporation. Five
years later a new shuffling of documents altered Erhard's corporate

alter-ego when Margolis switched tax havens from Panama to the Isle of Jersey and Switzerland, allowing est to reap millions of dollars worth of tax-free income. Between 1975 and 1981 Erhard's business earned more than $82 million in revenues but declared a mere $100,000 in taxable income in the United States.

Margolis himself had dodged a legal bullet during those years when he was acquitted in 1977 of all charges in the government's criminal tax fraud case against him. But the simmering controversy over est's bizarre financial structure hardly dissolved simply because Erhard's attorney had managed to stay out of prison. Instead, Erhard continued to rely on the same complicated shell game that had proven to be so profitable and rewarding both for him personally and for his business.

By the spring of 1980, however, Erhard and some of his management and legal advisors had convinced themselves of the need to remove the taint of Harry Margolis from the business of est. Though Margolis, in fact, would play a pivotal role in this latest transformation of Erhard's corporate structure, Erhard was urged to distance himself from the controversial attorney and his convoluted tax system. The plan for a new business structure for est certainly dovetailed conveniently with Erhard's own est-flavored philosophy about re-creating the present by burying the past.

In April, Erhard enthusiastically announced a sweeping new project to "create est anew." In truth, little was to change around the est offices; certainly Erhard himself had no plans to alter substantially the magic formula that had turned a smooth-talking salesman into someone who exerted mesmerizing powers over thousands of his faithful followers. Instead, Erhard was interested primarily in inducing others to believe that est was about to undergo a fundamental change.

"I personally feel a sense of joy, opportunity, and openness," Erhard declared when he first spelled out his plans for the new, though fuzzily explained, project. "The process of creating est anew has brought us to the threshold of a profound transformation."

One of the first signs of fallout from est's new transformation was Erhard's removal of longtime est executive Don Cox. For six years the former Coca-Cola official had brought solid business management skills to est, while also recruiting other experienced executives to help run Erhard's profitable business. But Erhard had never been satisfied merely with good business acumen from those around him; he always demanded complete loyalty as well, and had no use for anyone unwilling to surrender fully to his grandiose visions as a man destined to transform the entire planet.

Several months earlier Cox had had the audacity to write a confidential thirty-one-page report that criticized sharply Erhard's heavy emphasis on using est graduates to enroll new customers into the training. In a number-crunching analysis of est enrollments over the years, the portly Cox warned that the trends for continued growth looked ominous unless new ways were found to entice others into Erhard's courses. Among his ideas were advertising campaigns on radio and television, along with a new series of est programs to keep est graduates in the fold.

Some of Cox's proposals were anathema to Erhard, especially the recommendation of an expensive advertising campaign. Nor did Erhard have much use for an executive who dared to question his own approach to the mass marketing of est—or anything else for that matter. By early 1980 Erhard made it clear that Cox's days at est were numbered. Cox formally resigned his position as est's chief executive in April.

Erhard's power-driven plan to "create est anew" also prompted him in the spring to meet privately in San Francisco with a small group of former est followers who had earlier broken from the fold. In setting up the meeting, which took place at the home of a former employee, Erhard instructed his aides to explain that he wanted to hear suggestions for ways to improve the est organization. Once the meeting began, however, it became clear to everyone there that Erhard had little interest in listening to anyone's ideas. Instead, he quickly launched into an est-filled lecture about his own bold new vision for achieving global transformation.

This time Erhard's jargon-laced speech fell on critical ears. Among those in attendance was Landon Carter, the former est trainer who had been one of his most devoted acolytes. But Carter had since grown weary of Erhard's raw, authoritarian power and the unquestioning obedience he demanded from others. When Erhard sensed his words were falling flat, he lapsed into his old role as an est trainer, angrily cursing and berating those in the room who once had worshiped him as a source of enlightenment and transformation. Carter sat silently for a few minutes, shaking his head slightly as he listened to Erhard's tirade. Once the words of Werner Erhard had sounded so magical to Landon Carter. Now he simply sounded brutish and tiresome.

Finally the tall and muscular former est trainer decided it was time to challenge Erhard. He interrupted with some est jargon of his own.

"Werner, you're invalidating everyone, just like you taught us to do in the training," said Carter, staring intently at Erhard sitting across the room. "You taught me how to do it, and you're doing it now. You've just got to be right, don't you? Well, you're just an asshole!"

The two men bolted from their seats and rushed toward each other. "I'm not an asshole. You're the asshole," Erhard yelled.

As they began shouting at each other, everyone else in the room looked back and forth at each of them, as if they were watching two tennis players assaulting each other with pounding baseline shots.

"You're an asshole!" screamed Erhard.

"No, you're an asshole!" replied Carter.

"Well, fuck you, you asshole!"

"No, fuck you!"

Erhard and Carter now stood eyeball to eyeball in the middle of the living room, still hurling obscenities at one another until Carter, in angry frustration, grabbed Erhard by the lapels of his sport jacket and screamed one more time, "Fuck you, you're an asshole!"

"Get your hands off my jacket or I'll sue you," Erhard warned. Carter never intended to hit Erhard, knowing that a physical confrontation would accomplish nothing at all. Still, Erhard's final comment said it all. As Carter relaxed his grip on Erhard and backed away, never before had he viewed his former mentor in such a revealing light. Werner Erhard stood in the middle of the room, out of control and panting for air. For Landon Carter, it was a true moment of enlightenment.

While Erhard was confronting former followers, a team of legal advisors was insisting that Erhard replace Harry Margolis because the attorney's tax-shelter system exposed est to both public criticism and challenges from the IRS. A private memo given to Erhard by two of his advisors in September 1980 called for a new business structure that is "morally right, ethical and consistent with [est's] purpose." The easiest way to achieve the goal, the advisors said, was for Erhard to shed himself of the convoluted maze of corporate and "charitable" entities controlling est and replace it with a much simpler structure. Erhard agreed and decided to call his new company Werner Erhard & Associates.

By the spring of 1981 Werner Erhard's dramatic plan to "create est anew" was ready to unfold. But in the process of removing Margolis, Erhard actually found himself still enmeshed in the attorney's tax structure.

For years the two men had been insisting that Erhard had never owned the est business at all. Now Margolis was offering a new financial deal to allow Werner Erhard & Associates (with Erhard as the company's sole proprietor) to "buy" est back from the various Margolis entities that seemingly owned the enterprise. The deal Margolis had in mind featured his usual array of dizzying circular money movements. Some of Erhard's other legal advisors were skeptical, and at first tried unsuccessfully to warn Erhard away from a plan orchestrated by Margolis. Margolis, however, won over the advisors by insisting he had located a legitimate source of funds willing to "loan" Erhard the money he needed to acquire est.

The mysterious conduit for the money—which ultimately amounted to $14 million—was a prominent Zurich banker named Wolfgang Somary who had met Erhard in 1974 through a mutual friend and est enthusiast who sat on est's advisory board. Somary, in addition to his banking duties, presided over a dormant charitable organization that had never raised any funds or carried out any charitable activities.

Suddenly, in the late summer of 1981, Somary's foundation was awash in money. Funneled through a circular series of Margolis's dummy corporations and offshore bank accounts, the money ultimately destined for Erhard found its way into a bank account in Panama that Somary had opened just five days earlier. From there the money was transferred to an account at the same bank held by another obscure foundation headquartered in Costa Rica and controlled by a longtime friend of Erhard. The $14 million was then withdrawn from the Costa Rican account and deposited into Werner Erhard's newly opened account at the same Panamanian bank. From there the money was transferred electronically to a private bank chartered in the British Virgin Islands—and controlled by Harry Margolis.

Flush with the proceeds of his new "loan," Werner Erhard was now free to acquire a variety of est's assets technically owned by an assortment of corporate entities, all of which had been created over the years by Margolis. Three separate art appraisers in San Francisco were called in to review and price nearly 370 artworks and antiques, ranging from a $60,000 oil painting by Willem de Kooning to a series of African masks and carvings that adorned the Franklin House and other est offices. Now everything from est's real estate leases around the country and the valuable est mailing lists to a collection of gold coins and an expensive sailboat belonged—both in name and fact—to the company that Erhard, and Erhard alone, controlled.

For years the true details of Werner Erhard's curious $14 million "loan" remained one of the best-kept secrets inside and outside the est network. Erhard himself rarely talked about the real source of the money, nor that it had kept his new company firmly involved with the Margolis system.

One of Erhard's employees, however, had his own nagging doubts about the 1981 financing of Werner Erhard & Associates. Not long after he joined the staff in the fall of 1981, Mark Busse found that his duties in the finance department involved keeping track of a series of financial documents prepared by Harry Margolis's law office involving est's corporate makeover. Busse did not yet have much business experience, but the young employee feared that something might be amiss as he studied the financial documents that crossed his desk. The documents reflected a dizzying movement of money to and from bank accounts scattered around the world—Panama, Switzerland, the Netherlands, the Bahamas.

Several months after he began working at Erhard's company, Busse brought his concerns to his superior, Erhard's chief financial officer. After Busse outlined his suspicions about Margolis's curious money movements, his boss reached into his desk and pulled out a piece of paper. He drew two circles, one inside the other, and pointed to the inner circle.

"Everything inside that inner circle is 100 percent legal," Busse was told. "Lots of companies operate inside there." Then he pointed to the edges of the paper outside of the outer circle.

"That's where the illegal stuff is. And in between the two circles are the gray areas that haven't been proven legal or illegal. Those are the new areas." Erhard's financial officer pointed toward the lines of the outer circle. "We're operating toward the edge," he told Busse. The young man had heard enough and soon after announced that he was quitting.

During 1981, its first year in operation, Werner Erhard & Associates earned just under $21 million in revenues, but ended up with an operating "loss" of more than $60,000. In 1982 Werner Erhard & Associates increased its revenues to more than $36 million but somehow managed to show a $930,903 operating loss. Erhard reacted to the seeming poor financial performance of est that year by cutting salaries and laying off staff. For himself, however, Erhard took home a salary of more than $350,000. He continued to help himself generously to some of est's earnings, taking from his business an average annual "proprietor's draw" of $400,000 during the first four full years of its operation.

The years did not treat Harry Margolis nearly so kindly. After failing to convict the lawyer of criminal tax fraud in 1977, federal prosecutors continued their vigorous campaign to crack down on suspected illegal offshore tax shelters. The case against Margolis seemed to get a terrific boost after investigators discovered two tons of the lawyer's tax-shelter records stored behind a small grocery store in the British Virgin Islands.

Aided by thousands of pages detailing Margolis's complicated web of phony corporations and foreign bank accounts, a federal grand jury in San Francisco indicted the lawyer a second time in April 1985.

Charged with fraud, perjury, and obstruction of justice, Margolis's latest legal woes stemmed from his role in setting up tax shelters for nearly one hundred clients, Werner Erhard among them.

During a five-month trial that began in early 1986, prosecutors portrayed Margolis as a shrewd attorney who had defrauded the government out of millions of dollars in taxes. But in July the federal judge hearing the case stunned everyone by tossing out all the charges against Margolis even before the defense had begun presenting its case. By then a frail and weak Margolis was seriously ill with cancer. He died a year later. In the end, the government had failed twice to put Margolis behind bars. Unfortunately for his clients, Werner Erhard included, the government would have an easier time winning back taxes from them as a result of their own participation in the lawyer's tax-avoiding schemes.

DIVORCE, EST-STYLE

Ellen and I, from my perspective, had

a very successful marriage. The marriage was

certainly nurturing for me.

—WERNER ERHARD

Y ears earlier, a young Philadelphia secretary named June Bryde had fallen in love with a smooth-talking Philadelphia car sales-man named Jack Rosenberg. By the early 1980s, those distant mem-ories seemed like a different lifetime to Ellen Erhard—as if the new identities the clandestine couple had chosen for themselves after se-cretly marrying and leaving town had changed not only their names but their characters and destinies as well. In the years that followed, Ellen played the dutiful role that her husband both orchestrated and demanded of her. Once Werner Erhard began est, his wife assumed yet another role, this time as half of a marital relationship that, in Erhard's words, "worked" and was "complete."

Erhard was keenly aware that his own image as the creator of est and its transformational message required him to be viewed as a successful family man able to enjoy successful and fulfilling relationships. "Jack Rosenberg could botch a marriage," he once told an interviewer, referring to his broken relationship with his first wife, Pat. "But Werner Erhard had to make it work." The irony was that the est culture was filled with the victims of busted marriages, both among Erhard's staff and among plenty of est graduates as well. Divorce was not an uncommon result of the training for many couples. In some cases the training caused husbands or wives to become aware of problems in their marriages. In other instances, est participants found themselves speaking a strange new language and preferring the company of like-minded others who spoke the same fuzzy jargon.

Ellen Erhard, though she was careful to keep her thoughts and emotions to herself, always had her own reasons for remaining the obedient wife of Werner Erhard despite all the grief he had caused her. She had even rejoined him in the months after her "rehabilitation" program that followed the horrific abuse she had endured at the Franklin House in the fall of 1977, showing up as a smiling member of Erhard's car racing team that crisscrossed the country throughout most of 1979. Though the Erhards returned to their pattern of living apart at the end of the racing adventure, Ellen's insistence on providing for her children—and the fear of what might happen to them if she divorced her manipulative husband—kept her locked inside a tightly controlled world of silent suffering.

Relieved to stay in the shadows whenever she was allowed, Ellen Erhard remained in the dark as well when it came to the financial details of both her husband's business and earnings. She received what she needed to run the household and care for the children; otherwise she left money matters to Erhard and his business and personal financial advisors. From time to time Erhard used his wife as a convenient figurehead in some of the Margolis-created entities, typically without her knowledge. In the late 1970s an est official happened to mention casually one day that he noticed Ellen was a member of a supervisory panel that oversaw the activities of the Werner Erhard Charitable Settlement, the Isle of Jersey group that nominally owned est at the time. Ellen was puzzled by the news since she had never attended any panel meetings or participated in any decisions concerning the charity group's activities.

Ellen's disinterest in financial matters extended to the Margolis-engineered activities that had occurred throughout 1981 as est was being converted into the new company of Werner Erhard & Associates. On July 16, 1981, Ellen—accustomed over the years to signing tax returns and other documents prepared by her husband's lawyers—dutifully attached her signature to another piece of paper placed in front of her. The document, a "separate property agreement," officially relinquished any claim on her part to the earnings of Werner Erhard & Associates.

In requesting Ellen to sign the agreement, as Erhard explained later, he insisted that he was acting only to ensure that his cherished body of knowledge, along with the value of his ongoing work, pass into "charitable hands" rather than be inherited by his wife in the event of his death.

But there were other reasons for Erhard to remove any claim his wife might someday make on a business now generating tens of millions of dollars in revenues each year. During the summer of 1981, Erhard began accusing Ellen of trying to undermine him in the minds of their children.

One incident erupted during a sailing trip to Hawaii taken by the Erhards and their thirteen-year-old son St. John. The family, along with a four-man crew, set sail in July, taking about two weeks to reach the islands. During their stay, Werner and Ellen learned from an Erhard aide that one of their daughters had been injured in a serious accident while driving in a boyfriend's car. The bad news was compounded by the fact that the girl had been using drugs.

After returning to San Francisco, Erhard used his daughter's auto accident as evidence that his wife was not taking proper care of their children. Now, Erhard decided, the time had come once again to take decisive steps regarding his family. That fall he decreed that Adair and St. John were to be sent off to private boarding schools. (Celeste, the Erhards' oldest daughter, already was attending college at the time.) In September Adair was packed off to the exclusive Emma Willard School in upstate New York while St. John was enrolled in a boarding school in Ojai, California, not far from Santa Barbara. A month later Erhard put up for sale the house in Marin County in which Ellen had lived for several years. Erhard himself had never spent more than a few dozen nights at the house, preferring instead the discreet privacy provided by the Franklin House.

By the time Erhard sent his two youngest children away to boarding schools, he had grown more convinced than ever that Ellen had been conspiring behind his back to turn the children away from him. Using the same badgering techniques inflicted upon est graduates, he began accusing her of telling the kids about his abundant sexual affairs over the years and his use of drugs. Intent on painting Ellen as a spiteful woman bent on destroying his fatherly image, Erhard also tore into her for reporting to the couple's teenage daughters his occasional habit of inducing his wife to participate in sexual escapades involving himself and other women in his black-painted bedroom at the Franklin House.

The time had come once again, Erhard decided in the fall of 1981, to lay down the law to Ellen. This time he responded not with physical violence as he had done during the 1977 family meeting, but with the threat of a crippling financial blow unless she changed her ways.

Erhard, through his attorneys, presented his hapless wife with a nine-page document spelling out in precise terms the financial support she could expect to receive from him. But the document placed restrictions on Ellen's role in raising the children as a condition for receiving her husband's support. Written in legalese, the agreement gave Erhard the primary right to decide on schools for the children, where they would live, and who could serve as their rightful "guardians." Straying from the terms of the agreement would result in Ellen's losing the crucial financial support of her husband. The incredible document made it clear that Ellen would suffer if she did anything to "injure any child's respect for Werner."

The agreement set up an elaborate scheme under which Ellen could appeal her husband's decision to terminate the agreement if he felt that she had breached any of its provisions and no longer deserved, as a result, the financial support he was offering. The appeal process included the authority of a three-member arbitration panel to render a binding opinion, a panel that would be comprised of one member chosen by Werner, a second by Ellen, and a third chosen by the first two.

Werner Erhard's formula for settling any disputes with his wife was never tested. For a few months in 1982, Ellen tried once again to live at her husband's side. Though he still owned the Franklin House, Erhard had taken to living on a 58-foot motorboat, the *Exuberance*, that he kept docked in the Sausalito harbor. Ellen consented to join him on the boat, but only if his fawning assistants who had long been waiting on him hand and foot were kept away. Erhard at first agreed, but soon enough the assistants returned, along with Erhard's extramarital sexual appetite. By the end of the summer, Ellen Erhard finally had had enough. She told her husband she had decided to seek a divorce.

A month later it was Erhard's turn to hit Ellen with a new decision regarding one of the children. Disappointed in St. John's performance at his private school in Ojai, Erhard in the fall of 1982 enrolled the boy in South Kent School, a private boarding school in Connecticut. Unhappy about being so far from home, the Erhards' youngest child paid little attention to his schoolwork, which resulted in a few warning notes from school officials to his parents. Around Christmas 1982 a school official wrote to the Erhards that he hoped St. John would return to school after the holidays "with his mind made up to go to work." But St. John's grades only suffered further in the weeks ahead. In March, South Kent's headmaster wrote to the Erhards that it was "painful" to see their son doing so poorly in school. Erhard already knew about his son's faltering academic record. Helping to keep track of the children was part of the est duties assigned to Erhard's first wife, who still worked faithfully for her former husband in

San Francisco. Her job included typing up periodic one-page reports for Erhard that summarized St. John's performance at school.

Anguished over her young son's unhappiness, Ellen Erhard was determined to bring the boy home, even if it meant acting without her husband's approval or even his knowledge. Before St. John's spring break, Ellen wrote to Erhard telling him of her plans to fly to New York, where she would pick up Adair (who was still attending school in New York) and St. John before taking them on a brief vacation to see her brother in Florida. Although Adair returned to New York to finish her last semester at Emma Willard, St. John never returned to his Connecticut school. He flew instead to California with his mother and enrolled in a public junior high school in Marin County.

Though a few of Erhard's personal aides were fully aware of the increasing turmoil and bitterness inside his family, Erhard himself insisted that the news of his pending divorce from Ellen be couched strictly in the jargon of est. In March 1983 Erhard distributed a three-page memo to the est staff casting his marital separation almost as a successful capstone of his long relationship with Ellen. In the memo, Erhard acknowledged that he and his wife had not been living together for some time. He attributed that arrangement to the demands of his work while adding his opinion that it met with the satisfaction of both him and his wife. Now, he said, it was time to bring his twenty-two-year marriage to an end. Using the language of est, Erhard declared that his relationship with Ellen "is now complete and will continue to be complete." He added that his years with his second wife "contributed profoundly" to his life and that he intended fully to provide her with "what she wants in life" in the course of dissolving the marriage.

Behind the scenes, Werner Erhard had in mind a dramatically different scenario for putting an end to a marriage that had, in truth, been little more than a cruel charade for many years. He was not about to share willingly with Ellen much of the financial spoils est had reaped for him. Instead, he and his lawyers embarked on what would turn out to be a bruising, nearly six-year legal battle through the divorce court in Marin County. Werner Erhard would spend what-

ever it took to leave Ellen Erhard with as little as possible by the time
the dust finally settled.

At the outset of the divorce case in 1983, Erhard's strained relations with his children had all but reached the breaking point. His
daughter Celeste had turned into the most rebellious of all his children. Now enrolled at the University of California at Santa Cruz, she
adamantly refused to attend "family days" at the Franklin House, even
ignoring a traditional Easter gathering that year. Although Erhard's
three youngest children sent him a Father's Day card in June, none of
them showed up to celebrate the occasion at the San Francisco house.

Over the next several months, Erhard sent a stream of letters to
his children, most of them dictated to his ex-wife Pat or another one
of his aides who would type them and mail them to the children. In
the fall, after St. John began a new school year in Marin County,
Erhard worked out an agreement with his son, which required the boy
to call once a week and submit weekly school reports. Erhard instructed his son to ask each of his teachers to fill out a form every
Friday including their comments on his progress in school. St. John
then was to mail the reports to his father, though Erhard soon stopped
receiving them.

As the divorce case proceeded, Erhard dropped his earlier pre-
tense of a successful "completion" of the couple's marriage. Instead,
he portrayed his estranged wife to est trainers and other est officials
as a vengeance-seeking woman "hellbent on destroying me" and the
entire est enterprise. In his mind, it was always Ellen out to manipu-
late facts and distort reality to suit her own view of the situation. He
remained insistent that she acted that way to turn his children against
him.

In August 1983 Erhard appeared for the first of three long days
of a deposition he gave at the San Rafael offices of Ellen's attorney,
Verna Adams. Erhard detested such surroundings, accustomed to
years of wandering around stages and ballroom podiums, free to ramble on at will in the est jargon. Sitting at a table surrounded by
lawyers, Erhard was moody and edgy as Adams put question after
question to him about his stormy marriage to Ellen.

Though Erhard acknowledged he may have hit his wife at the

Franklin House in 1977, his account of what happened during that episode was far different from those of others. He explained that he had hit his wife "to shake her out of hysteria," which had been brought on at the time because "Ellen was very deeply troubled about something and not able to say what it was."

"I took Ellen by the shoulders when she was sitting down," Erhard told Adams, "and shook her and subsequently pushed her when she was sitting in the chair. And she fell over either from the push or from moving away from me and fell on the floor. I may have struck her with my open hand during that interaction, and I don't remember for sure, but I may have done that."

During his deposition, Erhard was asked as well about his sexual affairs over the years.

"Isn't it true," Adams asked during the first day of Erhard's deposition, "that [Ellen] told Adair that she objected to your extramarital affairs?"

Erhard remembered no such conversation. "I recall something about that she had talked to the children about our sex life and something about—I just remembered [her saying something about] my forcing her to use dope." Erhard quickly denied ever doing so, but acknowledged other experiments with drugs over the years. "Certainly I had experimented with hallucinogens, and I believe Ellen did at one time as well at her request."

Under Adams's persistent questioning, Erhard began to remember other things Ellen had told the children about their father's sexual habits. Some were true, others were not, he claimed.

Adams then asked Erhard if his wife had ever been afraid of him.

"I think from time to time, Ellen has been afraid of me, yes," Erhard replied in an icy tone.

Was the same true of the children? Adams wanted to know.

"Well," Erhard replied, "what I think is that when you've got a lot of lies, it generates a lot of fear. When you've got a lot of things you don't want to have somebody find out and they're afraid you're going to find out, yeah you're afraid they're going to find out. Yeah, I think the children were afraid that they were going to be found out. But once the finding out was over, I think the fear left."

"So the children aren't afraid of you now?" asked Adams.

"Oh, they may very well be afraid of me now," said Erhard, almost casually. "As a matter of fact, I would suspect that they're afraid of me now. I would suspect that Ellen has spoken to them in such a way as to encourage that fear and re-create that fear."

On October 27, 1983, Erhard appeared one last time in Adams's office to finish a deposition that had begun two months earlier. For hours, Erhard had answered questions put to him by Adams or one of his own attorneys. Throughout his lengthy testimony, Erhard offered his version of the couple's marriage, of his work habits, of his relations with his children. As she reached the end of her questions, Adams asked Erhard if he thought his wife had ultimately been helped or hurt through her exposure to the culture he had created.

Erhard hardly was ready to admit that Ellen had ever been harmed by himself or est. Instead, he said that Ellen had "benefited" greatly even though she now appeared to be denying that. All in all, Erhard testified, "I would say Ellen got lots of value out of my work."

As the bitterly contested case of *Erhard* v. *Erhard* dragged through the court, the attorneys on both sides clashed over Werner Erhard's complex financial dealings and the true extent of his wealth. When Erhard raised the separate property agreement Ellen had signed in 1981, her lawyers threatened to march into court with arguments that she had been pressured into signing the document. Soon after Erhard was forced to concede the document was no longer valid.

In the end, Erhard's second divorce cost between $2.5 and $5 million in legal fees, surely enough to make it one of the most expensive matrimonial lawsuits in the divorce-rich state of California. Though all the records in the divorce suit were promptly sealed shut by the judge, sources reported afterward that Ellen Erhard finally accepted about a $5 million settlement offer from her former husband. It was hardly a victory for Werner Erhard, since at the outset of the divorce he had offered his wife a far smaller amount.

Before putting an end to the contentious divorce case, Werner Erhard had one last demand of Ellen. She had to agree that, for the rest of her life, she would never discuss publicly any details of the marriage and the couple's curious private life. Ellen chafed at the idea of having it appear that her silence had been bought, but she realized that she had no choice. After signing the papers, Ellen Erhard retreated quietly to her new ranch-style home on a serene cul-de-sac in a shrub-filled suburban community in Marin County. At long last, she thought to herself, her ordeal with Werner Erhard was over. The long and dark journey out of Philadelphia had ended, and it was time to put back the pieces of her life.

At the office of Werner Erhard & Associates, the ending of Erhard's marriage was described a little differently. In early November 1988, the staff received a one-page memo announcing that Werner and Ellen Erhard had settled all the issues in their divorce case.

Although the terms of the settlement were confidential, the staff was told that all issues in the divorce had been "amicably resolved." The memo pointedly reminded the staff that any further gossip about the divorce was not acceptable. Werner Erhard's divorce was now declared a "fully complete" matter that belonged in the past. Now, the staff was told, the time had come to press ahead with Werner's work, with the opportunity to "make a difference to what it is to be human."

Sixteen

EST GOES TO COURT

If you send a hundred people to the grocery store,

a certain percentage of them will have psychotic episodes.

And if you send a hundred people to est, a somewhat

lower percentage will have psychotic episodes.

—WERNER ERHARD

D r. Michael Kirsch listened with curious interest one day in 1975 while one of his colleagues at San Francisco's Langley Porter Psychiatric Hospital presented the details of a patient's case to a team of doctors practicing at the hospital. In particular, Kirsch was intrigued when Dr. Leonard Glass mentioned that his patient had recently participated in an est training session. Kirsch remembered a medical journal article from a few years earlier that discussed psychological problems suffered by people who had participated in 1960s-style encounter groups. After hearing about Glass's patient, Kirsch asked him if she might be some kind of "casualty" of the est training.

"That's an interesting idea. I hadn't thought of that, but it's quite possible," Glass replied. He told Kirsch that the question about est might be worth pursuing, but Glass quickly found himself preoccupied with other matters at the hospital. In fact, the est connection faded away completely in his mind until Kirsch came to him several months later with another psychiatric patient who seemed to fit the same profile as Glass's first patient. The two doctors sent around a notice to others on the hospital staff asking about other patients with mental disturbances possibly stemming from est.

Glass and Kirsch decided to write an article describing est-related cases and arranged for it to appear in the prestigious *American Journal of Psychiatry*, which is published by the American Psychiatric Association. Shortly before sending the article to the journal in the summer of 1976, Kirsch got a phone call from Dr. Enoch Calloway, Langley Porter's research director who also happened to be an est enthusiast and a member of est's advisory board. Calloway told Kirsch that est officials were "very interested" in seeing a copy of the article before its publication. Kirsch quickly declined Calloway's request; thereafter est officials tried to convince the journal's editor not to publish the article on the grounds that its research could not be authenticated. Persuaded by est's arguments, the editor informed Glass and Kirsch that the article would not be accepted. She changed her mind, however, after hearing from three other medical experts who argued for the article's publication.

In March 1977 the psychiatric journal published the first of two articles by Glass and Kirsch (the second one appeared the following December) that described five patients who had developed psychotic symptoms, including paranoia, uncontrollable mood swings, and delusions in the wake of taking the est training. In one case, a thirty-year-old man had ceased his group therapy treatment immediately after completing est in 1973 because he was convinced that the training supplied all the answers he needed for his own mental health. Six weeks later he abruptly broke off contact with his family, confined himself to his house, and spent his days praying. Later, after arming himself with a bow and arrow and a handgun, he accidentally shot himself after brandishing the weapons at a group of men on the street.

Another case reported by Glass and Kirsch involved a twenty-six-year-old high school teacher who was admitted to a psychiatric hospital five days after completing the first weekend of the est training. While in the training, the man had risen from his seat and tried to take over the trainer's position on the stage. Later he told his doctors that during the training, he did not know who he was or that he could be anyone at all, for that matter. He was unable to sleep and began to believe that he was possessed by demons. After further hallucinations and escalating delusions of grandeur, the patient was confined to a locked ward. Convinced by then of the est principle that "nothing is real," the patient during his first day there punched his hand through a window, severing several tendons in his very real wrist.

In their article, Glass and Kirsch reminded their readers that "no assertion can be made on the basis of this evidence regarding the critical issues of causation and rate of occurrence of the serious and sometimes tragic outcomes that are reported here." Nor were they arguing, they wrote, "that the est experience per se is necessarily noxious to all participants." In other words, Glass and Kirsch were reluctant to point an accusing finger at est for directly causing the severe psychotic behavior they had seen in some of their patients.

Still, the two psychiatrists said they had seen enough evidence to speculate that est's "psychodynamic mechanisms" bore at least some responsibility for the psychotic episodes they had observed. "We are impressed," they wrote, "that an authoritarian, confrontational, aggressive leadership style coupled with physiologic deprivation fosters an identification with the aggressor. The inability of this defense mechanism to contain overwhelming anxiety aroused by the process may lead to fusion with the leader, ego fragmentation and psychotic decompensation." In plain English, Glass and Kirsch at least thought it likely that est could be terribly damaging to some of its participants.

Following the publication of the March and December articles,

Glass and Kirsch then asked for est's cooperation in carrying out additional research into the psychological effects of the training. During a meeting with Dr. Bob Larzelere, head of est's "well being" department, Glass and Kirsch explained that they continued to hear about cases involving mental breakdowns possibly related to est. Larzelere heard them out patiently, but called afterward to say est still was unwilling to assist in their research. Earlier, est had supported a Langley Porter study of the results of the training.

At the same time, Erhard and others at est were anxious to refute Glass and Kirsch's suggestions that est training might trigger psychotic outbreaks among some participants. Even before the two psychiatrists first published their findings on est-related psychiatric incidents, a state board in Hawaii decided in November 1975 that est amounted to a form of psychology and, as a result, had to comply with a state law requiring that either a certified psychologist or a physician supervise every training taking place there. Two months later, after est wrote to the board stating it would not comply with the board's decision, the matter was turned over to the state's Office of Consumer Protection for enforcement.

As est's popularity continued to spread across the country, psychiatrists and therapists began to encounter other cases of a seeming cause-and-effect between the training and psychotic behavior. "Most of the people I've seen at our clinic—and they come in after the training in fairly substantial numbers—have suffered reactions that range from moderately bad to dreadful," the executive director of New York City's Lincoln Institute for Psychotherapy reported in 1978. "They are confused and jarred, and the same pattern—elation, depression, feelings of omnipotence followed by feelings of helplessness—are repeated over and over again."

But Erhard, who hotly denied any damaging effects from the est training, also had the support of friendly psychiatrists and other mental health professionals, some of whom not only enjoyed the training themselves but regularly referred their own patients to est as either a substitute or adjunct to more traditional forms of therapy. In June 1978 Dr. Justin Simon, a Berkeley psychiatrist, responded to the Glass and Kirsch articles by publishing in the *American Journal of*

Psychiatry his account of sixty-seven of his patients who had taken
the est training. Simon himself had taken the training in 1973, a year
after detecting "unexpected positive effects" in one of his patients
who had gone through est over his objections. Soon he began "cautiously" referring more of his patients to est. "I have an unusual suggestion," he would tell some of his patients. "On the basis of my
experience I have reason to believe that our work together might be
facilitated by your taking the est training." The same year he took the
training, Simon received a $5,000 grant from est to study the train-
ing's effect on chronic alcoholics. Simon performed the study and
contributed the money to the Salvation Army.

In his 1978 article, Simon reported that five of his patients suffered a "regressive episode" during or shortly after going through est,
though he hastened to add that the episodes were "relatively short-
term and reversible." Otherwise, he concluded that the est training
represented a positive approach to helping people cope with an assortment of emotional problems. He wrote: "It may be that issues of
personal responsibility and choice, clarified as they are during est
training in the searing light of consciousness, are powerful medicine
and that Werner Erhard has discovered an unconventional route to
approach these psychotherapeutic goals with large numbers of people."

In the summer of 1979, a shy and reserved mother of three
named Evangeline Bojorquez had no psychotherapeutic goals in mind
when a girlfriend gushed about how "my whole life had been
changed" as a result of her recent est training. "This is really something you ought to do, Vangie," her friend Angela told the dark-eyed
Bojorquez, who lived in a modest working-class neighborhood in the
San Jose suburb of Morgan Hill. Bojorquez gave her friend a curious
look; est, after all, did not sound like anything that a forty-one-year-
old housewife needed in her life. Besides, she couldn't imagine why
she would sit voluntarily in an uncomfortable hotel ballroom chair for
hours at a time without being able to go to the bathroom when she
wanted.

Her friend persisted until a reluctant Bojorquez finally agreed at
least to stop by a small guest seminar at Angela's home where some-

one from est would answer questions about the training. As she listened that evening, Bojorquez slowly began to think that going through est would be like taking a college course "where you go to learn to do something." She also thought that est might help her sort out various problems in her marriage. Before the night was over, she enrolled in the next training to be held in San Francisco, paying a deposit on the $350 tuition for the training. On the way home, she wondered what her husband would think about spending so much money for such a strange-sounding course. She also was wary of attending the training alone and convinced a friend to enroll with her. Knowing how late the sessions would run, and not wanting to make the hour-long drive back to San Jose then, the two women booked a room together at a Holiday Inn, just down the street from the Jack Tar Hotel where the est training would take place.

When they arrived for the first Saturday of the training, Bojorquez and her friend, Susie, were disappointed to learn they could not sit together, since that violated one of the rigid est rules. Later, during one of the infrequent breaks, Susie admitted to Vangie that she had slept throughout the first half of the day. Bojorquez, however, was very excited about the day's events, although she didn't like it when the trainer yelled so much or the way she called everyone in the room assholes. During the afternoon of the first day, after she had been seated for several hours, Bojorquez suddenly felt a pressing need to use the bathroom. A stern-faced "assistant" guarding the door would not let her leave the room.

"You can't go," he told her.

"But I have to go. I don't think I can wait until the next break," Bojorquez replied.

"Well, you can't."

"I'm afraid I'll wet my pants if I don't go."

"Okay," he said, with the same stern expression. "Go ahead and do that."

Bojorquez, however, continued to insist that he let her out, and he finally relented, moving aside so that she could hurry to the bathroom. He was waiting for her when she returned to the training room.

"You know you weren't supposed to go," he told her. "You broke the rules."

Bojorquez apologized, but the assistant did not let up. "You definitely are not a person that can keep an agreement," he said before finally letting her take her seat. Despite the altercation with the dour-faced door guard, Bojorquez felt exhilarated by the end of the first long day, barely able to sleep and eager for Sunday's session to begin, now only a few hours away.

By the middle of the second day, however, Bojorquez's giddiness had given way to some discomfort, particularly when the trainer led the participants through the est "danger process." During the exercise, small rows of trainees were led to the front of the room where they were told to stand at rigid attention, not saying anything, while everyone else in the room looked back at them in equally stony silence. At the same time, a group of training assistants, playing the well-rehearsed role of "confronters," would march up to the front, each one standing toe to toe in front of the trainees, staring intently into their eyes for a few minutes, totally silent, before marching off in lockstep and making way for another row and another group of confronters.

Bojorquez, like many others taking the training with her that day, had no idea what the danger process was supposed to accomplish. It didn't matter, though, since one of the est rules that had been read to everyone the day before was not to question any of the exercises or processes used during the training. They worked because they worked, everyone was told. After the danger process, the trainer led everyone through a closed-eye exercise in which the trainees were to imagine that they were deathly afraid of everyone else in the room, and then everyone else in the city, and finally everyone else in the entire world. Then the training ended for the first weekend. On their way back home, Vangie Bojorquez and her friend Susie stopped at a restaurant for coffee. The exhilaration that Bojorquez had felt the night before had returned, and all she could tell her friend was how excited she was about returning to San Francisco the following weekend to complete the training. Although it was nearly dawn before she finally got home, Bojorquez woke up her husband to tell him about her incredible weekend. Half asleep, he barely heard a word she said, and she finally crawled into bed herself, only to wake up a few hours later, bright-eyed and eager to begin the week.

Not long before, Bojorquez had begun a new job as a bookkeeper at a kitchen and bath remodeling company in San Jose. At work on Monday morning, she could not keep her mind off the training, telling her boss about the weekend and rehashing in her mind what she had been thinking about during the various training exercises. She found herself preoccupied with thoughts about some of her marital problems. That quickly gave way to a deep sense of depression, and suddenly Bojorquez began to cry uncontrollably in the little office she used at the remodeling shop. She had hallucinations about drowning and began to talk in the high-pitched tones of a little girl. A few minutes later her boss came into the office 'and found her on the floor, screaming. He asked if she was all right, and after she managed to calm herself, he suggested that she take the rest of the day off. Before she left, she called her friend Angela, who had first talked her into the est training, and who now told her that she was having a "normal reaction" to the first weekend of est.

Bojorquez drove herself home, took off her clothes, and climbed into bed. Her husband was scheduled to work that night, and she did not feel like spending the night alone without him. Feeling another anxiety attack coming on, she called Angela again, who invited her to spend the night at her home. As a precaution, Angela called the est office in San Jose, only to be told that Bojorquez's behavior was "normal" and that Angela should just "be" with her friend until she settled down. That night Bojorquez woke up screaming for her friend to bring her some water. Later still, she began to crawl across the floor like an infant, bruising herself when she banged against the walls of the house.

By the time Bojorquez's husband arrived early the next morning, his wife was running around the house, screaming "let's play, let's play" while turning somersaults in the living room. After he brought her home, he called his sister who worked at a nearby medical clinic. After hearing about Bojorquez's condition, the woman immediately advised her brother to call for an ambulance to take his wife to Good Samaritan Hospital.

Ironically, one of the psychiatrists on call at the hospital when Bojorquez arrived the morning of September 11, 1979, knew a good deal about both Werner Erhard and est. In fact, Dr. Lloyd Moglen had taken est himself, during a special VIP training that Erhard had given a few years earlier in San Francisco. At the time, he was positively impressed with much of the training and had even suggested that some of his patients consider it for themselves. Moglen, who hosted a weekly radio call-in show in the Bay Area that focused on soothing personal advice, had been on a panel that had interviewed Erhard during a four-hour radio program in January 1975.

Since then, however, Moglen had seen and treated some apparent est casualties. One man from Fremont, California, imagined that he was God after taking the training. Another patient had shown up at Good Samaritan Hospital displaying signs of acute psychotic behavior and suicidal tendencies immediately after taking the est training. A year later the man walked out of a board-and-care facility in Santa Cruz at one in the morning and was struck and killed by a passing car while he aimlessly crossed the coastal highway which cut through the center of town. Over the years Moglen had begun to revise his initial feelings about est.

"Why am I feeling like this?" a frightened Evangeline Bojorquez cried, when Moglen first attended to her at Good Samaritan Hospital. As he began to treat her, he quickly realized that her psychotic behavior was taking the shape of both sides of a running conversation between an est trainer and an est participant.

"What the hell is wrong with you?" Bojorquez screamed. "I don't know. Yes, you do. Come on out, let it out. No, I don't. You're full of shit!" Hours later Bojorquez was found in her locked hospital ward curled up under her bed. "Come watch her commit suicide," she yelled to the walls. "Look into my eyes so I can stare through your body as I die!"

Moglen decided to call Larzelere at the est office in San Francisco. "This often happens," the est official told Moglen, after the psychiatrist described Bojorquez's behavior. "What I do, and it often works, I just say to people, 'Snap out of it.' "

Unconvinced that such a prescription would help in this case, Moglen, after visiting Bojorquez a second time, diagnosed her condition as an "acute psychotic reaction secondary to est training" and ordered her to be given the tranquilizer librium four times a day. Four days later he noted that her condition had deteriorated and admitted her to a two-week hospital confinement on the grounds that she was "gravely disabled and a danger to herself." At the end of the two weeks, Moglen extended Bojorquez's confinement another fourteen days after she tried to rip off the curtains in her room and jump out the window.

Released from the hospital twenty-five days after she was first admitted, Bojorquez remained at home for the next four months, usually confined to bed and kept heavily sedated on tranquilizers. By early 1980 she felt well enough to take a part-time job; it would be more than a year before she returned to full-time work. In April 1980 a young San Jose attorney named David Rude filed a lawsuit against Werner Erhard and est, claiming that Evangeline Bojorquez's hospitalization and emotional injuries resulted directly from her est training seven months earlier.

That same year Erhard had boasted to a group of est seminar leaders in New York that est had never been sued, nor were lawsuits possible given the way that est operated. Anyone would be a "fool and an idiot" to take est to court, Erhard said at the time. "We tell people that they're responsible [and] to expect nothing. And we take responsibility for any damage."

For nearly five years, the case of *Bojorquez* v. *Erhard* dragged slowly through the legal process. Eventually filling six volumes of documents at the Santa Clara County superior court, the case pitted against each other legal and medical experts who battled over est's responsibilities for Bojorquez's mental breakdown.

Moglen, the onetime est enthusiast, bluntly blamed est for causing her psychiatric condition. "What est did was to break down Mrs. Bojorquez's defenses and concept of reality," he said in a court document. "Then they left her. They left her to put herself back together again. This she was unable to do."

Lawyers for est, however, brought in their own experts to refute the argument that the training had anything to do with Bojorquez's psychotic behavior in 1979. One of those experts was Dr. Justin Simon, the Berkeley psychiatrist who had received an est research grant and had been sending patients to est since 1973. After examining Bojorquez, who had no prior record of any mental disorders, he concluded that it was only coincidental that her breakdown occurred immediately after the first weekend of her est training. And where Simon had once written about Erhard's "unconventional route" for achieving psychotherapeutic goals, he now insisted in a deposition that people should go to est for "educational purposes."

One of Bojorquez's lawyers, a Seattle attorney named Richard Stanislaw, challenged Simon during his deposition on the educational value of est.

"Are you aware of any educational setting where barf bags are available for the participants?" Stanislaw asked.

"No," Simon replied.

"Are you aware of any other educational settings where people throw up in the normal course of their educational course?"

"No."

"Are you aware of any other educational institution where people go through cathartic reactions in the same or similar sense as you have observed people going through the est training?"

"Not directly," replied the psychiatrist.

Bojorquez's case, meanwhile, turned on other matters besides a medical battle over the connection between the est training and psychotic behavior. David Rude, the San Jose lawyer who had originally filed Bojorquez's lawsuit, had turned to Stanislaw for help after learning that the Seattle lawyer was litigating another est-related case in Denver in behalf of a plaintiff named Mark Blair. Blair, like Bojorquez, had suffered a mental breakdown after taking the est training in May 1981. In particular, both Rude and Stanislaw were concerned that est's corporate transformation into Werner Erhard & Associates in 1981 would allow Erhard's lawyers to argue that the new organization assumed no liability for any legal damages caused by the old corporation.

Once again Harry Margolis emerged as a key player in the long-standing drama of est's shadowy corporate and financial dealings. After discovering that Margolis officially remained the attorney for the now-defunct entity known as est, An Educational Corporation, Rude and Stanislaw quickly asked him to allow them to inspect documents that they thought might be relevant to the Blair and Bojorquez cases. Surprisingly enough, Margolis casually dispatched one of his assistants to meet the two lawyers at a San Jose storage facility, where they soon found themselves staring at what Rude later described as "the lawyer's equivalent of King Tut's tomb"—hundreds of boxes containing Margolis's files that provided a roadmap to his interlocking network of dummy corporations and offshore entities.

Erhard's lawyers, aghast at what Margolis had done, rushed into federal court in Denver seeking an order compelling the return of the revealing documents. Instead, the judge presiding over the Blair case ordered the Margolis records turned over to the court, with indexes provided to Stanislaw for purposes of locating documents relevant to his case. Armed with evidence of a close link between est, An Educational Corporation and Werner Erhard & Associates, Stanislaw and Rude felt increasingly confident as they approached a February 1985 trial date in the Bojorquez case.

But the case never went to a jury. On the day before the trial was to begin, Erhard's lawyers offered to settle the case, just as they had done earlier in the Blair litigation. Though the terms of the settlement were confidential, Bojorquez probably received a six-figure amount as compensation for the traumatic episode she experienced after her est training session in September 1979. As late as two weeks before the trial was supposed to start, Erhard's lawyers insisted that they would not settle the case on the grounds that hundreds of thousands of people had gone through est without any apparent damage. Behind the scenes, however, the est lawyers had staged a mock trial to see for themselves how a jury would respond to Bojorquez's claims. When the simulated jury ruled solidly against Erhard, the lawyers had the powerful incentive they needed to settle the case quietly, before a real jury was given the opportunity to reach the same conclusion as its mock counterpart.

Alarmed by the prospect of a rash of lawsuits, est officials as early as 1981 began to take steps aimed at reducing what they described as "severe emotional upsets" during est training sessions. Erhard's trainers had observed dozens of incidents in which est participants exhibited strange and bizarre reactions to various portions of the training. And while the official est policy was to discourage anyone from taking the training if they were already involved in psychotherapy, in many instances there was little emphasis placed on weeding out anyone who was intent on going through est.

A confidential memo distributed to est trainers in February 1981 outlined a series of new procedures to minimize severe emotional upsets by adding new ground rules to the training. Foremost among the changes was a more detailed informed consent agreement that each participant would be required to sign before every training began. In addition, the trainers were instructed to carefully monitor their sessions with an eye toward heading off any incidents and to have a therapist on call during the training. The memo also stressed the necessity of having a staff member available to answer any questions that trainees might have between the two weekend sessions. The purpose of the new policies, according to the memo, was to ensure that est participants "eliminate going crazy" in keeping with est's message of having everyone take responsibility for their lives.

But Erhard insisted as well that each of his est trainers assume their own responsibility for the well-being of everyone undergoing the training with them. Casting the issue of severe emotional upsets in the parlance of est's philosophy, Erhard drilled into his trainers the theory that training "incidents" reflected as much on the well-being and integrity of the trainer as on the participants themselves. The fact that est trainers were not trained therapists was no excuse, according to the memo, for not handling est-related incidents. The trainers were instructed to "deal with what is in front of you."

At times, est trainers and enrollment officials found themselves torn between their obligations to draw paying customers into the training while trying to keep out those who might very well be harmed by

203

est. Even after the 1981 "going crazy" memo was in effect, an est staff member in New York was advised by a manager to take a creative approach to the rules against enrolling people with a history of psychiatric problems. "If you were in a psychiatric ward but weren't treated, that doesn't constitute being hospitalized," the staff member was instructed to tell prospective customers. The same staff member also was told to advise participants who thought they were exhibiting signs of emotional breakdowns that they were probably suffering only an "adrenaline high" as a result of the high-powered training.

One of the most manipulative exercises during the est training occurred when the trainer divided all of the participants into pairs and instructed them to rehearse the invitations they would be asked to extend to others to attend an upcoming posttraining session in which guests would themselves be "invited" to enroll in a future training. A few days after Irving Bernstein once led an est training in Miami, he got an anxious call from an est official in San Francisco whose job was to keep track of severe emotional upsets occurring around the country. He was calling to tell Bernstein about a woman who had just completed the Miami training and who had been found naked in a nearby playground by two policemen. When the officers approached her, all she could tell them was "Would you come to my posttraining with me? Would you come to my posttraining with me? Would you come to my posttraining with me?"

By the time Vangie Bojorquez settled her case against est, about a half-dozen lawsuits had been filed by others seeking similar damages for a variety of psychological injuries. All had either been dismissed in est's favor or settled out of court for confidential sums. Although Erhard continued to claim, accurately enough, that est had "never lost" a legal battle, he had been forced to spend more than $1 million defending the integrity of the est training in the lawsuits that dogged him around the country. He spent at least $460,000 in legal fees and expenses on the Bojorquez case. The Blair lawsuit in Denver cost Erhard another $200,000, while a case that eventually settled for an undisclosed amount in New Jersey had eaten up more than $400,000 in legal expenses.

In 1984, meanwhile, yet another lawsuit was filed against Erhard and his company, this time adding a dramatic new wrinkle to Erhard's ongoing legal woes. This time a man—a seemingly healthy twenty-six-year-old at that—had dropped dead during a particularly stressful portion of the est training. Far beyond causing a "severe emotional upset," the man's family now was claiming that Werner Erhard was responsible for the est-induced death of Jack Slee.

A year earlier, Slee seemed to have a bright future. A 1978 graduate of the University of Connecticut, he had been accepted to law school at the University of Vermont but decided instead to pursue a career in the financial and business world. After working for a while at a loan company, Slee took a job at the Farmers and Mechanics Savings Bank in Middletown, Connecticut, where promotions and advancement came quickly. Soon he had been selected to become manager of one of the bank's new branches in town.

One of his friends at the bank, Howard May, began encouraging Slee to take the est training in the spring of 1983. Another friend who had taken the est training similarly talked it up with Slee and brought him to a guest seminar in New Haven in May. The sales pitch worked like a charm on Slee, who decided that evening to pay a $50 deposit to reserve a spot in a New York City training the next month. A few weeks later, however, he switched his enrollment to a training scheduled for New Haven in the middle of August. On his registration form, Slee described the results he hoped to achieve in the est training:

> Relieve current difficulty in interacting with unknown people in a group setting, whether social or business meeting.

> Address difficulty of always avoiding interpersonal conflicts, rather than being frank about a problem and resolv[ing] it.

> I hope the training will facilitate the meeting and establishment [of] long-term meaningful relationship with a woman.

> More open communications, and better relations with parents, especially invalid father.

On June 11 Slee used his Visa card to pay the remaining $375 cost of the est training. The day before the training began two months later, he spent the day with his friend Howard stripping paint off a rundown house they had recently purchased as part of a plan to refurbish and sell old homes. Slee, shy and reserved by nature, seemed excited and enthusiastic about the next day's trip to New Haven for the first day of his two-weekend training. Howard assured him that he would not regret his decision to enroll in the training.

On the night of August 14, at around eleven-thirty at night, Jack Slee took his place on the stage of the Grand Ballroom inside New Haven's Park Plaza Hotel where trainer David Norris was conducting the danger process. Also taking his position on the stage that night was Kevin Flannigan, an est graduate who was assisting as a "body catcher." His job was to keep an eye on the participants in case anyone fell or collapsed during the exercise that often had a powerful effect on people, particularly those who feared having to stand up in front of strangers. In fact, est headquarters in San Francisco had prepared an eighteen-page manual that described each step of the danger process, including the responsibilities of the "people catchers," as est officially described assistants like Flannigan.

In precise detail, the manual explained that the purpose of the people catchers was to protect est participants from hurting themselves during the danger process. They were instructed to look for signs of anyone demonstrating "erratic behavior" and then to gently catch those who fell during the exercise. Once someone had fallen, the people catchers were instructed to stay with the person until he or she "moves through the space of falling."

Up on the stage, Flannigan turned his attention to one of the last rows of trainees standing up for the danger process. He watched as one man suddenly broke into uproarious laughter—perhaps a sign, thought Flannigan, that the man had just experienced just the kind of personal breakthrough that he himself had felt during his own est training. A few moments later he noticed another man, the one with the name tag that read JACK in bold black letters, starting to fall backward. Quickly Flannigan rushed over to catch Jack Slee from behind. In his haste, Flannigan did not have time to position himself directly behind the falling body and, as a result, was unable to withstand Slee's weight as he fell to the floor at the back of the stage.

Instead, the momentum of Slee's fall forced the body catcher to take a half-step backward to brace himself, and as he did he felt Slee's head bump against the wall behind the stage curtain. A startled Flannigan thought he felt the man suddenly jump, as if the jolt against the wall might have instantly revived Jack Slee. But then Flannigan felt Slee's body slacken to the floor. It did not look as if he were breathing.

Flannigan, growing more panicky, rushed out of the ballroom in search of another assistant, who happened to be a state-certified emergency medical technician. Earlier in the day the same assistant had been forced to come to the aid of another man who had suffered a seizure and had to be taken to a local hospital. By the time Flannigan returned back inside, two women were at Slee's side in an effort to provide first aid. The medical technician stepped in between them, putting his fingers on Slee's carotid artery. He felt no sign of a pulse. When he tried to open Slee's eyes, they rolled back in the man's head. Finally he began administering mouth-to-mouth resuscitation. For a moment, it seemed that Slee had resumed breathing, but then no more breaths came.

One of the other training assistants came up to Flannigan, telling him to return to his position at the side of the room. He heard the sounds of laughter wafting around the room and realized that most people had no idea what was happening on the stage. No one, except for a few people who had gathered around Jack Slee at the back of the stage, knew that something horrible had just happened.

Soon enough, however, it was clear that some kind of commotion was taking place. David Norris quickly instructed the half-dozen or so assistants scattered around the room to keep everyone calm and in their seats. "This is all right. Don't let this bother you. This has nothing to do with you," Norris shouted to everyone in the ballroom.

A New Haven fire emergency squad was the first to arrive on the scene, having been called by someone in the training. But when the first two fire fighters got to the ballroom entrance, they were held up by one of the assistants guarding the doors. One fire fighter asked whether anyone inside needed medical attention. The assistant turned her head back toward the door, peering inside for a moment, and then turned back to the two men. "No, not yet," she told them.

After another moment or two, the fire fighters brushed past the door guard and made their way to the stage where Slee still lay. Minutes later two more fire fighters arrived along with an ambulance crew of paramedics that had been dispatched to the hotel. Flannigan, who had returned to the stage, watched as the paramedics tried to revive Slee, but then he heard the ominous flat tone on the portable heart monitor they had set down beside the stricken man. No heartbeat. No vital signs. Someone came up and tapped Flannigan on the shoulder. Norris wanted him to count everyone in the room, to make sure that everyone was still accounted for. "Jesus, give me a fucking break," he muttered to himself. But est assistants were trained, above all else, to do what the trainer told them to do, so Flannigan proceeded to count. One hundred sixty-six. Precisely the right number. One of the other assistants counted alongside Flannigan just to confirm the tally.

Shortly before midnight, the paramedics carried Slee out of the room, after which Norris announced that the training would continue and that he would try to wrap up the session as quickly as he could. He then invited participants to "share" their experiences about what had just happened that night. Someone got up and suggested that everyone recite in unison the Lord's Prayer. One of the trainees later remembered hearing Norris asking everyone to consider the possibility that Jack Slee might have "willed his own death."

An hour later, at 1:03 A.M., doctors at Yale–New Haven Hospital pronounced Jack Slee dead of "undetermined causes." A subsequent autopsy report, following a more extensive medical examination of Slee's body, could shed no further light on the cause of death. However, the Connecticut state medical examiner's office, in its autopsy report issued in November 1983, found that stress might have caused Slee's death. "Available history," read part of the autopsy report, "indicates that Mr. Slee collapsed in a situation in which high emotional stress could be expected. Such emotional stress may have neural and hormonal effects which are deleterious to cardiac rhythm. . . ." In other words, the stress brought on by est's danger process might have caused Slee's heart suddenly to stop beating.

At first, Kevin Flannigan felt horribly guilt-ridden by the news of Jack Slee's death. After all, his job as a body catcher was to assist people, and somehow he felt at first that he had betrayed that duty by allowing Slee to fall so abruptly to the floor. But soon his feelings of guilt gave way to another realization more in keeping with his enthusiasm for est's view of the world. As the days passed, Flannigan began to see that the awful episode just may have turned out to be yet another transforming experience—for himself. Not long after Slee's death, Flannigan described his latest experience of transformation in a letter he wrote to Slee's friend Howard May. Written as a glowing testimonial to est, Flannigan's letter explained how Jack Slee's demise "transformed me in a sense" while providing an "ongoing purpose to experience life." Flannigan wrote that he might actually have helped to prolong Slee's life for a moment by causing his heart to beat after Slee's head hit the ground when Flannigan tried to catch him on the stage. In any event, Flannigan no longer felt any guilt about Slee's death and instead was now grateful "for the gift he gave to me."

In San Francisco, est officials for the moment had little interest in taking credit for a transformational experience growing out of the man's death. Instead, they hastened to disclaim any responsibility for Slee's death that night in New Haven. A statement issued within days of the incident from Jack Mantos, est's director of research and a Harvard-trained medical doctor, insisted that the training had nothing to do with Slee's fatal collapse.

> In any large group of people, medical emergencies do arise from time to time and this appears to be one of those. According to our reports, it was responded to quickly by trained professionals. Paramedics were notified within seconds of the collapse and were by [Slee's] side in minutes. Although medical authorities have not yet determined what caused Mr. Slee's death, it is evident that the est training could not have had anything to do with it.

A month after Slee's death, a fifty-eight-year-old man collapsed and died from a heart attack while undergoing est's rigorous six-day advanced training course in New York. Coming so quickly on the heels of the New Haven incident, the New York death made staff members understandably edgy when the subject of it came up in a San

Francisco staff meeting. Est trainer Jerry Joiner, a medical doctor who had once worked for NASA, sought to put everyone at ease by playing down the significance of such a tragic incident occurring during any kind of est program.

While reminding staffers of the precautions taken by the company for the safety of the more than 1,000 people attending est trainings and other Erhard programs each week, Joiner mentioned that some people die while shopping or on the street, while others could die while attending one of the company's programs. Joiner admonished the staff against blowing up the significance of the fatality in the six-day course. "That's what's going to ruin things. . . . People are going to die from time to time in the courses we do."

A year after Slee's death, his family filed a $5 million lawsuit claiming that est was directly responsible for the tragic events that August night at the Park Plaza Hotel. Nine years after his death, the case finally went before a federal jury in Connecticut. In October 1992 the jury ruled that Werner Erhard and his company had been negligent and were responsible for inflicting severe emotional distress on Jack Slee. But the jury found that the est training itself did not "proximately cause" Slee's death. As a result, his family walked away emptyhanded, left only with the painful memories of a young man with a bright promise who thought that est might have had something to teach him.

Seventeen

THE SELLING
OF THE FORUM

There are only

two things in the world—

nothing and semantics.

—WERNER ERHARD

A s Werner Erhard bounded onto the stage, the spotlights shining
down from the rafters at New York's Avery Fisher Hall bathed him
in a soft, amber light, illuminating his brown wool suit, cream-colored
shirt, and corporate silk tie. In the audience, more than two thousand
est graduates and guests greeted his arrival with customary loud
cheers and a long standing ovation. Settling back into their seats on a

cold, snow-blown evening in January 1985, they were eager to hear about a new "breakthrough in transformation" that Erhard had in store for them. They were ready to follow his lead.

For a few glorious moments, Erhard's nagging problems seemed millions of miles away. On this night, at least, the demons of divorce, of taxes, of lawsuits, would have to wait in the wings of the packed, applause-filled auditorium. Once again Werner Erhard was ready to resume his rightful spot as the master of his own fate, the creator of his own reality—a New Age prince of transformation.

His words punctured the air with stiletto sharpness. "I invite you tonight to stand in a new possibility for living," Erhard told his receptive audience. He paused for a moment, waiting for the vague-sounding words to settle across the hall. "A NEW POSSIBILITY FOR LIVING."

Over the last few weeks, Erhard had taken the same well-rehearsed message to other cheering throngs across the country. From Seattle and San Diego to New York and Boston, he had walked onto stages, glowing in the spotlight, elaborating on the official announcement he had made to the news media in the middle of December. After nearly thirteen years of est-induced transformation, Werner Erhard decided the time had come to retire the est training. According to his accounts, some 500,000 transformation seekers had "gotten it" over the years—clearly making est one of the most widely marketed programs in the long history of America's fascination with consciousness expansion. But Erhard had other news for the reporters gathered around him at the offices on California Street in San Francisco.

He was there to announce a bold new program that he called the Forum. It promised new breakthroughs in transformation. It relied on new groundbreaking "technology." It cost $525, or $50 more than the now-defunct est training.

"There is a much different mood among people today than when we started the training in 1971," Erhard declared in announcing the new Forum. "In the 1970s people concentrated on 'getting it together,' while in the 1980s people are more interested in 'making it happen.'"

Within six months of his that-was-then, this-is-now proclamation, Erhard and his staff at Werner Erhard & Associates unveiled an entirely new catalog of "transformational" courses along with correspondingly increased tuition costs. Along with the Forum, Erhard's new centerpiece course, there was the advanced six-day course ("you will make a non-linear/non-logical quantum leap to another way of being alive") with a $1,000 price tag. A similar seven-day course aimed at business managers and executives was priced at $1,200.

In truth, there was little difference between the bottom-line message of est and the Forum. Instead, the changes were largely cosmetic, such as the elimination or revision of a few of the est processes and the noticeable departure of at least some of the straitjacket rules that once had rigidly controlled the behavior and bladders of est trainees. Erhard grandly boasted that "what I designed [est] to accomplish had been accomplished. Its value had become part of the mainstream." Est had resulted, he insisted, in a major advance in human transformation, but now "the training is obsolete."

Actually, Erhard had already been earning considerable sums of money from an earlier version of the Forum that began long before it officially replaced the est training. As early as the summer of 1983, Erhard had teamed up with a business partner, Bay Area accountant Arnold Siegel, to begin marketing new programs aimed at pumping new vitality into the flagging est training. it was Siegel who first conjured up the idea of turning Erhard's own staff meetings into a source of revenue for the company. The imaginative Siegel envisioned the new program as a "forum," much like the ancient days of Rome when the public would gather to watch noble senators debate great issues and carry out the solemn duties of governing the empire.

In the fall of 1983, Siegel and Erhard were ready to launch the new plan with a slick brochure that heralded the new Forum as a "breakthrough in transformation." Using the same jargon that filled est trainings, Siegel described the $700 course (or $5,000 for a complete series) as an opportunity to watch "masters at work" and to discover that the "source of Werner's mastery is his willingness to be the stand that he takes."

By the time he teamed up with Siegel, Werner Erhard had plenty of compelling reasons to concoct and market, using his same tried-and-true sales techniques, a course aimed at breathing new life into the est-created phenomenon. In San Francisco, est's business managers had been grappling with a declining growth curve in the company's revenue prospects. The dollars were still flowing in at a healthy level—Werner Erhard & Associates racked up some $35 million in gross revenues in 1983—but the enthusiasm for est was waning. During the halcyon days of the late 1970s and early 1980s—est's golden years—anywhere from 1,000 to 1,500 people were enrolling in the est training each week. But the arc had been heading downward ever since, forcing Erhard to scramble for new ways (such as an ever-increasing price tag) to translate transformation into hard cash while doing whatever he could to keep heavy pressure on his employees to ensure that customers kept signing up.

Weekly enrollment memos distributed to staff people around the country served as stern reminders of the constant need to sell, sell, sell. The memos contained an eye-glazing litany of statistics, management projections, quotas, and other details as part of an ongoing pressure campaign to sign up more paying customers.

The constant pressure to produce sometimes resulted in staff members simply making up phony names of people supposedly enrolling in est training sessions. An est staffer in Minneapolis, for example, once added forty-five false names to an est training session scheduled there in July 1982. After the staff member was fired, another est employee in Detroit was abruptly placed in charge of the Minneapolis operation. But as soon as she flew there to sort out the registration problems, she was berated and called a "righteous cunt" by one of her superiors, who ordered her to work harder on producing more enrollments in est seminars.

Throughout Erhard's company, nothing ever assumed more importance than the fulfillment of ever-present quotas for new enrollments. Quota production often was measured every few hours, with staff members pressured in the morning to sign up new customers before an early-afternoon staff meeting. As the pressure mounted, so did tempers and emotions in est centers across the country. Far from being considered unacceptable behavior, temper tantrums and angry outbursts were justified as part of the zealous commitment to Werner Erhard and his work. Those who worked closest to Erhard often wit-

nessed his own tirades and yelling bouts, and sometimes felt free to
mirror his own behavior when they were in charge.

By the end of 1984, est's declining enrollments plummeted even
further in the wake of media accounts that chronicled Erhard's ongoing divorce suit with Ellen and est's Margolis-related tax battles
with the Internal Revenue Service. Complicating matters for Erhard
was the fact that most of the staff found themselves reading gritty
details about his personal life they had never known before. In guest
seminars and other est sales pitches, they had long been instructed
to say that Erhard earned only modest amounts of money from est and
that he had never carried out "the work" to gain personal enrichment.

The lavish life-style he led painted a different picture of Erhard's
attitude about money. In 1981 Werner Erhard & Associates spent
more than $47,000 on Erhard's wardrobe expenses. The following
year he acquired the *Exuberance*, the $300,000 motorboat that served
as his floating residence though he still owned the Franklin House.
Although the days of the sumptuous salons there were past, Erhard
now looked for other ways to win recognition and acceptance into the
highest circles of San Francisco society. He tried repeatedly, for example, to win a coveted membership in the city's blue-blood St. Francis Yacht Club, assigning teams of staff people to figure out a way to
be invited to join. He was never successful. His bid for acceptance
into society circles prompted Erhard to contribute hundreds of thousands of dollars to organizations such as the opera and the symphony.
Though the beneficiaries of his patronage certainly savored his largess, his aggressive and expensive campaign to win society status
clashed with his public insistence that he had little interest in the
rich spoils est had provided.

As he prepared to launch the Forum and boost sagging enrollments, Erhard also took new steps to prop up staff loyalty. Several
weeks before unveiling the Forum, Erhard proclaimed that each staff
member was now a participant in an "advanced program in the mastery of transformation" that he had developed for their benefit. That
program, in turn, required everyone to adhere to a new litany of promises, the fulfillment of which, they were told, would hasten their own
transformation as human beings inside the culture of Werner Erhard.

Many of the "promises" boiled down to the same proscriptions that long had been part of Erhard's pervasive campaign to influence and control the thoughts and actions of everyone who worked for him. Staff members had to promise not to complain or gossip and to stop others from doing likewise.

The new rules sought to confirm the same personal dedication and devotion to Erhard that had always been a crucial part of the est culture. Along with promising to "personally represent Werner" in their work, staffers pledged themselves to a code of conduct consistent with the "honor and privilege" of carrying out their assignments.

This time, however, Erhard added a new twist to his list of staff promises by requiring everyone to work in tandem with a fellow staff member, a curious kind of buddy system for enforcing ritualistic rules of behavior. Each staff member and his "committed listener," as the other person was called, were now responsible for carrying out the obligations of Erhard's employees. Among other responsibilities, each staff member was required to give to their partner a daily report on each day's activities to ensure that the staffer was "complete, whole and satisfied" at the end of each work day.

The new rules, in practical terms, amounted to a stringent commitment required of everyone working for Werner Erhard. By the mid-1980s Erhard had extended to the general staff the same vows of eternal service that once had applied only to the elite corps of his personally trained and designated est trainers. In Erhard's centers around the country, staff members were led through "Each and Every" meetings, so named because each and every staff member stood up and pledged to perform "Werner's work" forever. In New York one est employee received a stern lecture from her supervisor after feeling a sudden impulse to bolt from her job. "Sit in here until you close the door on the option called leaving," insisted the supervisor.

In San Francisco Erhard's renewed campaign to ensure staff loyalty led him to fire many of the company's professional managers whom he himself had installed to run Werner Erhard & Associates after Don Cox's forced departure in 1981. Now Erhard put in place a new management team headed by those who had proven to be unquestioningly subservient and yielding to him through the years. One of the new executives was Stewart Esposito, who once had been bailed out of debt by Erhard after losing several thousand dollars selling Mind Dynamics franchises.

Another one of Erhard's new executives was an est trainer named Steven Zaffron who years earlier had been a door-to-door salesman for the Fuller Brush Company and later sold speed-reading courses. Three years after first joining Erhard's staff in 1979, Zaffron had been indicted on mail fraud charges for participating in a scam to collect phony unemployment checks. Zaffron agreed to a plea bargain in the case and was placed on three years' probation shortly before Erhard conferred on him the coveted "lifetime" designation to do Werner's transformational work.

Above all else, Erhard craved respectability and prestige, and not only among the fawning multitudes of est graduates who would soon be flocking into a warmed-over version of est called the Forum. While the Forum would serve as the bedrock of Erhard's business, in the 1980s he also embarked on other ambitious efforts to bolster his public image as a transformational guru intent on changing the face of society.

In July 1984 a company named Transformational Technologies was incorporated in the state of New York. The corporate charter listed a successful management consultant, a small, wiry man named James Selman, as the company's chief executive officer, but the sole owner of the new firm was Werner Erhard. Selman was a longtime est enthusiast, having gone through the training in 1975 while he was a partner at the prominent management consulting firm Touche Ross. He later quit to work for Erhard, and now he was ready to put into place one of Erhard's long-standing objectives—applying the principles of est to the world of big business.

Together Erhard and Selman embarked on a plan to sell, at a handsome price, franchises in Transformational Technologies to independent business consultants who then would be licensed to utilize Erhard's est-influenced "technology." Within eighteen months nearly fifty franchises had been sold at a cost of $25,000 apiece. The franchise agreement also required each independent consultant to pay a portion of his or her revenues to Erhard's company.

As part of its sales campaign, Transformational Technologies boasted that Erhard's expertise in management consulting had grown out of "research over the past fifteen years, conducted in live situations, with more than a half-million people." The disingenuous claim simply counted up everyone who had ever attended the est training. Not that a more revealing explanation would have mattered much to the franchise owners—all but one of them were est graduates themselves.

Likewise, some of Erhard's business programs appealed to corporate officials who themselves had undergone the est training. In the mid-1980s, TRW Corporation, the Los Angeles defense and aerospace company, paid $50,000 to Transformational Technologies for a five-day training session led by Selman. Within two years of its formation, Erhard's profitable company could claim an impressive roster of Fortune 500 corporations doing business with his franchise owners, among them AT&T, Ford Motor Company, Lockheed, Procter & Gamble, and General Motors. Several government agencies also utilized the Erhard-flavored training services of the company's franchises.

Though Erhard typically remained behind the scenes, he occasionally hired himself out to meet with clients. In late 1984 NASA paid Transformational Technologies $45,000 for three sessions in which Erhard and others lectured forty-seven space agency officials on est-style management theories. "What surfaced," a NASA official later wrote in an estlike memo, "is the need for a whole new arena of mastery in management, one that comes to grips with the phenomena of the dance between an organization's cultural capacity and the unfolding of program accomplishment. It's not a problem that needs to be fixed. It's an opportunity." Others had more critical reactions to Erhard's management theories.

In December 1988 several former employees of the DeKalb Farmers Market, a huge produce and seafood mart near Atlanta, claimed in a federal lawsuit that they had been forced from their jobs after protesting their coerced attendance at the Forum along with another similar training session put on by an Erhard-licensed franchise firm in Florida. The market owner denied the allegations, saying that the employees were encouraged but not coerced to attend the sessions. Among the suit's allegations were claims that employees were programmed in the training sessions to adopt certain beliefs and forced to talk about highly personal matters such as relations with parents and spouses. The lawsuit, which did not include Werner Erhard & Associates as a defendant, eventually was settled out of court.

As part of his strenuous effort to shape his public image in this period, Erhard also underwent something of a physical makeover. Gone was the old casual est look that Erhard had sported during the 1970s, with his informal sweaters and open-throated shirts with the collars flared out. He replaced them with tailored suits, silk ties, and button-down shirts befitting a serious-minded businessman tending to matters in the corporate world.

But little else had changed about Werner Erhard. In private, he maintained the same loyalty-demanding personality that had always defined him during the years of est. His expectations of intense devotion even extended in one instance to former employees, whom he included as honorary members of his own extended family. Raz Ingrasci, Erhard's original "communicator" and longtime aide, had quit the est staff in 1982, though he continued to attend occasional social events as a member of Erhard's "family." Four years after his departure, both Ingrasci and his wife, Liza, took jobs as part-time consultants to Lifespring, the California self-awareness company run by John Hanley that offered its own estlike training programs.

In March 1986 Stewart Esposito wrote a stinging five-page letter to the Ingrascis, castigating them for their involvement with Lifespring. In his letter, Esposito warned the Ingrascis that their work for Lifespring "does not support" Erhard's work.

Esposito accused Ingrasci, through his work with Hanley, of helping to "steal" information used in Erhard's programs. According to the letter, Lifespring was using in its programs the concept of "intention," among other innocuous Erhard-favored phrases.

Two weeks later Raz Ingrasci wrote back to Esposito in a seven-page handwritten letter, reminding Erhard's loyal lieutenant that he hardly had reason to complain about Lifespring stealing Erhard's precious material. Ingrasci, after all, had known Erhard back in the days of Mind Dynamics and was well aware of the true origins of much of the est training.

While he was unable to exercise much control over former employees, Erhard and his most loyal aides continued to perpetuate a culture inside the organization that, for its employees, equated a commitment to human transformation with unquestioning service to Werner Erhard.

Michael Breard had taken the est training in Dallas in 1979 and then spent the next few years as a volunteer assistant, enthusiastically leading guest seminars and harboring the dream of one day becoming an est trainer. In the summer of 1984 he felt he had taken a step closer to that goal when he joined the est staff in San Francisco. Asked on his application what kind of position he preferred, Breard said he would take on any assignment "as long as it's working closely with Werner Erhard." Soon after Breard eagerly agreed to train to become one of Erhard's personal aides. He was told to show up one morning on board Erhard's latest Sausalito houseboat, the 96-foot *Canim*, which had replaced the smaller *Exuberance*.

"What we want you to do is clean these bilges," one of Erhard's aides told Breard when he showed up to begin his training aboard the 1930s-era vessel. Breard had heard stories about est trainers getting down on their hands and knees to clean toilets and scrub floors, willingly accepting the lowly assignments as part of their own service to est. Given his own aspirations, at first he considered it an honor to be invited to work at Erhard's side.

In the weeks that followed, Breard discovered there was little honor in the menial tasks he was ordered to perform in the service of Werner Erhard. In the predawn darkness, he scrambled aboard the polished decks of the *Canim*, careful not to make any noises as he slipped stealthily into the boat's small galley at around five in the morning. After putting on the coffee, Breard made his way into the bathroom, seeing to it that the room sparkled. Then Breard meticulously arranged Erhard's toiletries, lining up his shampoo, dental floss, razor, and shaving cream so that nothing was out of place. Breard knew there was a price to pay if he overlooked any of the details. Even the slightest miscue had sometimes resulted in a torrent of shouted obscenities from Erhard himself, who would stand within inches of Breard while he vented his anger. So Breard made sure the colognes were lined up in perfect order and that the toothpaste was spread evenly across Erhard's toothbrush. After finishing in the bathroom, Breard repaired to the boat's small galley, inspecting the glass of orange juice for signs of too much pulp that displeased Erhard. Finally Breard was ready to pad softly into Erhard's bedroom. Kneeling at the foot of the bed, he slipped his hands under the covers until they reached Erhard's feet and began a gentle massage.

"Werner," Breard whispered in a singsong voice, "it's five-twenty." After more massaging and another five minutes passed, Breard's chiming voice updated the time. "Werner, it's five-twenty-five." At five-thirty, Erhard arose to begin his day.

Other staff members found themselves performing equally menial tasks as part of their own service to Werner Erhard. In the middle of 1985, some est staffers began volunteering in their off hours to work in "Werner's closet." The closet turned out to be a spacious storage facility in Sausalito in which Erhard kept his clothes, a wine collection, and portions of his valuable art collection acquired over the years. A detailed manual instructed the est assistants how to polish Erhard's 150 pairs of shoes and iron his French-cuffed shirts. A rack of suits and other items of expensive clothing were arranged by season. As always, assistants were constantly reminded what a rare privilege it was to help further the goals of "Werner's work" by tending, free of charge, to the upkeep of his lavish personal life-style.

Outside of Erhard's tightly controlled world, however, doing Werner's work did not always produce the kind of results it intended. In March 1986 Erhard's thirty-three-year-old brother Nathan Rosenberg suddenly announced his decision to run for Congress in a conservative district in Orange County, California. Nathan, who bore a striking resemblance to his famous older brother, for years had been deeply involved in est and the Hunger Project but tried to play down those connections during his campaign. His opponent, an incumbent congressman named Robert Badham, was quick to remind voters about Rosenberg's ties to Erhard and how that might affect his role in Congress. "I imagine that would be the outreach for power [and] the tenets of the est program, to create a different world by mind revolution," Badham told reporters during the campaign.

Erhard remained on the sidelines during his brother's campaign, though Rosenberg relied extensively on est-trained campaign volunteers along with financial contributions from several Erhard staff members and supporters. On election day conservative Orange County voters gave Badham a huge victory over Rosenberg, who tried to win the same congressional seat two years later after Badham announced his retirement. Once again Rosenberg was attacked as an "est advocate" who tried to conceal ties to his controversial brother. Once again Rosenberg went down to defeat—ending his political ambitions and frustrating Werner Erhard's own private desire for increased political influence.

Despite such setbacks, Erhard continued to carry out the same type of warlord relationship with those among the former corps of est trainers who now had been transformed into Forum leaders. Actually, Erhard relegated the trainers to the status of "Forum leader candidates," a psychic demotion reminding them that, once again, they would have to prove their loyalty to Werner Erhard before he would recognize them as full-fledged leaders of his new transformation-promising course. Talking in San Francisco to a group of Forum leader candidates in July 1986, Erhard spoke, as he always had done to his est trainers, of the rights they were giving up in exchange for the privilege of carrying out his work.

To those who gathered around Erhard that July day in San Francisco, the true meaning of his blunt words all but vanished in their own dizzying excitement about the missionary zeal they felt for serving him and the work carried out in his name. Some of them, like Laurel Scheaf and Charlene Afremow, had traveled the est circuit with Erhard for years, throughout all or most of its thirteen-year existence. For years they had lived and thrived in a culture defined by a charismatic and authoritarian leader whose every action and word was accepted without question.

When one of the new Forum leader candidates got up to speak on that summer day, she echoed the words of everyone who had been dazzled by the man who once again had summoned them to pledge their loyalty and devotion to him. She spoke the words she knew Werner Erhard wanted to hear.

After promising to perform Erhard's work for her entire life, she added in a voice gushing with enthusiasm, "And I really love you very much."

Erhard had one more thought to share with the Forum leader candidates. Was it a confession? Or just an enigmatic riddle to keep them wondering about his mystery and power? Did they even hear the telling words he spoke?

> It may all turn out to have been a sham, and bullshit. . . .
> It may even turn out to be evil. . . . You may have given up
> your life for something evil. Only time will tell.

For Werner Erhard, as it turned out, time was beginning to run out.

Eighteen

NEW SIGNS OF TROUBLE

The end is the end,

or it isn't. The end justifies the

means, or it doesn't.

—WERNER ERHARD

W hile Werner Erhard continued to command and receive the adoration and loyalty of most of his staff, some of them slowly began
to conclude that they had seen and heard enough about him to free
themselves from his grasp on them.

In 1980 Irving Bernstein, the former accountant, had pledged to
do "what Werner asked forever" when he received his coveted lifetime

designation as an est trainer. A few years earlier he had left a successful New York City practice, along with a handsome six-figure income, in favor of a $25,000 salary and an uncertain future on Erhard's staff. But as he moved cross-country to San Francisco, Bernstein had no doubt at the time he had made the right decision, for he viewed Erhard almost as a god who had the raw power and the energetic commitment to transform the world.

By 1985 Bernstein no longer could tolerate the conditions he and others had been subjected to inside est. While Erhard helped himself to hundreds of thousands of dollars and lived a first-class life-style everywhere he went, life for est trainers and later Forum leader candidates was dramatically different. In the mid-1980s a new travel policy aimed at clamping down on expenses required Bernstein and other trainers to stay in the homes of local staff people or volunteers when traveling outside of San Francisco. At first, the policy provided five dollars per night to the host, though it was later boosted to ten dollars.

A nine-page list of travel rules, originally issued in 1980, spelled out the rigid conditions placed on est trainers (and later Forum leaders) while they were on the road. There were strict limits on how much to tip everyone from baggage porters (fifty cents per bag) to hotel doormen (fifty cents to hail a taxi). No tipping was permitted for hotel maids. Traveling staff members were allowed only one ten-minute personal phone call at company expense each evening away from home.

With his background in accounting, Irving Bernstein had long wondered about the bizarre financial structure Harry Margolis had set up for Erhard. As an est trainer and Erhard acolyte, however, he had been conditioned to justify all of Erhard's actions, viewing them as necessary to carrying out the enlightened goals of transformation. For years Bernstein's devotion to Erhard simply crowded out his lingering doubts about Erhard's corporate affairs. Ultimately, however, he found himself unable to justify Erhard's lavish ways. The image of Erhard flying around the country first class or in his own privately leased plane while staying in luxury hotels bumped up too harshly against the discomfort of his faithful employees sleeping on living-room couches while worrying how to make their mortgage payments.

Erhard, of course, had no such financial worries of his own. In

June 1985 he sold the Franklin House for $715,000 in favor of permanent residence aboard the *Canim*. By then a handful of Erhard's closest disciples had formed a partnership that purchased the boat for about $750,000. The partners then leased the vessel to Werner Erhard & Associates, allowing Erhard to use it for both personal and business affairs.

The new owners of Erhard's cherished Franklin House, meanwhile, discovered a multitude of problems after moving in. With leaking gas ranges and a termite-infested deck, the house that once had symbolized Erhard's fanatic insistence on perfection turned out to be another part of est's illusionary façade. Only on the second floor, where Erhard had spent huge sums of money on his own private quarters, did the new owners, a local attorney and his wife, find the house in mint condition. A subsequent lawsuit was eventually settled after Erhard agreed to reduce the price of the house by more than $30,000.*

The financial realities of Werner Erhard's world revealed themselves as well in the always-increasing pressure on est trainers and Forum leaders to produce "results" measured only in the number of customers signing up for courses. Throughout his career as a salesman, Erhard had learned the importance of goals and statistics as the only truly effective way to motivate people to sell more. He carried that lesson to est, constantly evaluating and managing his trainers and other employees on the basis of their success or failure in packing bodies into hotel ballrooms.

Around the est offices in San Francisco, trainers found their "results" posted on the walls for others to see. The results were reflected in a litany of statistics—not only the numbers of people in each training, but how many completed the training, how many left before the end, how many signed up for posttraining seminars. Adding to the pressure, Erhard ordered the est trainers to sit through "clearing" calls with their supervisors in which they would make a commitment to produce a specific result—nothing more than an enrollment quota—at an est event they were scheduled to lead.

---

*In 1989 the owners of the Franklin House sold the property to actor Nicolas Cage, who undertook his own expensive renovation of Werner Erhard's onetime est pleasure palace.

Still, leaving the service of Werner Erhard was not an easy thing to do. Irving Bernstein still believed passionately in the power of human transformation, even recognizing that est had played an important role in his own evolution. After deciding to leave in 1985, Bernstein received a letter from Erhard reminding him he had broken his word about doing "the work" forever. Yet even in accusing Bernstein of such a serious transgression, Erhard formally forgave the former est trainer for his broken promise. Others who remained on Erhard's staff did not prove to be so accommodating. A Forum leader who had invited Bernstein to his wedding called back to rescind the invitation after learning of Bernstein's traitorous decision to break his oath to Werner Erhard.

A year or so after Bernstein broke away, the former est trainer finally realized just how well founded his longtime suspicions of Erhard's financial affairs had been. On October 23, 1986, the U.S. Tax Court in Washington, D.C., handed down two intricately detailed opinions that stripped bare the tax-avoiding façade that Harry Margolis had so elaborately built for Erhard and est dating back to 1971. The two rulings—directed against Erhard Seminars Training Inc. and est, An Educational Corporation—did not involve any charges of criminal wrongdoing. However, the court wiped out millions of dollars' worth of phony tax deductions claimed by est during the first several years of its existence. After tracing the convoluted maze of offshore corporations and bank accounts through which est's profits had been funneled, the tax court ruled that the Margolis scheme added up to a series of "sham transactions" aimed solely at escaping any taxes.

Armed with the court's opinions, the Internal Revenue Service now moved in to collect nearly $14 million in back taxes from Erhard's business. But it was too late. The court rulings were directed against two est corporate entities that no longer existed. And since Werner Erhard, legally speaking, did not "own" either company, he was off the hook personally for paying back taxes. All the IRS could do was place a lien against any assets that might still be held in the name of the defunct est entities.

Still, the exposed details of Erhard's deep involvement in the Margolis system challenged his repeated assertions that est never made much money or that he had never been motivated by the desire to acquire great wealth. "None of my associates or I have ever operated in the work with the notion of making money," Erhard told a magazine interviewer in 1985.

The plain truth was that Werner Erhard profited handsomely from the mass marketing of human potential. Between 1982 and 1984 alone, Werner Erhard & Associates earned just under $113 million in gross revenues, out of which Erhard took as his "draw" more than $1.2 million. Nor did Erhard depend on his company's earnings alone for his income. During the same period he received more than $2 million from a variety of other est-related business ventures.

While his battles with the Internal Revenue Service continued, Erhard found himself facing some polite but persistent protests from some of his own staff members concerned about their financial future.

Throughout est's history, Erhard always had paid his employees as little as possible, while relying on the armies of smiling volunteer assistants to do much of the legwork—from secretarial and cleaning chores to leading est seminars and making sales pitches for Erhard's other courses. Even after est gave way to the Forum, Erhard continued to benefit from his swollen ranks of free laborers. By 1987 there were 30,000 of them, compared to a paid staff of about 300 people in San Francisco and other Erhard centers around the country.

Others inside the est culture were unaware of Erhard's lucrative earnings. For his part, Erhard merely reminded everyone that the enlightened business of human transformation revolved around sacrificial "service" rather than financial gain. Although salary levels began to rise with the arrival at the company of professional business managers, Erhard continued to stress the need for financial sacrifices from the staff along with relying on masses of unpaid assistants.

With the exception of a few executives, the Forum leaders had become Erhard's highest-paid employees by the mid-1980s, earning annual salaries anywhere from $30,000 to $60,000. For some the privilege of doing "the work" was payment enough, but others— though they shared the same commitment to Erhard—thought the time had come to nudge Erhard gently in the direction of improving their own financial security. Every time the issue was raised, however,

Erhard responded with little more than another one of his patented motivational speeches that revolved around the need to enroll more customers.

In July 1987 at a meeting in San Francisco between Erhard and the Forum leaders, the discussion once again turned to money. Again Erhard did his best to sidestep any responsibility for boosting their financial well-being. Instead he treated everyone to a bit of est-speak that had some in the room wondering just what he had in mind.

Erhard rambled on vaguely about "a proposal I would make if I thought it would make any difference to make that proposal." A moment later, he scrambled logic and syntax even more furiously by offering a plan, but only if doing so would allow the Forum leaders to consider it in such a way "that this could be said as a proposal." Ultimately, he had left them only with a string of confusing words.

Later in the meeting, Erhard returned to the perpetual bottom line. It was pointless, he told the Forum leaders, to be discussing raises or retirement plans or any other financial matters without corresponding increases in the company's revenues. He offered a vivid example by mentioning that the company's Los Angeles center had recently increased its Forum enrollment quota by ten. "I don't give a rat's ass if it's ten ahead," barked Erhard, adding that he would "smoke the same number of goddamn cigars" regardless of enrollment levels. He made it clear, however, that producing more enrollments meant everything for the rest of the staff.

By the time the meeting ended, Erhard had steered the discussion away from a concrete plan to boost salaries to one that offered only the vaguest commitment on his part to listen to a four-person committee he had just "empowered" to consider the financial issue. Indeed, Erhard had trained his Forum leaders well, for now they stood up one by one to acknowledge the generosity of his mushy promise. They all spoke the same language, a jargon-filled string of words that could mean anything to anybody. It was, more than anything else, a language without any real meaning.

One Forum leader solemnly declared that he was now taking on responsibility for his own financial future. "And given that I am that declaration . . . I declare my responsibility for that." Erhard looked on approvingly, assuring everyone that here was one Forum leader "serious about a financial future."

"I'm transformed," another Forum leader announced to Erhard, "in the possibility of delegating to you the accountability of a financial future for us." Though Erhard, of course, had easily deflected his own responsibility, this Forum leader had been convinced that Erhard would handle the matter in such a way that "empowers our relationship to you."

Six months later Erhard had done nothing to resolve the ongoing financial concerns of the Forum leaders. But now there were new concerns being raised about the increasingly burdensome travel schedules that often required leaders to be away from their families and homes for weeks at a time. Aggravating the grueling travel schedules were the omnipresent cost-cutting policies requiring less expensive red-eye flights and other budget-minded steps. Erhard stalled for time, telling the Forum leaders in December 1987 to "shut up and do what you are asked to do with regard to the schedule."

Two months later Erhard offered another blunt response to the continuing concerns about the demanding schedules maintained by Forum leaders. "Before, I made a request to shut up about it and make it work," he told them. "Now, my request is to make it work and shut up about it."

Later that month Erhard left San Francisco for a two-week Caribbean cruise with some of his assistants. During the trip, Erhard learned that Jack Mantos, a Forum leader and one of his close aides, had died suddenly of a heart attack at the age of forty-three at his home in Marin County. Other Forum leaders naturally expected Erhard to cut short his Caribbean vacation to attend the funeral in Boston. But Erhard remained on the cruise, even after Mantos's family postponed the memorial service.

In San Francisco, Charlene Afremow could not understand Erhard's decision not to return immediately after hearing about Mantos's death. For years Afremow had been one of Erhard's most loyal and effective est trainers and Forum leaders, but now she wondered aloud to another leader about Erhard's absence. Almost immediately, Afremow received a stinging message from one of Erhard's "communicators," letting her know that second-guessing Erhard's actions was not appropriate behavior for anyone truly committed to him. Afremow was told bluntly that it was none of her business what Erhard did, and that she should "get the fuck out" of the organization if she had the audacity to even question his actions.

A few weeks later it was Erhard who pounced on staff members like Afremow (though he mentioned no names) who seemed to call into question his integrity in light of his actions surrounding Jack Mantos's death. A meeting of Forum leaders in March 1988 turned tense when Erhard angrily brought up the death of his friend.

With the Forum leaders listening in awkward silence, Erhard berated those who took Mantos's death as a "fucking signal to produce some kind of shit in the space." Erhard's eyes were blazing as he exclaimed that Mantos was now less important to him than were those sitting around the room. "I was nice to Jack when he was alive," Erhard told the group. "I don't need to be nice to him when he's dead. And I don't need to honor his memory either. I may choose to do that, but I don't need to do it."

Erhard wasn't the only one at the meeting in a hot-tempered mood about some of the staff's perceived rebelliousness. Earlier during the discussion, his brother Harry launched into an angry tirade against what he saw as subtle challenges to Erhard's absolute authority.

Chiding others on the staff for making "snide remarks" about Erhard, Harry also criticized anyone for "trying to make Werner human." Harry made sure everyone understood his brother's unique status among the Forum leaders, telling them Erhard "is not like you or I."

For Afremow, by the spring of 1988 listening to this type of discussion had become increasingly burdensome. For the past several months she and other Forum leaders noticed a sudden increase among the staff, and throughout the organization, in "upsets" and "well-being" problems—in other words, more people on the staff were getting sick more often, and more participants in the programs seemed to be reporting problems as well. A year earlier, during a staff conference call, Steve Zaffron, as head of the Forum leaders, had issued a stern warning about a "massive rash of serious incidents" that, in his view, reflected directly on the integrity of the leaders and seminar directors. The staff had learned that, in recent weeks, there had been two suicides among seminar participants—one in Toronto and another in Arizona—while a few others had been hospitalized.

Zaffron warned that such episodes threatened to undermine the credibility of the Erhard enterprise. Erhard himself, Zaffron told the Forum leaders, had recently complained to him about having to spend "millions of dollars" in legal fees defending the company against lawsuits arising out of "severe emotional upsets" occurring during the Forum and other programs. One of the Forum leaders reminded the rest of the group that publicity about any of the new incidents could put the company out of business.

But Zaffron, keeping with Erhard's tradition of avoiding responsibility for problems inside the company, pointed an accusing finger at staff members for getting sick themselves. He offered their illness as obvious evidence of their own lack of commitment to their work and believed that it was connected directly to the "incidents" among program participants. Zaffron sternly reminded the Forum leaders it was still "unacceptable" to be sick.

Besides their concerns about demanding travel schedules, Afremow and a few other female Forum leaders urged the company to consider expanded responsibilities for women and address some of their needs, such as more generous expense policies. In line with Erhard's usual response to such requests, Zaffron and Esposito agreed to listen to a committee delegated to address the "women's issues."

In March 1988 Afremow put in a tiring twenty-nine days of work, of which nineteen days were spent out of town, with portions of an additional four days spent traveling to or from San Francisco. Her April schedule had her on an equally rigorous travel program. At the time, Esposito reissued an existing policy aimed at reducing such heavy travel schedules for Forum leaders. Although the policy was designed to limit employees to working no more than twelve hours per day and six days per week, Afremow later claimed that the policy had rarely been followed or enforced.

In late April, Afremow was in New York leading a weekend Forum and a Tuesday night wrap-up session that did not allow her to get to bed until nearly two in the morning. A few hours later she was up to catch a morning flight to San Francisco in order to attend a two-day meeting of Forum leaders. On the first day of the meeting, there was a lengthy discussion about the new travel policies. Although she was exhausted by the end of the day, Afremow had trouble sleeping that night. She returned to the offices on California Street the next day determined to voice her concerns about the demanding policies.

Erhard wasn't at the meeting on April 28, which was led by Steve Zaffron in a fifth-floor conference room. Two floors above, Stewart Esposito was able to tune into the meeting whenever he wanted by switching on a closed-circuit television monitor. One of the staff members began the meeting with an update on "well-being" issues, mentioning that some 10 percent of the company's 300-person staff was out sick at the time.

In Afremow's mind, there was a direct connection between the collective health of the staff and the increasing workload demands which, according to Afremow, required employees to work longer than the official twelve-hour daily limit.

"Yesterday was disgusting to me," said Afremow, referring to the desultory debate a day earlier on the company's official policies. "I'm not going to do those policies. . . . And you can fire me, kick me out. I am not going to live those policies."

Charlene Afremow was tired, angry, and frustrated when she spoke to Zaffron and the other Forum leaders. For years she had worked inside a culture that, in the name of selling transformation, often produced fatigue and anger and frustration. Maybe she should have simply sat down, collected her thoughts, and let the tenseness of the moment pass. But Afremow did not do that. Instead, she continued her testy exchange with Zaffron.

"What are you going to do?" Zaffron asked the veteran est trainer and Forum leader.

"I'm going to do what I know works," Afremow replied. "And you can fire me. . . . Those policies are to protect somebody, not to take care of us. They do not take care of us."

As Afremow became more agitated, Zaffron tried to placate her by telling her how productive she had been. But Afremow was not willing to back down this time, even when Zaffron insisted she was mistaken about the company's work policies.

"You're making something up," he told her.

"Don't handle Charlene," Afremow replied testily.

"You are going to comply with the policies like everyone else," admonished Zaffron.

"No, I'm not," she replied tersely.

Zaffron responded, cutting her off. "Then you won't work here."

"Steve, I'm not going to support people—"

This time Zaffron cut her off in midsentence. "You are going to comply with the policies."

"Fine," she said wearily. "So, should I leave now? Are you firing me?"

"If you are not going to comply with the policies, you should leave," Zaffron said.

She stared at him for a moment. "Are you firing me?" she asked again.

"Yes."

For thirteen years Charlene Afremow had carried the words and work of Werner Erhard from one end of the country to the next, even conducting est events as far as London and Israel as part of her missionary work in spreading the gospel of transformation. Before est ever existed, of course, it was Afremow who had taught Werner Erhard a program called Mind Dynamics, showing him how to sell it to others and then sponsoring his first entry into the mind business as an instructor himself. Now, almost two decades later, it was Afremow's turn to learn the consequences of standing up to Werner Erhard.

It wasn't until months later that Afremow finally began to realize how things could have turned out so wrongly for her. How such a strong-willed woman as herself had managed to fall under the spell of a charismatic former car salesman. "It was disgusting," she said in court documents that accompanied a wrongful termination lawsuit she filed against Erhard after her firing. "Nobody could think for themselves. We were a bunch of zombies. I was too. I was so addicted to my commitment, I couldn't speak out. And when I did, I was called on it."

Nineteen

TIME IS
RUNNING OUT

Obviously the truth

is what's so. Not so obviously,

it's also so what.

—WERNER ERHARD

O n a bright, sun-splashed day in the fall of 1988, Stewart Emery
and Werner Erhard sat down on the deck of the *Canim* to a lunch
of fresh salmon, salad, and a crisp white wine. It had been awhile
since Emery had seen Erhard, who delighted in impressing the former
est trainer with a tour of the gleaming vessel. As they looked out
across the boats moored in the Sausalito harbor, Emery could see that

Erhard's mood was pensive, much different from the buoyant and jovial times they had shared together in the past. The memories of sunny beaches in Hawaii and giddy nights in Aspen now seemed like they belonged to other people. After they finished their lunch, Erhard looked out across the water, gesturing to a flock of seagulls perched on some boat cables overhead.

"You see those seagulls out there," Erhard solemnly told Emery. "Well, I wake up some mornings and I look out there and I see them as vultures."

Emery glanced curiously at Erhard. They had just finished a luscious meal and now Erhard was talking about vultures? With a rare look of resignation on his face, Erhard pointed up at the birds.

"One's the IRS, and another are all these lawsuits. One of the vultures is this whole thing with Ellen. And then there's the loan in Switzerland."

Erhard looked back at Emery for a moment and then turned away to gaze once again at the seagulls. "I always used to believe that the vultures would never get me. But I'm really not sure anymore. So if you wake up one morning and notice the boat's gone from its moorings, you'll know that a couple of those vultures left their perches and headed in this direction. And then I'll decide that wisdom is the better part of valor and that it's time to depart."

To his followers, and to the public at large, Werner Erhard in the fall of 1988 managed to maintain the image of a successful, though quirky, New Age leader. Despite bouts of critical attention over the years, he still stood at the helm of a self-awareness and corporate consulting empire that earned more than $40 million annually. With twenty-six offices throughout the United States and another nineteen foreign branches stretching from Tokyo to Tel Aviv, Werner Erhard & Associates seemed to have confounded cynics and skeptics who always were so eager to dismiss est as little more than a kooky California fad back in the disco days of the 1970s.

By the late 1980s Erhard seemed as determined as ever to present himself as a reputable figure, not only in the New Age field of transformation but in education, social welfare, and other worthy endeavors through programs such as Youth at Risk and Prison Possibilities, a spin-off group that sponsored Forum sessions in prisons around the country. Erhard had even begun to make some forays into the Soviet Union, following up on contacts he had made there earlier in the decade. He had no doubt that his impact had been felt on the society he had set out to transform nearly two decades earlier.

"In the daily newspapers, you find people talking about 'space' and today everyone knows what that means," Erhard told an interviewer in late 1988. "In the last few months, there have been four major business books talking about transformation. There's no question that a lot of the principles that we developed in our work in the '70s have found their way into the mainstream."

But the demons that had long lurked in the shadows and corners of Erhard's life and career were ready to emerge yet again. He thought of himself as someone destined to make a mark in the world, based on a tantalizing vision he had been able to sell to eager audiences for years. But Werner Erhard had never been able to separate the vision from the secrets of his own past. And now the past was about to intrude on the future.

On November 1, 1988, seven lawyers—three representing Erhard and four representing the Internal Revenue Service—sat down at opposing counsel tables in a second-floor courtroom at the Jacob Javits Federal Building in lower Manhattan. Once again the matter before a special trial judge of the U.S. Tax Court was the curious financial structure of Erhard's transformational business and its connection to a deceased attorney named Harry Margolis.

The specific issue facing the court this time was the validity of the globe-circling financial transactions out of which Werner Erhard & Associates had emerged in 1981. The IRS for years had taken the position that Wolfgang Somary's $14 million "loan" to start up Erhard's new company was illusory, engineered by Margolis solely for its tax benefits for Erhard. In response, Erhard's team of lawyers attacked the IRS's position as nothing more than frustrated retribution against Erhard prompted by the government's failure to convict Margolis in either of his two criminal tax fraud trials.

"This case is an effort to vindicate, to reclaim those losses and criminal prosecutions of Margolis," Michael Saltzman, Erhard's lead tax attorney, told the special tax judge when the trial in New York opened. "Harry Margolis died. Werner Erhard is alive. Werner Erhard is the vehicle for prosecuting the dead Harry Margolis."

The IRS readily agreed that its case against Erhard revolved crucially around Margolis and the system he had used for years to help his clients avoid paying taxes. Unfortunately for Erhard, IRS attorney Craig Connell was ready to remind the court of thirty previous tax court rulings that went against Margolis's tax-planning methods.

"This case," Connell told the judge, "looks like another Margolis case. It walks like another Margolis case. It even quacks just like another Margolis case. Your Honor, it is a Margolis case."

While the tax attorneys quarreled in a New York courtroom, presenting a series of opposing witnesses and introducing thousands of pages of documents into evidence, a lawyer in San Francisco was preparing his own legal battle against Werner Erhard. He had no idea at the time that the legal drama about to unfold eventually would help to expose some of the most damaging secrets ever revealed against Erhard and the est culture.

A couple of days after Charlene Afremow was fired, she walked into the Montgomery Street office of Andrew Wilson, whose small firm occupied a fourth-floor corner of the stately Russ Building in the heart of San Francisco's downtown financial district. Afremow had heard of Wilson, whose firm primarily practiced securities law, through her boyfriend, who had worked in the securities business for a time. Since the firm occasionally handled wrongful termination cases, Wilson agreed to an appointment with Afremow so that he could hear her account of her firing from Werner Erhard & Associates.

Werner Erhard certainly was a familiar enough name to Wilson, who grew up in Marin County and had heard plenty about the est training in earlier years. One of his former law partners was an est graduate who often talked up Erhard around the office, while urging Wilson to enroll in the training. But Wilson let his partner know that the chances of his ever signing up for the program decreased markedly every time the other lawyer even brought up the subject.

After listening to Afremow and jotting down some notes on a yellow legal pad, Wilson thought the case sounded intriguing despite the strange-sounding jargon Afremow relied on in recounting her experiences as one of Erhard's longtime employees.

"That's all very interesting, Charlene," Wilson told her politely. "And no offense, but the first thing you're going to have to learn to do is speak English because if you talk like that, nobody is going to understand a thing you're saying."

Over the next several weeks, Afremow received a series of phone calls from other Forum leaders, most of whom fully expected her to return to work at Erhard's company. After all, they explained to her, it had been a common practice over the years for employees to be "fired" from their jobs only to be asked back a few days later after the heat of the moment had subsided. Toward the end of May, Stewart Esposito also called Afremow to let her know that she could "request" to come back on staff, and that, as far as he was concerned, the "sky was the limit" in terms of what she could ask for. But Afremow curtly rebuffed Esposito's offer, angry that the company now seemed to be taking the position that she chose voluntarily to leave rather than was fired. Afremow also felt that if she now "requested" to be given her job back, she would bear the painful stigma of a woman who had demonstrated disloyalty toward Erhard only to be forgiven and welcomed back into the culture.

Esposito responded to Afremow's icy reaction during their phone call with an angry letter sent later the same day. In his letter, Esposito said he saw no further reason to maintain friendly feelings toward Afremow in light of her "hostile" and "aggressive" actions. Whether Afremow chose to return to Erhard's company is irrelevant "because you're not here," wrote Esposito.

Erhard himself had maintained a cautious distance from Afremow ever since her firing in late April. Finally, in early July, after Afremow made it quite clear she had no interest in returning to work for him, Erhard wrote her a compliment-filled two-page letter that praised her years of "extraordinary" service during which she had led est trainings and Forums attended by nearly 100,000 people.

Telling Afremow that he was writing to "validate" her years of service, Erhard offered his thanks for her contributions to himself and others. He closed his letter by saying he was confident that Afremow would continue on in life "happy, satisfied and fulfilled." With bold strokes of the pen, he printed "I Love You" and signed his name at the bottom of the letter.

In late December 1988, Andrew Wilson filed a $2 million civil lawsuit against Werner Erhard & Associates, Werner Erhard, Stewart Esposito, and Steve Zaffron, claiming that Charlene Afremow had been wrongfully terminated from her position as a Forum leader. The suit largely was based on Afremow's claim that she had been fired only after objecting to working conditions she considered to be unreasonably harsh.

Wilson hoped to settle the case quickly, assuming that Werner Erhard would have little interest in airing publicly the strange behavior and internal disputes of his organization. But Erhard's attorneys gave no indication that a settlement was likely. A year after the lawsuit was filed, it looked like the case was heading for a trial.

Privately, Afremow's lawyer was never very optimistic about his client's chances in front of a jury. There was something about the whole affair—perhaps it was the seemingly cultlike behavior of everyone involved, including Charlene—that might prevent a jury from deciding in her favor. As the trial approached, Wilson knew he had to devise another strategy to force Erhard to settle the case out of court.

Wilson made his move in the middle of March 1990. He filed with the court a series of legal declarations—statements made under penalty of perjury—submitted by former Erhard employees that carried sensational allegations of harsh treatment at the hands of Erhard and others around him. Erhard's lawyers immediately requested the court to seal the declarations from public view, arguing the allegations were irrelevant to Afremow's case. The judge agreed to do so, but not until after several copies of the damaging documents had been picked up by the media.

One of the declarations came from Vincent Drucker, est's former financial officer, who had worked for Erhard for five years from 1975 until 1980. Drucker said Erhard had long postured himself as a "godlike figure" whom others in est had to acknowledge as the "source of their lives."

In another declaration, Michael Breard, who had once trained to be Erhard's personal aide aboard the Sausalito houseboat, described how he had been sworn to secrecy about "confidential information" regarding Erhard.

Erhard flatly denied the damning allegations contained in the court documents, dismissing them as "ridiculous fabrications from a few disgruntled former employees." Once again, however, he had been forced into a hasty damage-control effort sparked by the sudden new media interest in Charlene Afremow's lawsuit and the accusations of other former employees. He immediately issued a three-page memo aimed at quelling any nervousness among est and Forum graduates, along with new customers in Erhard's courses. The memo politely described Afremow as a "valued and trusted employee" whose legal claims were "simply untrue."

Inside the offices of Werner Erhard & Associates, there were other problems brewing besides a new round of nasty headlines in the newspapers. In 1989 the company had earned $45 million in gross revenues. But Erhard's executives—led once again by Don Cox—were keenly aware of the vast sums of money that Erhard was spending to support his own expensive life-style and personal projects, such as his ongoing efforts to export human transformation programs to the Soviet Union. By spring 1990 the company's bloated overhead costs, coupled with a drop in new enrollments in the Forum, forced Cox and other executives to take dramatic steps. Cox himself had a powerful incentive to maintain the company's financial health. In April he negotiated a contract with Erhard to assume management control of Erhard's entire business enterprise. The contract called for Cox to receive $300,000 annually plus 20 percent of the increased profits from each of Erhard's corporate entities.

On April 25, 1990, Cox received a dramatic two-page memo from Bob Curtis, the company's former in-house lawyer who now headed the international division of Erhard's enterprise. Curtis painted a grim picture of the company's financial health, telling Cox that weekly expenditures exceeded revenues by anywhere between $75,000 and $100,000. He noted that Forum enrollments had declined 20 percent between 1988 and 1989 and were expected to fall another 5 percent in the first four months of 1990. All in all, warned Curtis, the financial structure of Erhard's company "isn't viable."

In a no-nonsense manner, Curtis suggested several ways of addressing the company's fiscal crisis, starting with a budget-slashing program to reduce overhead expenses from $13 million annually to less than half that amount. But Curtis knew perfectly well that such cuts would be nearly impossible to make, given the huge amounts that Erhard had been taking out of the business. At the time, Erhard's personal office (set up within the "network" as a separate entity) was spending about $35,000 each week, or more than $1.8 million annually. Curtis recommended that payments to Erhard's office drop to $100,000 per month, saving more than $600,000 over the course of the year.

In his memo, Curtis told Cox about several other plans to cut costs and produce more revenue for the company. Chief among them was the elimination of the Forum's two-weekend format in favor of a shorter three-day course "which lowers the entry barrier and utilizes less Forum leaders and facility resources." In other words, the company had found a way to save money by trimming the time it took to transform human beings. In addition, the company had decided to hasten the development and marketing of a new advanced post-Forum course described by Curtis as a "major revenue/cash producer."

Although the steps outlined in Curtis's memo were aimed at restoring financial vitality to Erhard's company, he added one more suggestion in his message to Cox. Faced with mounting financial shortfalls, unresolved lawsuits, and the expected repayment of the $14 million Swiss loan, Curtis suggested that the company consider "financial reorganization through the court system." Bob Curtis was suggesting that Werner Erhard think about filing for bankruptcy.

Curtis was not really serious about the bankruptcy option, including it in his memo largely to call dramatic attention to the company's precarious condition. Certainly he and other executives with knowledge of corporate finances knew that Erhard, as a sole proprietor of his company, would have difficulty seeking bankruptcy protection as long as he also controlled other financially lucrative businesses, including Transformational Technologies and the profitable international arm of the Erhard enterprise. At the time of Curtis's doomsday memo, in fact, Werner Erhard & Associates International had been generating more than $2 million in annual revenues, fueled largely by the Forum's popularity in Japan. Other countries in which Erhard presented his programs included Germany, Sweden, Australia, Switzerland, Canada, India, Israel, and Brazil.

Armed with Curtis's dire financial warning, Don Cox embarked on a vigorous campaign to cut as many overhead expenses as he could while concentrating on a new marketing plan for Erhard's catalog of transformational courses. From his previous years as est's chief executive, Cox knew that increased enrollment in the cornerstone program (once the est training, now the Forum) was crucial to boosting the company's overall revenues. The company's internal statistics revealed that each Forum participant, on average, spent another $1,000 to $1,500 on additional programs, not to mention the valuable recruitment function each one played in enticing others into the course.

"The Forum is equivalent to selling a razor, the other programs are equivalent to selling razor blades," Cox later wrote to Erhard. "The more (or less) razors you sell, the more (or less) will be your razor blade revenues."

By the end of 1989, Forum enrollments had dropped to an average of 250 per week. If he managed to increase that number to 1,000 per week—matching the high-water mark of enrollments into the est training a decade earlier—Cox estimated that Werner Erhard & Associates could generate an additional $50 million in revenues over the next five years.

But even as Cox turned his attention toward the future promise of a new and profitable business plan, Werner Erhard was about to be engulfed by even more dark accounts of his own past. While Charlene Afremow's case slowly wound its way through the court system, some of the salacious details stemming from the lawsuit that had first sounded only as whispers were about to be heard in a series of loud roars. Intrigued by the tantalizing tidbits contained in the Afremow court declarations, newspaper and magazine reporters around San Francisco, who not long ago had thought of Werner Erhard as old news, now picked up the scent of a juicy story. Fifteen years earlier

Erhard had turned to a private investigator in an abortive attempt to derail a critical magazine article. This time he had to find other tactics to divert attention from the public exposure of a personality cult he had maintained for two decades.

Between June and November 1990, Erhard found himself the object of damning articles in a variety of local publications, including the *Marin Independent-Journal*, the *San Jose Mercury-News*, and *Focus* magazine, published by San Francisco public television station KQED. The first story to appear, a two-part series in the Marin County newspaper, recounted in vivid detail some of the same incidents described by former Erhard employees in their declarations in Charlene Afremow's case. Though Erhard declined to talk to the reporter who wrote the articles, one of his public relations advisors arranged for interviews with some of Erhard's loyalists, each of whom had only positive things to say about him.

Three weeks after the articles appeared, Werner Erhard & Associates countered with a full-page advertisement in the newspaper that sought to portray Erhard in a flattering light. The ad touted Erhard's record of "compassion and humanity" while lauding his "record of extraordinary contribution to people, the community and the world."

At his office in San Francisco or from his quarters on board the *Canim*, Werner Erhard now spent hours of his time crafting elaborate strategies for attacking the credibility of his critics and challenging the accuracy of the latest stories. Consumed by the latest assault on his image, Erhard conducted long conference calls with some of his executives that ended up accomplishing little after he began to ramble about matters having little to do with the original purpose of the call.

In the summer of 1990 one of Erhard's original media critics showed up in the Bay Area again, intrigued by the new charges and mysteries swirling all these years later around Werner Erhard. It had been more than fourteen years since Jesse Kornbluth had written a word about Erhard. In fact, the New York writer—who now was a contributing editor to *Vanity Fair* magazine—had long assumed that nobody cared much anymore about a pop guru from the forgotten 1970s. But Erhard indeed was in the news again, which brought Kornbluth to California, where he spent weeks interviewing current and former Erhard employees, finally making arrangements to talk with Erhard aboard the *Canim*.

Kornbluth, like other writers looking into Erhard's past, had heard by then some of the stories surrounding Erhard's harsh behavior toward his wife and children. He had read the declarations filed in the Afremow case and now was ready to confront Erhard when the two met in Erhard's comfortable study on the boat in Sausalito. He was not, however, prepared to see a coltish young woman dressed in a pretty black linen dress breeze casually into the room ten minutes after he and Erhard began the interview.

"Hi, sweetheart!" Erhard said as he kissed the brown-haired woman gently on her cheek. She apologized for interrupting the interview and said she'd be happy to call him later. Erhard cheerfully waved aside her apologies, asking her to sit by his side and introducing her to Kornbluth as his daughter Adair.

"I'm going back to school, and I wanted to talk to you about it," Adair told her father. "I'm not sure what to study."

"That's a good reason to go back to school," he replied, "to find out what you should study." After a few more moments of casual conversation with his daughter, Erhard explained that he was busy with his interview but assured her he wanted to continue later their conversation about her college plans.

Adair got up to leave the room, kissing her father again before walking out. When Erhard turned his attention back toward Kornbluth, he made a few pleasant comments about his daughter, a bemused smile crossing his face. Kornbluth immediately wondered about the accuracy of the stories he had heard about Erhard's harsh behavior toward his own family. The gentle moment he had just observed certainly seemed at odds with the image of an uncaring parent.

Later in the day, Kornbluth was comparing notes with a *Vanity Fair* photographer who had spent the morning photographing Erhard. The photographer mentioned that Adair had shown up at the end of the photo session, after which Erhard excused himself to go off to lunch with her. Kornbluth was curious about the episode, wondering why she would have returned an hour later with her innocuous ques-

tion about college. A few months after his meeting with Erhard, Kornbluth received a phone call from Adair, who explained what had happened on the boat.

"For so long, I wanted to have a father, for him to be there, to
love me," a solemn-voiced Adair told the journalist. "He said you
were interviewing him, and he asked if I'd do this scenario. It's sick-
ening but I agreed. I would have done anything to have the relationship." The whole episode on the *Canim* had been scripted, plotted in
advance with Adair and two of Erhard's aides. The morning of Kornbluth's interview with Erhard, Adair and the aides had figured out the
best subject that she could convincingly bring up after her on-cue
entrance into Erhard's study. Afterward, Adair had been offered a
"reward" for her convincing performance—the honor of setting up
some of Erhard's dinner parties.

For almost twenty years, Werner Erhard had been telling transformation seekers around the world to take responsibility for their
lives, to stop complaining about being victims when they had only
themselves to blame for the circumstances of their lives. But Erhard
had never shown much interest in following the tenets of his own jargon-filled theories that he eagerly mass-marketed to hundreds of thousands of others. Once again, by the end of 1990, he cast about for
someone else to blame for his endangered image. This time he
dwelled endlessly on a story about an elaborate conspiracy out to get
him. In staff meetings, he began launching into hours-long tirades
about how he had become the victim of a malicious "disinformation
campaign" waged by the Church of Scientology.

In fact, Scientology officials for years had been keeping files on
Erhard's est activities out of anger toward his generous use of Scientology material in the est training. L. Ron Hubbard himself had once
decreed that his opponents could be "tricked, sued, lied to or destroyed" in order to protect Scientology's shadowy reputation. Now
Erhard was alarmed by the news that a few Scientology-hired private
investigators were snooping around the Bay Area, collecting critical
information about him and apparently making efforts to spread it
around. But even if others were eager to seize on Erhard's misfortunes, his problems were entirely of his own doing.

For Erhard, time was running out on his dream of a worldwide empire built on a foundation of innocent enthusiasm for his mass-marketed ideas about human transformation. Nearly two decades after est's arrival, Erhard reached the inescapable conclusion that the "vultures" he had once pointed out to Stewart Emery aboard the *Canim* were now hovering too close for comfort. It was time to seek safe harbor elsewhere.

Twenty

ERHARD'S FINAL DOWNFALL

I say that people who

are destroyed create their

own destruction.

—WERNER ERHARD

H al Bertram, the owner of the Mandrake Bookshop, a used bookstore in San Rafael, received a curious phone call from one of Werner Erhard's employees toward the end of 1990. The caller told Bertram that Erhard was offering for sale his vast collection of books stored in a Sausalito warehouse. A few days later Bertram found himself staring at thousands of books covering almost every imaginable subject, from art history to Zen Buddhism. There were books by writers that included Hemingway, Steinbeck, and Shakespeare. There was a huge selection of sailing books and another large collection of titles suggesting myriad ways to get rich quick. Most of the hardcover books were in very good shape, and Bertram couldn't help but notice that few looked as if they had ever been read.

Bertram filled a one-ton truck with more than two thousand books, leaving a vast amount behind inside the warehouse. Before he left, he also noticed hundreds of other items scattered around the place—kitchenware, household items, pieces of sculpture, vases, a few pot-bellied Buddha figurines. Every item had a price tag affixed to it.

Local residents of Sausalito already had been hearing about Erhard's cash-only warehouse sale, and some began wandering by to gawk at the expensive pieces of African art, Pierre Cardin socks, and the assortment of boating supplies available for purchase. There was even a white, one-piece fire retardant driver's suit left behind from Erhard's race-car driving days.

A few weeks after Bertram's book purchase, Paul Gutfreund, the former environmental engineer and disgruntled Hunger Project volunteer, had his own reasons to be curious about Werner Erhard's warehouse sale. For more than two years now Gutfreund had been pressing a lawsuit against Erhard and the Hunger Project, claiming he had suffered disabling mental injuries as a result of Erhard's programs. Since then, Gutfreund had turned into something of a one-man vigilante squad, monitoring Erhard's activities in an effort to assist his own legal case. From his car, which was parked outside the Sausalito warehouse, Gutfreund watched three burly men load nearly one hundred boxes and trunks into a Tokyo Express moving van. When the movers were finished loading the huge truck, Gutfreund followed them to a storage facility near the San Francisco airport.

He's leaving, Gutfreund thought. That bastard Erhard is simply going to vanish from sight and leave others to clean up the mess. Unknown to Gutfreund, Erhard already had taken steps to do just that.

The moving van that Gutfreund trailed to the airport contained more than $150,000 worth of antiques, pieces of art, video cameras, computer equipment, and other Erhard belongings. Among the items moved out of Erhard's warehouse was a set of Baccarat crystal glassware, a collection of Steuben wineglasses, and several sets of silver serving dishes, including an espresso Thermos. According to subsequent court documents, Erhard instructed that the items be shipped to Japan where they were either to be sold with the help of a former employee, or kept aside for his personal use. Included among Erhard's inventory set aside for his continued use were a flight simulator, several fishing rods, and a $6,000 wrist watch.

On January 14, 1991, Erhard agreed to sell his New Age enterprise to a group of his most loyal employees, among them his brother Harry, Forum leader Steve Zaffron and others. In doing so, Erhard rejected a competing bid to purchase the operation put together by a group led by Don Cox and Bob Curtis. One day later Erhard relieved Cox of his duties as chief executive officer and turned the position over to Harry Rosenberg.

Cox was outraged when he learned what had happened, and wrote to Erhard ten days later telling him of the myriad problems facing the new company. Using the blunt language of a bottom-line business manager, Cox told Erhard that, in his opinion, Erhard was leaving behind a company with "virtually no chance of succeeding." Cox told Erhard that the sale of the company would place in control a group of individuals whose collective management, as a group, was disastrous in the 1980s, when Erhard had fired his team of experienced executives in favor of his most loyal acolytes.

But Erhard had no interest in Cox's stark business analysis. Instead, he was concerned only with the hasty completion of the terms of a lucrative business deal that promised to put millions of dollars in his pocket.

Throughout the previous fall, during the latest rash of critical stories in the Bay Area media, an investigative team from the popular CBS news program "60 Minutes" had been preparing its own version of the Erhard story. While earlier media accounts had appeared only in local publications, Erhard and others around him quickly realized that a damaging exposé on "60 Minutes," with its millions of viewers, could all but put an end to Erhard's reputation and the future of his organization.

Don Cox, in particular, was acutely aware of the disastrous financial consequences that might result from nationwide exposure of Erhard's dirty laundry. In one small area alone—San Jose—Forum enrollments had dropped a whopping 77 percent in the aftermath of two hard-hitting Sunday magazine stories in the *San Jose Mercury-News.* Erhard himself was growing more despondent about the upcoming broadcast, telling his staff weeks before the show aired that it might well destroy his reputation.

By the time Erhard was ready to announce publicly the sale of his company, he already had quietly moved off the *Canim* and out of the Bay Area. He said he had taken up residence in Windsor, Massachusetts, a tiny town in the northwest corner of the state where the wife of one of his New York lawyers owned some property. Erhard made it clear that he no longer expected to reside in California.

On January 31, 1991, Werner Erhard signed a twenty-one-page sales contract that officially turned over the assets of Werner Erhard & Associates to the new owners, who called their company Transnational Education Corporation. Shortly after, the name changed again, this time to Landmark Education Corporation.

The carefully worded contract provided Erhard with a $3 million payment, with the cash provided by a $300,000 deposit and the eventual sale of two pieces of valuable real estate the company owned in California's Sonoma County and upstate New York. Landmark Education further agreed to pay Erhard a long-term licensing fee for the material used in the Forum and other courses. Werner Erhard stood to earn up to $15 million over the next eighteen years.

In part, Erhard's sale of his company provided some of the final pieces of the puzzle that Harry Margolis had created for him twenty years earlier. The new sales contract specified how the licensing payments were to be made to Erhard over the years. Forty-four percent of each installment was to be paid directly to Wolfgang Somary's mysterious Intercultural Cooperation Foundation in Zurich, Switzerland. Technically, the payments to Intercultural were designed to pay off Somary's 1981 "loan" that had financed the initial creation of Werner

Erhard & Associates. Of course, the loan was nothing more than an illusory transaction. Now Erhard was completing part of the around-the-globe loop that Margolis had begun years earlier. During the first few months of 1991, for example, the coffers of the Swiss "foundation" were enriched by some $700,000, nearly half coming from the new owners of Erhard's old company and the rest from one of Erhard's bank accounts in San Francisco. Erhard was finally ready to pay himself back for an offshore loan that never existed in the first place.

The remaining licensing payments to Erhard, according to the sales contract, were to be divided between a tax trust account (40 percent) through which Erhard would pay back taxes owed to the IRS and a separate trust account (16 percent) to pay Erhard's other creditors.

While the terms of the sale included the purchase by the new company of Erhard's international operation, Erhard shrewdly insisted on retaining ownership of the Japanese branch, which accounted for more than 70 percent of total international earnings. Other assets retained by Erhard included a valuable art collection and a handsome villa in Puerto Vallarta, Mexico.

In February 1991 Erhard released a written statement officially announcing the sale of his company to his employees. Without mentioning any of the financial details, Erhard said the transaction "puts the future of the work that I and others started into the hands of people who have dedicated their energy, their heart and their talent to serving the people who have participated in these programs."

A few weeks later, on the evening of March 3, millions of television viewers across the country tuned their sets to CBS to watch another edition of "60 Minutes." Each week the program began with short teasers—a few seconds of excerpts from each segment—so that viewers knew what to expect over the next hour. On that evening, the first teaser showed CBS correspondent Bob Simon describing his harrowing tale of captivity in Baghdad while covering the war against Iraq. Simon had just been freed, and the show had rearranged its schedule so that he could report on his experience.

A few seconds later Erhard's face filled the screen, and he was heard briefly touting his est-flavored philosophy about making "the world work for everyone." Then the scene switched to a woman named Dawn Damas, who once had been hired as a governess to take care of the Erhard children. "He beats his wife and he beats his children and he rapes a daughter, and then he goes and tells people how to have marvelous relationships," Damas said solemnly. "I'm sorry. That's what I have against Werner Erhard."

All across America, thousands of est graduates, Forum participants, Erhard employees, and other faithful acolytes—not to mention countless others who may have remembered only vaguely the man with the strange-sounding name of Werner Erhard—watched as "60 Minutes" correspondent Ed Bradley related a dark story of Erhard's past. The camera dramatically focused its gaze on a few of Erhard's former followers such as Bob Larzelere, est's onetime "well being director," who had left in the late 1970s, and Wendy Drucker, the wife of former est executive Vincent Drucker, as they described their own harrowing accounts of life inside Erhard's world.

Bradley then turned his attention to two of Erhard's daughters by Ellen—Celeste and Adair—who choked back tears as they recounted the ugly stories of their father's violent temper and relived the night their mother had been beaten and abused years earlier at the Franklin House.

"Does your mother know you're talking to us?" Bradley asked Adair after informing viewers that Ellen's divorce agreement prohibited her from telling her own side of the story of her relationship with Werner Erhard.

"Yeah," Adair replied. "Before we left tonight, I talked to her and she's just—you know, she said, 'I can't thank you enough for doing this, for saying these things that need to be said.' And I know that she wishes she could do the same."

So far, the "60 Minutes" broadcast had not included anything about Erhard that had not already appeared in other stories. But Werner Erhard knew there was more to come. He knew the most damning charge against him was about to be made from another one of his daughters.

The screen pictured a well-dressed woman with a self-assured expression and the same penetrating eyes as her father. Deborah Rosenberg, the youngest of Erhard's four children from his first marriage, had never spoken publicly about Werner Erhard since her well-orchestrated interview years earlier for a book about children of celebrities. She had long since retreated into the shadows, preferring to live quietly in Honolulu with her husband and infant son while trying to put her father out of her mind. Now, the blond thirty-one-year-old had a more solemn story to tell about what it was like to be the daughter of a man named Werner Erhard.

"I don't have a problem saying that it happened," Deborah told Bradley, choosing her words carefully. "I don't like describing it, but I don't have a problem admitting that he molested me."

Deborah then added that her father had forced sexual intercourse with one of her older sisters, a charge that Erhard vociferously denied in a portion of a taped interview played by Bradley on the air. Deborah, however, offered a different version of her father's response to the alleged incident during a family gathering aboard Erhard's boat in the mid-1980's.

"What he did say when I confronted him about it was that there had been sexual intercourse and that it had been a nurturing experience for my sister," she said.

"He admitted it?" asked Bradley, an incredulous tone in his voice.

"He admitted there was sexual intercourse and that it was a nurturing experience," she replied softly. "He said he did not rape her."

As the "60 Minutes" segment came to a close, Bradley read to viewers a statement from Erhard, who otherwise had declined to be interviewed by the program. "There is only one appropriate response to these allegations: to heal and restore my family," read Erhard's statement. "And that is what I will do. To respond to the accusations at this time would only further publicly exploit my family and there has already been enough of that."

One year after the "60 Minutes" piece aired, Erhard filed a lawsuit against CBS and a variety of other defendants, claiming that the broadcast contained several "false, misleading and defamatory" statements about Erhard. However, Erhard dropped the lawsuit a few months later before any court decision had been reached on its claims.

By the time of the "60 Minutes" broadcast, Werner Erhard had already decided that the United States no longer provided a very hospitable place in which to live. Two weeks before the broadcast, a travel agency in Sausalito issued to Erhard an $8,490 first-class airline ticket that included some exotic destinations. Erhard's itinerary began on March 1, two days before "60 Minutes," with a flight from San Jose, Costa Rica, to Miami, connecting there to a flight to Zurich, Switzerland. A week later, Erhard planned to fly from Frankfurt, Germany, to Moscow, where he was scheduled to stay for two weeks before continuing on to Tokyo. The airline ticket included an open-ended return to San Francisco.

Insisting that a busy work schedule now required him to be overseas for much of the time, Erhard announced plans to remain outside the country for at least the rest of 1991. Though he was once spotted in San Francisco, picking up some suits at one of his favorite clothing salons, Erhard otherwise vanished for a while into the netherworld of his self-imposed exile. Following his globe-trotting adventure in early 1991 (in Moscow, Erhard appeared on a local television show discussing his transformational theories to an audience of enthusiastic Russians), he eventually settled into his villa in Mexico. There he undoubtedly wondered whether he could yet figure out a way to reappear in the public spotlight.

While the "60 Minutes" program once again riveted public attention on Werner Erhard, Charlene Afremow's long-delayed lawsuit against him was finally coming to trial. Andrew Wilson, Afremow's lawyer, claimed that Erhard was an essential witness in the case and asked the judge to order his return to San Francisco.

Wilson, it turned out, was still trying to bluff Erhard into settling the case out of court. In the wake of the furor over the "60 Minutes" broadcast, the lawyer was sure Erhard would rather settle than be forced to appear in public so soon after being the subject of such damning allegations. But Wilson's tactic failed when the judge refused to order Erhard's appearance at the trial.

Shortly before the trial began in April 1991, Erhard replaced his original lawyers in the case with San Francisco attorney John Keker, one of the nation's premier courtroom litigators. Keker's clients in the past included former Black Panther leader Eldridge Cleaver and film director George Lucas. His formidable legal skills were put to use in the Reagan administration's Iran-contra scandal, when he prosecuted former Marine Colonel Oliver North, one of the key figures.

Keker convinced the judge in the Afremow case to bar any evidence or testimony dealing with abusive behavior at Werner Erhard & Associates that was not directly related to Afremow's firing. Wilson had hoped to present the case against a backdrop of cultlike incidents within Erhard's company that might make a jury more sympathetic to his client's claims of harsh working conditions. Instead, the judge ordered Wilson to confine his case to the relatively narrow circumstances of Afremow's departure from Erhard's organization.

"She wanted to make a difference in people's lives. She wanted to help people," Wilson told the jury during his opening statement, almost three years after Charlene Afremow lost her job working for Werner Erhard. Wilson described his client as a woman devoted for years to her onetime student Werner Erhard, a man "of uncommon charisma and ability to motivate people. He had an idea, and he was better at it than anyone else ever was."

Keker responded to Wilson's opening statement by telling the jury the case before them was simply about "a woman who at one point liked her job very much, and then hated it. The job didn't change, she did." Keker, astutely aware of the negative image that many jurors might have had about Erhard, reminded them on the first day of the trial that Erhard's direct involvement in the case was "almost zero."

By then there was little else Wilson could do to salvage the case. Though Afremow presented her own emotional account of the events leading up to her firing, Keker kept returning to the contents of a tape recording made of the meeting in which she had been fired. She flatly insisted that she would not comply with company policies, and she had all but invited Steve Zaffron to fire her as a Forum leader. A few members of the jury nodded slightly as Keker challenged Afremow's version of the events.

After a two-week trial, the jury hardly surprised anyone when it

handed Erhard and the other defendants in the case a near-total victory. One juror said there was little doubt that Zaffron had been
"goaded" into firing Afremow. Neither Erhard nor anyone else at the
company acted improperly in dismissing Charlene Afremow, declared
the jurors.

They were not without a little bit of sympathy, however, toward
Afremow. They awarded her $28,400 in damages after deciding that
Werner Erhard & Associates interfered with Afremow's attempt, after
her firing, to start a "relationships" seminar with the wife of one of
Erhard's Forum leaders. Part of Wilson's case had included evidence
that Erhard officials intentionally tried to block the course on the
grounds that it competed with a similar seminar offered by Erhard's
company.

Not long after the trial ended, Afremow received a three-
paragraph note signed at the bottom with a familiar closing salutation
and distinct signature. Erhard said he was saddened by the way in
which his relationship with Afremow had been "defined" by the lawyers involved in Afremow's lawsuit and others rather than by his work
with her over the past two decades. Now, wrote Erhard, it was time to
put the "ridiculous and tragic" events of the past behind both of them
and restore a long-standing friendship marked by "dignity and mutual
respect."

Afremow did not respond to Erhard's note and received one further message from him a few weeks later. In it, he told her he was
willing to listen to anything she wished to tell him. Again, Afremow
did not reply to Erhard's brief note. She did notice, with a bit of
curiosity, that the note included a return address for Erhard in Zurich, Switzerland.

One other piece of the Werner Erhard puzzle was about to fall
into place. Twice before, the shadowy financial dealings of his business enterprise had been challenged by the Internal Revenue Service
and rejected by the U.S. Tax Court. On July 1, 1991, the court
released yet another lengthy opinion that tracked once again the familiar fingerprints that Harry Margolis had left on Werner Erhard's
lucrative "mind business." The court's decision, resulting from the
1988 tax trial against Werner Erhard & Associates, held squarely

against the "sham transactions" that Harry Margolis had engineered when the last incarnation of Erhard's enterprise was formed a decade earlier.

The court's detailed ruling focused on the $14 million "loan" that Margolis had arranged for the initial financing of Werner Erhard & Associates. Although Erhard's lawyers had insisted that the purpose of creating Erhard's new company in 1981 was to remove the taint of Margolis from the business of est, the court concluded that the controversial attorney "continued to play a significant role" in the pivotal financial transactions that spawned the new enterprise. But the court also ruled that Erhard himself had not been negligent nor had he intentially disregarded tax rules and regulations, but rather had relied on the advice of competent lawyers and accountants in the course of the disputed transactions. As a result, the court held that Erhard was not liable for additional tax penalties on top of the back taxes claimed by the IRS.

Even before the Tax Court handed down its decision, IRS officials in California had already imposed a lien worth nearly $7 million on assets held in Erhard's name, equivalent to the amount of money the IRS claimed he owed. Ironically, one of the IRS agents investigating Erhard's finances was himself an est graduate, having taken the training back in the 1970s. Although the amount of the lien would be adjusted to reflect subsequent court rulings that narrowed Erhard's liability, it still took its place alongside two previous liens amounting to nearly $14 million attached to the two Erhard-linked companies that had sold the est training during the 1970s.

There were other unpaid bills as well. In January 1988 Werner Erhard & Associates had signed a ten-year lease for 66,000 square feet of office space spread out over six floors in a building on the southern edge of San Francisco's financial district. By the spring of 1991, after Erhard's business had been transformed by the sale to the new Landmark Education Corporation, the owners of the office building began receiving less than the full monthly payments of $78,904 required under the lease. After June, the lease payments stopped altogether. The building owners responded with a lawsuit, charging Erhard with breaching the terms of the lease.

Landmark's attorneys responded to the lawsuit with the argument that the new company had no obligations or responsibilities for a lease between the building owners and Erhard's previous company.

In March 1992 a panel of three outside arbitrators in San Francisco ruled that Erhard indeed had breached the lease agreement, awarding the owners nearly $2.5 million in damages. The owners further were entitled under the ruling (which later was confirmed by a court order) to collect more than $600,000 following the eventual sale of a valuable piece of property once owned by Erhard's former company in upstate New York. In the meantime, Landmark moved its operations to a new set of offices in downtown San Francisco.

Werner Erhard's name surfaced in another lawsuit stemming from alleged damages suffered by a participant in his self-awareness program. In September 1989 Stephanie Ney, a forty-three-year-old artist from Silver Spring, Maryland, suffered a nervous breakdown three days after sitting through the Forum in nearby Alexandria, Virginia. Two years later she filed a $2 million lawsuit blaming Werner Erhard and Landmark Education Corporation for her emotional injuries.

Before Ney's trial began in July 1992, the federal judge hearing the case dismissed Landmark from the suit because it had not yet been created when Ney attended the Forum. A jury then ruled that the Forum leader who conducted Ney's session was not responsible for inflicting emotional distress on the woman. But Erhard himself was not off the hook. Because Erhard had never responded to the suit, the judge entered a "default judgment" against him, but waited for the case to finish before announcing Erhard's liability. Werner Erhard was then ordered to pay more than $500,000 in damages for the mental injuries suffered by Stephanie Ney.

But the judge's ruling against Erhard amounted to a hollow victory for the plaintiff in the case. With Erhard living outside the country, and with the IRS already trying to collect millions of dollars from him, there was little chance of Ney collecting much, if anything, from the man who promised such lofty results.

Epilogue

Laurel Scheaf planted her statuesque frame within a couple feet of the slim, middle-age woman and stared into her eyes for several moments. At first, the woman returned Scheaf's glare with her own blank gaze, but then averted her eyes completely, as if she could hide from Scheaf's relentless stare simply by focusing on some other object in the room. There were a few nervous coughs scattered around the hotel conference room, but mostly there was only awkward silence as everyone else watched the tense moment unfold before them. After a few more moments of staring, Scheaf turned away from the woman and took a few steps toward the raised dais at the front of the room. Suddenly she wheeled around on the balls of her feet and glared again at the diminutive woman still standing at her chair, gripping a microphone that she held at her mouth but not saying anything. Scheaf's face contorted into a deep scowl, and you could tell she was about to rip into the woman with the ferociousness of a Marine drill sergeant laying into a raw contingent of boot camp recruits.

"WHO ARE YOU KIDDING?" she yelled, her eyes ablaze in anger. "DON'T YOU SEE WHAT'S HAPPENING IN YOUR LIFE?"

The woman gripped the microphone a little more tightly in her hand, but otherwise remained a frozen figure as she stood there bearing the brunt of Laurel Scheaf's outburst. Her lips were pursed, and for just a moment it looked as if she would either break down in tears or lunge at Scheaf in desperation, like a trapped, helpless animal backed into a corner by a dangerous predator.

"ARE YOU LISTENING TO ME? YOU HAVE A DAUGHTER WHO DOESN'T WANT TO TALK TO YOU! YOU HAVE A DAUGHTER WHO DOESN'T EVEN WANT TO SEE YOUR FACE!!"

Scheaf was yelling even louder now, and the chords in her neck stood vertically at attention, accenting the rigidity of her at-attention posture as she stood in the middle aisle of the room and bore further into the silent woman's empty eyes. There were a few more coughs around the room and then silence again. Finally Scheaf was ready to finish her high-decibel analysis of the woman's problem. Once again came the throaty scream, as the muscles in Scheaf's face went taut and stretched themselves against her high cheekbones.

"DO YOU KNOW WHAT YOUR PROBLEM IS? YOU ARE NOT A LOVING MOTHER!"

Scheaf turned back toward the dais, swiveling away from the woman who looked as if she had been paralyzed by the angry torrent of words. Still clutching the microphone in the tight grip of her right hand, the woman finally managed to find a few words that she now muttered softly in Scheaf's direction. "I hear what you're saying," she almost whispered into the microphone. "I think you might be right."

She expected the accommodating words to bring a gentle response from Scheaf, who now stood just at the edge of the dais, not staring any more in the woman's direction but instead appearing annoyed and perplexed by the meek, almost apologetic tone of the woman's voice. The scowl on Scheaf's face let everyone know that she was not about to let the woman off the hook that easily. After all, there was some tough business to conduct here in this hotel conference room in downtown San Francisco on a cool spring night. A few minutes earlier Scheaf and the woman had been talking almost like two old friends would talk about things going on in their lives. There was compassion in Scheaf's voice as she gently questioned the woman about a problem she was having in her strained relationship with a grown daughter. After all, it was one of the reasons why the woman had enrolled in the Forum in the first place, since the weekend program was designed, among other purposes, to help its participants improve their relations with others.

Scheaf leaned against the edge of the dais and shot a quick glance at one of several volunteer assistants scattered around the room, nodding her head just slightly before turning back to stare yet again at the woman standing in the middle of the room. But then the angry scowl returned and with it came another torrent of verbal abuse flung at the hapless woman holding the microphone. This time Scheaf shouted so loudly that her screams strained the clarity of the wireless mike she wore clipped to the lapel of her blouse.

"YOU'RE SO BUSY BEING RIGHT ALL THE TIME THAT YOU CAN'T EVEN HEAR WHAT I'M TELLING YOU!"

"I think I do hear you," the woman replied in her muted voice.

"YOU DON'T HEAR ME! JUST LIKE YOU NEVER HEAR YOUR OWN DAUGHTER. NOW LISTEN TO ME! YOU JUST HAVE TO GET OFF IT! NOW!!"

There was dead silence, not even a nervous cough or a bit of awkward laughter to break the tense mood that permeated the room. Scheaf did not let the woman out of her boot-camp gaze for several seconds, during which time the woman managed only the slightest nod of her head—the barest acknowledgment that she accepted what Scheaf had told her. This time she offered no other response, and after another moment or two had passed she blankly yielded up the microphone to one of the assistants who by then was at her elbow, waiting eagerly to snatch it away so that it could be handed quickly to someone else waiting to "share" something about their own life in front of Laurel Scheaf and 150 other people seated in the straight-backed chairs in the hotel conference room.

When she spoke next, the feverish pitch in Scheaf's voice had vanished. She had walked back to the dais and settled into the director's chair, reaching over to a small table and sipping some tea from a stainless steel beaker that one of the assistants constantly kept refilled. The harshness and yelling was replaced now with a school teacher's gentle and reassuring tone.

"I think you know what you need to do," Scheaf told the woman from her podium perch. A broad smile had erased the menacing scowl, and the chords in Scheaf's neck had relaxed their rigid stance.

From the audience, the woman nodded her head a bit more confidently now, even returning a faint version of Scheaf's wide smile. "Okay, that's great. That's really great," said Scheaf.

Everyone in the room responded with a polite round of applause, just as they had been instructed to do at the beginning of the Forum whenever people got up to share something about their lives, something about their reasons for enrolling in the Forum. As the applause continued, Scheaf reclined for a moment in her director's chair and took another sip from the beaker of tea. She was still smiling as the applause died down and the woman took her seat. As she did, Scheaf winked at her and the woman answered with a thin smile. It was time for Scheaf to turn her attention to someone else in the room. It was time for someone else to benefit from the "extraordinary results" promised to those who signed up for the Forum.

It had been nearly twenty-one years since Werner Erhard first stepped forward as the "source" of one of America's most successful mass-marketed self-awareness programs, ultimately selling more than $430 million worth of gauzy transformation to more than 1 million customers. Before Erhard vanished into exile, his instruction courses in enlightenment and take-charge-of-your-life lessons were offered in more than one hundred cities around the world.

Werner Erhard was hardly the first self-appointed sage promising heady results to those seeking personal transformation. He will not be the last, for America's social history has been filled right up to the present with plenty of examples of authoritarian figures—some very silly, others downright deadly—offering sustenance to those hungering for spiritual or motivational nourishment. But Erhard certainly led the way in applying mass-marketing techniques to transformation. He hit his stride at the beginning of the New Age era, and his ideas have since been studied and copied by other New Age purveyors. Today's self-help landscape features an array of courses similar to est offered by organizations such as Lifespring, PSI World, and Insight.

With his charisma and self-assured salesmanship, Erhard also paved the way for other New Age promoters to achieve their own celebrity status. Erhard's fame had been boosted by a bevy of Hollywood stars rushing into est training sessions and emerging to sing his praises. Indeed, he stirred up Hollywood the way no other self-help master had ever done before, and the town has never been the same. Twenty years after Erhard appeared on the scene, America's glitterati fêtes a new generation of gurus—flocking to lectures by the likes of a former nightclub singer named Marianne Williamson or workshops led by a onetime drug company salesman named John Bradshaw. The harsh tones of est have vanished, replaced with soothing hymns about a "course in miracles" and "reclaiming your inner child." Steven Spielberg, Barbra Streisand, Cher, Oprah Winfrey, Peter Guber, and Elizabeth Taylor have been only a few of the marquee names seeking enlightenment from the latest versions of America's long-running self-help extravaganza.

There were no celebrities in the second-floor conference room at the ANA Hotel in San Francisco on a cool, overcast weekend in the spring of 1992. Erhard himself was only a ghost, now that he no longer officially had anything to do with the Forum, his successor to est now offered by Landmark Education Corporation. Even his name, once so revered among the legions who looked simply to "Werner" for transformational guidance, had been expunged from the slick brochures that advertised the Forum and the other self-awareness courses sold by Landmark. But the words and phrases bore his unmistakable imprint, for they had hardly changed from the days when Erhard was in control.

"The Forum," read the brochure, "provides a breakthrough in the technology of living powerfully, living effectively, living an extraordinary life. It is a penetrating, challenging and practical inquiry into the issues at the heart of our lives—communication, relationship, happiness and satisfaction. It results in an extraordinary advantage in performance, creativity and self-expression."

For more than two decades, Werner Erhard had taught Laurel Scheaf how to sell. First it had been books, and there had been no harder way to sell them than by walking door to door throughout the hilly streets of San Francisco. Next came Mind Dynamics and with it a new product for the former Ohio school teacher to peddle. Finally there was est—and with it, Laurel Scheaf was attached more closely than ever to the man who had been her mentor, the Svengali figure to whom she owed everything in her life. How many years had she sat on one of the Erhard-trademark high-legged director's chairs and sipped from the Erhard-trademark stainless steel beaker? How many years had it been since she had first dutifully memorized the words and phrases Erhard had taught her and his other disciples to repeat over and over again in front of the paying customers? On this cool, spring weekend in San Francisco, Erhard lurked in the corners of the room like a fallen spirit. Scheaf felt his presence and sat in his chair and sipped from his beaker of tea. And then she went about the business of the day—selling the enticing product of human transformation to yet another group of willing buyers.

The chairs had been lined up in perfectly straight rows. A black ballpoint pen had been centered underneath each chair, its tip pointed toward the front of the room. Outside the room, neatly lined rows of name tags were arranged on one of the tables, first names printed in large black letters. Smiling assistants ushered the Forum participants into the conference room, which quieted down as soon as a dour-faced woman named Kirsten marched to the dais and began to explain some of the rules that everyone had to agree to follow as a condition for participating in the Forum. There would be one meal break during the course of the fifteen-hour session, plus a few short breaks spaced throughout the day. No talking, no standing up and strolling about the room. Always wear your name tag. No sitting next to someone you know. A few people dozed off while Kirsten read through the rules. When she finished, she asked everyone to pick up the pen placed carefully beneath each chair and sign an agreement form that was being handed out by the team of assistants around the room. When the assistants collected the forms, they made sure to retrieve the pens as well. There was no note-taking permitted inside the Forum.

A few minutes later Laurel Scheaf emerged from the back of the room to the sounds of loud applause, much of which came from the assistants now gathered around the doors leading in and out of the conference room. After walking briskly to the dais, Scheaf picked up a piece of thick yellow chalk and began drawing a circular pie chart on one of the two large green chalkboards standing on either side of the stage.

"There are things that we know that we know," she said as she marked off one small slice of the pie. "There are things that we know that we don't know." She marked off another quarter slice. What was left, she said, as her hand swept across the remaining half of the pie, was everything "that we don't know that we don't know." That, concluded Scheaf, is "what the Forum is all about."

For the next three days, Laurel Scheaf treated the 150 transformation seekers to a steady dose of mystifying phrases and head-scratching mental exercises that had the participants tied up in knots as they made valiant efforts to attach even a shred of logical meaning to the strange language and bizarre goings-on in the room. "Languaging is the house of being," Scheaf declared at one point during the weekend. Moments later, without bothering to explain what she meant, Scheaf served up another piece of Forum wisdom by announcing that the weekend was all about "dancing with the listening in a conversation for possibility."

By late Saturday night, another round of linguistic gymnastics was touched off after Scheaf printed the deceptively simple word "I" on one of the chalkboards. A sly grin crept across Scheaf's face as she sat perched on her director's chair and glanced at the chalkboard, serving up another cryptic piece of Forum-speak. She suggested to those in the room that the word "I" is only a "superstition."

Within moments, the smiling volunteer assistants were passing microphones to the participants who wanted to express their own opinions on the puzzling meaning of "I." Scheaf nodded approvingly at most of the comments, while those who stood up to talk usually smiled back at her appreciatively and everyone else in the room applauded, just as they had been instructed after someone finished "sharing." But Scheaf's approving nods vanished in an instant when a man in his late thirties held the microphone in his hands and defined "I" to include someone's own sense of spirituality. In a flash, the drill-sergeant scowl returned to Scheaf's face. She glared at the man in the audience and then cut him off in midsentence with an acid-tongued retort that left him stunned.

"I'm not interested in your point of view," she told him sternly.

The man stood his ground, bringing the microphone up to his lips and looking at Scheaf. "But I don't see why my position about this—"

Scheaf angrily cut him off again. "Oh, so now you're being right, is that it? Now you've decided to be self-righteous about all this."

"I don't think I'm being right at all. I'm just saying that—"

"I say you're just being an asshole," Scheaf told him in a mocking tone of voice. "Now being an asshole isn't a bad thing to be. It's just another way of being."

The man continued to stand with the microphone to his lips, as a half smile stretched across his face. He looked as if he wanted to say something else, to challenge Laurel Scheaf's dismissal of him with one of Werner Erhard's favorite standby epithets. But before he could say another word, a few people scattered around the room hissed and muttered at him to sit down. A woman sitting a few seats away from him got to her feet and was quickly handed a microphone by one of the assistants. She reminded everyone in the room that the man only a few hours earlier had confessed that one of his problems in life—one of his "rackets"—was that he liked to argue. And here he was, said the woman, arguing with Scheaf and "being his racket." Applause rang throughout the room, and Scheaf grinned from ear to ear while the man stood frozen at his seat. A few moments later he shrugged his shoulders in a gesture of resignation and yielded up his microphone to one of the assistants.

At one of the dinner breaks, a gentle-faced Asian man in his early sixties explained to a few other Forum participants eating together at a nearby restaurant how surprised he was when he learned after registering in the course that it used to be connected to Werner Erhard. "I had no idea that this had anything to do with est or with Erhard," he said. "They never volunteered any of that information when I signed up."

Of course they didn't. For Werner Erhard, the past had always been something to run away from, to render invisible by pretending that it barely even existed. Erhard and est for years advocated a convenient culture of amnesia, which certainly served the needs of so many thousands of his most loyal followers. In their zeal to discover the innocence of enlightenment, they savored his message of "completing" the past by casting it into a dark abyss. Many of Erhard's followers also cheered est's satirical rejection of traditional psychotherapy for similar reasons. Most forms of therapy have aimed for transformation by mining the individual's past. Erhard's own experiences in life were reflected in est's formula for achieving transformation by avoiding the past.

"That's not an issue," Scheaf replied curtly when one Forum participant wondered what he should tell others if they asked about the Forum's connection to est. "Est no longer exists," she added. The only reason to mention it "is if you like talking about the past."

When leading the Forum, Laurel Scheaf managed whenever she could to drop est from the disappearing past, as if it had never been one of Werner Erhard's strongest selling points through the years. Scheaf no longer mentioned once having served as est's first president in those early years when Erhard first turned his booksellers into mind-sellers. Instead, she vaguely boasted two decades later only of having served as president "when this work was first presented" without going into any of the past-reminding details. Years ago Scheaf talked proudly about enrolling her own solidly midwestern parents in an early est training and how their lives were forever changed by the experience. Now, in the aftermath of Erhard's fall from grace, she simply switched course names, telling 150 participants inside the San Francisco hotel about her parents' "incredible" experience in a course—the Forum—that did not even exist until twelve years after Oral and Mildred Scheaf supposedly sat through the same program in 1973.

By Saturday evening, more than midway through the three-day Forum, the conference room inside the ANA Hotel reverberated with the sounds of transformation. One by one dozens of participants reached for the microphones to announce their own pending rebirth, triggered by Scheaf's probing questions into the intimate details of their lives. Though she had made it clear earlier that she held no therapy credentials and that Landmark Education Corporation most certainly was not in the therapy business, Scheaf worked the room like a talk-show psychiatrist, digging up all those repressed emotions and burrowing deep into individual psyches in order, she insisted, to rip out the weeds of the past and clear the way for a transformed future.

Everyone in the room listened with rapt attention while a woman sitting in the front row shared a bit of her own past. She described her father who had committed suicide when she was a young child, part of a "homework" assignment handed out by Scheaf the night before in which every participant had been asked to write a personal letter as part of an exercise in "completing" an unresolved personal relationship. Most of the letters had been written to mothers and fathers, and now the tears welled up in the woman's voice as she read her letter, with a sobbing catch in her voice, to a deceased father.

Scheaf sat in her director's chair a couple of feet from the woman, sipping from her beaker of tea while she listened, along with everyone else, to the sorrowful words that the woman had written. As the tears began to stream down the woman's cheeks, Scheaf reached over and handed her a couple of tissues to dry her eyes.

"How was that for you?" Scheaf asked in a gentle voice after the woman had finally gotten through her letter. "Tell me what happened when your father committed suicide."

The woman spoke slowly, sounding very nervous and tentative. "I really don't remember anything about it."

Scheaf was out of her chair now, standing close to the woman. Her voice hardened a bit, and she stared directly into the woman's moist eyes. "Oh yes, you remember all right. It's all there. Now tell me about your father's suicide."

Other confessionals followed. A young man in a tank-top shirt confided that he'd been in therapy for the past three years, paying $90 for weekly sessions but feeling as if he'd made little progress after all that treatment. Scheaf laughed loudly and turned toward the rest of the room with a theatrical tell-me-all-about-it nod of her head. Her point was clear—the man was much better off bringing his problems to the Forum, where transformation could be had in the course of a weekend. Underscoring the point, Scheaf tartly reminded everyone that psychiatrists have one of the highest rates of suicide in the country.

All through the evening the telltale stories of people's lives continued. A young woman rose with a gut-wrenching story of being abused as a child. Another woman recounted how her father often beat her over the head with a rolled-up newspaper, calling her a "shithead" who never would amount to anything.

"That's just the way he was," counseled Scheaf. "He was being an asshole." As if to offer some comfort, she reminded those in the room that everyone does things "that make us assholes every day of our lives." Throughout the Forum, Laurel Scheaf dropped several references to parents who abuse and molest their children, reminding everyone how common such incidents are. Though she acknowledged that such parental behavior "never works," Laurel Scheaf made it clear that such abuse certainly did not prevent a mother or a father from being a loving parent. The veiled reference to Werner Erhard's own alleged behavior as a father—allegations which Scheaf certainly knew about by then—served as a cryptic reminder that she, in her own way, was intent still on protecting Erhard's damaged image.

There were more tears, and more tissues from the director's chair. More applause after each dark secret had been laid bare. After five or ten minutes, it was time to move on to the next case, since there were now so many hands raised around the room. The smiling assistants scampered among the rows of chairs, thrusting microphones into the hands of the participants so quickly that Scheaf barely had time to pause after each new round of applause before turning her attention to the next confession.

On Sunday evening, a mood of gaiety and celebration filled the conference room as previous Forum graduates streamed inside to congratulate the latest group of entrants into the transformational fold. There were balloons and flowers and hugs and smiles, everyone wearing the ubiquitous name tags, all of them coded with different colored strips to identify the wearer's status (graduates, assistants, staff) inside the world of the Forum. For most of the evening, Scheaf delivered a strong sales pitch for the Forum's advanced course, normally priced at $700 but available with a $100 "scholarship" for any Forum graduate who signed up that evening.

The remainder of the evening reflected Erhard's long-standing reliance on the aggressive approach to marketing his self-awareness courses. Now that the Forum had "empowered" their own lives, Scheaf reminded everyone it was time to "live that empowerment" by introducing others to the Forum as well.

"Take a stand in the possibility that your life is," she urged everyone, by making a solemn commitment to bring ten guests to the post-Forum "guest evening" two nights later. As the volunteer assistants scribbled down their names, a handful of new Forum enthusiasts stood around the room, announcing their intention to round up plenty of guests for the midweek session. Every time a new person stood up, the rest of the room broke into applause.

The guest evening began with a quick introduction to the Forum given by Scheaf. Largely free of the confusing jargon that marked much of the Forum itself, Scheaf's brief remarks were followed by a round of applause-filled testimonials delivered by several newly minted Forum graduates. After an hour or so, the guests were divided into smaller groups and directed to other rooms around the hotel, where they were "invited" to sign themselves up into the next session of the Forum. Back inside the main conference room, Scheaf continued with her aggressive sales pitch for the advanced course. The $100 scholarship was still available, but only until the end of the evening.

Laurel Scheaf was all smiles as the evening session came to a close, basking in the loud applause that now echoed around the room in her honor. How many times had she savored such a moment, knowing always who deserved the real credit for the cheers and the clapping? But now, on this night and on other nights to come, it was up to Laurel Scheaf and a few dozen other disciples of Werner Erhard who led the Forum to accept the applause they knew really belonged to him. They would continue to serve him as they always had—by imitating him, copying his gestures and his style, subtly planting in the mind of each new customer a rationale for the dark acts that Werner Erhard had been so publicly accused of. A rationale for the behavior of a man who humiliated his wife and had been accused of beating her and abusing his own children, while claiming to invent a world-changing "technology" of personal transformation. Finally the demons had caught up with the man, and he no longer was able to accept the delicious applause that had once greeted his name wherever he went. On a cool spring night in San Francisco, no one even wondered what ever happened to Werner Erhard.

Acknowledgments

A first-time author needs an abundance of encouragement and support while traveling along the path that culminates in a maiden
book's publication. Fortunately, I was the beneficiary of both from my
agent, Jane Dystel, whose belief in my abilities as a journalist and
writer led to my taking on a book about Werner Erhard. At St. Martin's
Press, senior editor Charles Spicer shared from the very outset my

vision and enthusiasm for the book. He further deserves my thanks for improving upon that vision through his insightful suggestions for shaping the book so that it remained squarely focused on its subject. I also appreciate the diligence and good-natured attention to this project paid by Charlie's editorial assistant, Liz Weinstock.

My background as a legal journalist has resulted in a healthy cynicism aimed at our legal system and those who practice law. Nonetheless I want to thank David N. Kaye, general counsel at St. Martin's, for his patience, understanding, and good humor that were required in connection with the preparation of this book. The same applies to Paul Sleven, at the New York law firm of Szold & Brandwen, who helped steer me through some of the potential legal rapids that confront authors writing these days about controversial subjects.

In San Francisco, the law firm of Jaffe, Trutanich, Scatena & Blum provided an altogether different kind of support, which helped to make this book possible. The firm generously provided me with office space and other facilities during the many months of research and writing, and always made me feel welcome as I went about my business. To Fred Blum and his partners, associates and staff, I extend appreciative thanks—though I reserve the right to remain cynical about attorneys as a class.

Two former colleagues of mine at *California Lawyer* magazine in San Francisco played an invaluable role in sustaining my work on the book. Peter Allen and Pamela Feinsilber offered superb comments on an early draft and followed them up with an endless amount of moral support and keen advice. I'm afraid I may never be able to repay Peter for all the lunches he treated me to while I rambled on about Werner Erhard and est. I also want to thank Eric Effron, editor and publisher of *Legal Times* in Washington, D.C., for his warm friendship and interest in the book, even when my writing unwittingly entangled him and his newspaper. I owe a large debt of gratitude to Jesse Kornbluth, who wondered why anybody would want to write a book about Werner Erhard but then provided me with a treasure trove of Erhard-related materials he had gathered over the years. For reasons too numerous to detail here, I thank Ronald Collins and Susan Cohen. Suffice to say they provided nurturing assistance that far exceeded the bounds of friendship.

Certainly this book could never have been written without the cooperation of scores of individuals who provided me with their candid recollections and revealing records of their dealings over the years with Erhard.

A note is in order here about my use of quoted conversations throughout the book. In some cases, conversations have been recounted based on the recollections of participants or witnesses. In other instances, I have relied on previously published accounts, court transcripts, depositions, and other documents in which various individuals have recounted earlier conversations. Many of the sources I relied on for information are named throughout the book; many others are not. They all deserve equally my thanks for contributing to this disturbing story of Erhard and the movement he created.

Lastly I want to acknowledge my wife, Tracy Salkowitz, for her unlimited support and unwavering faith in me that began long before I embarked on this project. Her own roots as the daughter of a writer served to cushion us both against the foreboding feeling that we were jumping off a cliff together when I went to work on my book. I hope she agrees with me that it has turned out to be worth the fall.

Index